Odd Bits

Odd Bits

HOW TO COOK THE REST OF THE ANIMAL

Jennifer McLagan

Photography by Leigh Beisch

TEN SPEED PRESS
Berkeley

Copyright © 2011 by Jennifer McLagan
Photographs copyright © 2011 by Leigh Beisch

All rights reserved.
Published in the United States by Ten Speed Press,
an imprint of the Crown Publishing Group, a division
of Random House, Inc., New York.
www.crownpublishing.com
www.tenspeed.com

Published in Canada by HarperCollins Canada

"Rillons, Rillettes" from COLLECTED POEMS
1943–2004, copyright © 2004 by Richard Wilbur,
reprinted by permission of Houghton Mifflin Harcourt
Publishing Company.

Ten Speed Press and the Ten Speed Press colophon are
registered trademarks of Random House, Inc.

Library of Congress Cataloging-in-Publication Data

McLagan, Jennifer.
  Oddbits : how to cook the rest of the animal /
by Jennifer McLagan.
     p. cm.
  Includes bibliographical references and index.
  ISBN 978-1-58008-334-8
  1. Cooking (Variety meats) I. Title.
  TX749.5.V37M35 2011
  641.3'6—dc22
                                          2011011575

ISBN 978-1-58008-334-8

Printed in China

Cover and text design by Betsy Stromberg
Food styling by Dan Becker
Food styling assistance by Emily Garland
Prop styling by Sara Slavin

10 9 8 7 6 5 4 3 2 1

First Edition

For my mother, Claudine, who, with her Sunday night dinners,
unknowingly planted the idea for this book.

_____

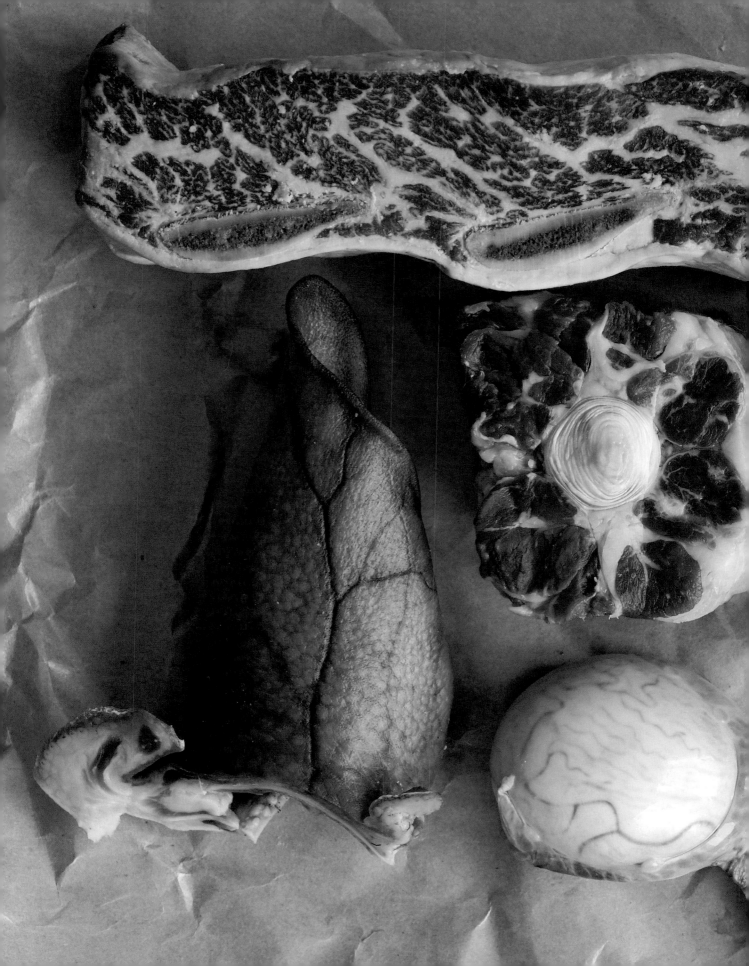

Contents

INTRODUCTION

Not So Odd After All

Just what do I mean by this strange title, *Odd Bits*? Most of the meat we eat—the tenderloins, the racks, the steaks, the legs, and the chops—is only a small percentage of the animal carcass. These prime cuts, once expensive and special, are now, thanks to industrialized farming, very cheap. Simple to cook, these familiar and common everyday cuts fill our butcher shops and supermarkets. What were once uncommon and prestigious pieces of meat have become banal and boring.

Well, I'm not interested in these cuts and you won't find them here. This book is about the rest of the animal: the pieces we once enjoyed and relished but no longer bother with. Unfamiliar and odd, they have become the "*odd bits.*" I am not talking just about offal or variety meats. Yes, I am interested in the strange wobbly bits and they're here, but alas these pieces are not the only animal cuts considered odd today. So, I chose this term because it is broader and more inclusive. *Odd Bits* covers everything from tongues to tails, cheeks to shanks, brains to bellies. They are all animal parts we have forgotten not only how to cook but also how to eat. This book, *Odd Bits,* is an introduction to cooking and eating the rest of the animal.

Today we are so removed from the sources of our food that we rarely think of meat coming from living, breathing animals. The steaks, chops, and ground meat we buy shrink-wrapped in the supermarket give no hint of the animals they came from, while an ear, a kidney, or a tail all remind us very tangibly that they were once parts of a living creature. These pieces of the animal now seem odd and strange to us, something we don't want to eat. But why is it stranger to eat a beef cheek than a cow's back? Why do people chew a rib chop but recoil at roasted marrow bones? Why do we happily eat lamb chops but overlook lamb neck? And why do so many people know, without a doubt, that they hate brains? Should we care that these odd bits go unappreciated? Isn't there more than enough cheap meat for us to buy and eat?

As a percentage of our income, food is cheaper than it has been at any time in the past—especially meat. We spend much less of our income on our food than our grandparents, and we spend less time sourcing it, cooking it, and eating it. The application of industrial principles and economies of scale to farming have lowered the cost of our food dramatically. (Still, while factory farming has reduced the cost of meat, it hasn't improved its quality or taste.)

However, dirt-cheap food is not sustainable and, in the long term, it can only be a blip on our culinary landscape. We are already rethinking our relationship to our food and recognizing that there are other costs incurred with this type of farming: polluted and infertile land, shrinking biodiversity, and, worst of all, wretched treatment of animals. Those of us who care about what we eat—and we should all care—must demand that the animals we eat are raised naturally and humanely, treated with respect in both life and death. This is the only way a thinking carnivore can continue to eat meat.

> *Scared? Intimidated? Grossed out? Put off by memories of Mom, or some long ago lunch lady, coming at you with a slab of ineptly and indifferently fried liver, or by some comedian's jokes about haggis? Does the phrase 'Eat IT! It's good for you!' still strike fear into your heart?*
> ANTHONY BOURDAIN

Yes, the meat produced this way costs more, but that in turn has its benefits. By paying the true costs of production, we no longer rely on factory farms that pollute the countryside, the animals can be well cared for, and we will have better quality and better tasting meat. Paying more for our meat is good in other ways. If our meat costs more, we will not waste it, we'll take more care when we cook it, and we will eat less of it—a good thing because most of us eat too much meat. My time in France has shown me that where meat is more expensive, portions are smaller and waste is less. I also see the way meat is handled and displayed there—with care and respect. More expensive meat forces us to look beyond those now familiar prime cuts for less popular and often cheaper cuts, the odd bits—it encourages us to cook and *eat* the whole animal. All these positive results come from keeping our side of the bargain we made when we domesticated animals: in exchange for their meat, eggs, and milk, we provide them with food, protection, and care.

Recently, in the world of professional cooking, there has been a renewed interest in odd bits. When it comes to food, often the impetus is top down: chefs discover "new" foods and "new" techniques, which then migrate into home kitchens. Fergus Henderson, the English chef-owner of St. John restaurant in London, has become a cult figure for his philosophy of "nose to tail" eating. This is good, and I love Fergus's cooking, but I am sure he would be the first to say that he is just making proper English food, cooking dishes that have a long history in England's cuisine. My mother, whose roots are Scottish, cooked many similar dishes when I was young—not with Fergus's skill, perhaps, but there is not much in his books that she doesn't recognize. Unfortunately, as with many new trends, this enthusiasm for odd bits can lead to excess and one-upmanship. Cooks compete to create the weirdest dishes that anyone would want—or more often *not* want—to eat. This doesn't help. It makes people already unfamiliar with odd bits think that they are difficult to cook—that only trained chefs know how to handle them—and strange to eat—something to be tried only in a restaurant. This is the reverse of true. At cooking school, chefs get very little exposure to odd bits, apart from the fashionable sweetbreads and calf's liver, and few of them understand the art of butchery and where on and in the animal a given odd bit is found. Most know less than my mother about cooking odd bits—and if she can cook them, so can you.

But where do you turn for advice in cooking odd bits? As odd bits have disappeared from our consciousness and our kitchens, so has our savoir-faire with them and our recipes for them. So in the following pages I hope to coax you into cooking odd bits by giving you some basic information and techniques. I want you to think beyond the familiar chops, steaks, and roasts when making dinner, and to realize there is a panoply of delicious, tasty morsels waiting for you to welcome them into your kitchen. At present, many are relegated to pet food: they all deserve a better fate. I am not trying to shock, although I am sure I will: my goal is simply to demystify the rest of the animal, to give you sound advice and to show you that cooking odd bits is really not that difficult.

Odd Bits Past and Present

When man began hunting, he consumed all of his kill. First he enjoyed the animal's heart and brain. People of many cultures believed that by eating them they would acquire the animal's strength, bravery, and intelligence. Next the intestines, liver, kidneys, and sweetbreads, the most perishable odd bits, were enjoyed, either by the hunter as reward for his success, or reserved for an honored elder of the group. The Romans enjoyed lavish banquets that included bird tongues and stews of goose feet and cockscombs. The ancient Greeks delighted in eating *splanchna*, the animal viscera. There was less of it, so it was more precious than the animal's meat, and merited respect and special handling. In Greece, *kokoretsi*, skewered lamb offal wrapped with intestines, remains a popular dish. In France these odd bits are still

called *les parties nobles,* the "noble's pieces" or "prized parts," and odd bits like liver, tongue, feet, and tails, were popular with the great cooks Taillevent (1398), La Varenne (1651), and Grimod (1803–1812), who all included recipes for them in their books. Odd bits' prestige still remains high in Europe, Asia, and South America, Africa, and the Middle East, but their fortunes have fallen in the Anglo-Saxon world.

One argument put forward to explain why odd bits aren't popular in the kitchens of the English-speaking world is that we don't appreciate their taste and texture. This is nonsense. Sausages and puddings made with intestines stuffed with mixtures of blood, liver, lungs, heart, marrow, brains, and tongues then simmered in stews were part of the early English diet. They were not perhaps gourmet treats, but with the arrival of the Normans in 1066, the range of odd bits used and the methods of cooking them became more varied and sophisticated. Liver, giblets, and sweetbreads along with testicles, tripe, palates, and cockscombs graced the royal table. King Henry II feasted on boar's head and the Elizabethans enjoyed bird tongues. Later, Hannah Glasse described how to cook ox tongue and udders and how to stuff a calf's head in her *Art of Cookery Made Plain and Easy* (1747).

At the end the eighteenth century, the growth of abattoirs in Britain facilitated the killing of large numbers of animals in a single place, which resulted in an oversupply of odd bits. As they were very perishable and difficult to ship, they were given to the poor instead of being thrown away. The result of this generosity was that many odd bits came to be seen as food for the poor, and their prestige fell. The arrival in England, starting in the late eighteenth century, of French chefs displaced by the French Revolution made odd bits fashionable again. Eating marrow with special spoons became popular among the aristocracy, and the middle classes enjoyed oxtail soup and tripe stew. Odd bits remained popular until the Second World War, when, as one of the few protein sources not subject to rationing, they became a regular part of the English wartime diet. Then, when the war was over, eating them reminded many of hard times, and so they were often passed over for now-affordable, and more sophisticated, steak.

In a past that I can remember, odd bits were still widely eaten. Dorothy Hartley's *Food of England* (1954) includes recipes for giblets, pig's ears, cow heel, brawn, and oxtail. These dishes were part of my childhood culinary horizon, eaten at home and in restaurants and pubs. My aunt never missed an opportunity to order crumbed brains and bacon at the local watering hole, and she was famous in our family for her oxtail stew. My first job as a cook was in a large Melbourne hotel, where I was in charge of making breakfast. One of the most popular dishes was a mixed grill that included lamb's kidney. So until quite recently, English cooks at home and abroad were eating and cooking odd bits. It is the drop in price of other cuts and the association of odd bits with hard times and poverty that has led to their decline.

But what about North America? It's true that there is more squeamishness around eating odd bits on this continent than elsewhere, despite strong culinary traditions of using the odd bits. Native Americans ate the entire animal, and early colonists could not afford to waste any part of the animals they slaughtered. As the West opened up, son-of-a-bitch stew (see page 167) and bone marrow (see page 189), called prairie butter, were common dishes. Buffalo tongues (see page 58) became a delicacy featured on restaurant menus along with ox heart, pig's feet and kidneys.

Irma Rombauer's *Joy of Cooking* (1936) has recipes for tripe, liver, oxtail, sweetbreads, brains, tongue, kidneys, and even testicles and cockscombs. While not every American was eating odd bits, a good percentage of the population was, as noted in the *Joy of Cooking:* "Variety meats provide welcome relief from the weekly round of beef, pork, veal, chicken, and fish." The author goes on to note a rise in their popularity, which she attributes to her compatriots' broadening culinary horizons due to the new American passion for travel. Americans, like Australians and the English, did travel more as airfares became affordable in the 1970s, but there was no parallel surge in the eating and cooking of odd bits. Despite Rombauer's assertion, odd bits continued to disappear from Anglo-Saxon kitchens in the late twentieth century. What happened?

Loss of Food Literacy

The way our food is produced changed dramatically in the second half of the twentieth century. The family farm nearly vanished, swallowed up by industrial farming based on fossil fuels and monocultures. This has led to a dramatic drop in food prices—we now spend a third of what our grandparents did on our food. Chickens, once a prized bird reserved for Sunday dinner, are now cheap and ubiquitous. Steak is inexpensive enough for us to eat every night, and it's quick and easy to cook. So why bother with the odd bits that often took time and effort to prepare? With a few exceptions, odd bits disappeared from the marketplace. To a great extent, this is because when an animal is slaughtered, the odd bits must be carefully separated from the carcass, and many require further processing before they can be sold. With meat prices so low, these cuts were no longer viable. Except for calf's liver and sweetbreads, with their special cachet, most odd bits are not worth processing and the result is that many never find their way out of the abattoirs or often end up as pet or animal food.

The US government has also helped create and reinforce prejudices against odd bits by banning some of them from sale for human consumption, notably lungs and blood. In Europe both can be purchased from a butcher, and in some countries blood is available in the supermarket. Other, temporary bans, such as the removal from sale of oxtail, brains, marrow, and sweetbreads during the outbreak of mad cow disease (BSE), have further stigmatized odd bits. It is interesting to note that if we had allowed our cattle to graze instead of feeding them ground up animals, the ban wouldn't have been necessary.

At the same time as farming was being industrialized, the food supply chain was being centralized. Supermarkets became our prime source for food, and small food shops, notably independent butcher shops, closed. Without someone to recommend a cut, save us a set of brains, brine a tongue, or share an odd bits recipe, we were left to our own devices. Even the most informed shopper must rely on the advice of experts, but supermarkets rarely provide any skilled personnel to help us shop, and they don't employ butchers, as the meat arrives precut. This is also the situation in some of the remaining butcher shops, where there are no real butchers left: they've been replaced by meat slicers. We are all easily seduced by the convenience of buying everything in one place, but with no one to ask, and less and less knowledge of our own, it is hard for us to make good choices. We don't, and often can't, use our sense of smell or touch. Even our common sense leaves us, and we shop by price and appearance, believing these are more important than taste.

Our supermarkets prefer uniform foods that look good on their shelves, and as a result numerous apple and tomato varieties that didn't fit these parameters have vanished. Odd bits are also victims of this need for durability and perfection, as many of them are extremely fragile and require careful handling. They cannot linger in the supermarket or in the consumer's refrigerator, and few of them could be described as photogenic morsels. Our growing distaste for linking the meat we cook with the animal it came from has badly hurt odd bits' popularity: some odd bits, like the head, tongue, or heart, instantly remind shoppers they are buying a part of a dead animal—something the dismembered, plastic-wrapped supermarket meat does not do. With loss of knowledge and no one to guide us, we turn for help to the new "experts": the government, meat processors, nutritionists, and even celebrities, and we rely on the health and nutritional claims on the package to make our choices.

> 'Tell me,' she said, her voice sympathetic as she leaned over the table and restored control of the sausage casing to my clumsy fingers for the fifth time. 'I've been wanting to ask you ever since you and your family arrived, but I did not wish to seem inquisitive. Please forgive me, but did your mother teach you nothing at all?'
> ELISABETH LUARD

We do, as Rombauer noted, travel more than previous generations and many of us try exotic foods in foreign places. Globalized culture is marked by a fascination, almost an obsession, with the new. Cuisines the world over are in a constant state of flux, always incorporating new ingredients into their cooking. The tomato and potato in Europe are famous examples of the impact of new ingredients on established cuisines. However, these two did not conquer overnight, but took decades and longer to be accepted. Today the pace of change is much faster: an ingredient unknown to us last year is in every supermarket this year, and it seems that we can't cook without it, whether it is balsamic vinegar or an exotic sea salt. Tantalized by the new, we neglect and forget the past. Food media aggravates the situation, with magazines promoting the hottest trends in food and cookbooks filled with banal recipes that provide little information and don't teach the reader any skills or techniques. More and more, we are eating variations of the same dish. It seems that we talk more about food than ever before, and the proliferation of food on television reveals that we are interested in food, but the more time we spend watching food programming the less time we spend in the kitchen cooking. The idolizing of chefs has left home cooks thinking that cooking is a specialized skill. It's true that cooking in a high-end restaurant requires training and dedication, but making dinner is something we can all do.

The Future for Odd Bits

Despite some bleak periods in the recent past and continuing strong prejudices against them, I believe the future for odd bits is bright—not least because many of the forces that worked against them are now supporting and promoting them.

Increases in the price of food and earthquakes in our economies make people reassess their food choices. In France, long a bastion of odd bits, there was a dip in their popularity—until the recent shakiness of the global economy resulted in a 15 percent increase in sales, demonstrated by the long queue every Friday morning at my market *tripèrie*. In the United Kingdom, sales of odd bits rose by 25 percent in a year and in North America and Australia, where meat is still cheaper than it is in Europe, there have been increases, albeit less dramatic, in the demand for odd bits. Food television can have a positive effect. In an episode of *Iron Chef America,* the secret ingredient was offal, which sparked an interest among viewers; and when contestants on

the hugely popular cooking program *MasterChef Australia* dueled with lamb shanks, that odd bit sold out across the country the next day. People are rediscovering odd bits.

In the last decade, food has become an increasingly politicized issue, with many voices raging against the industrial food system and raising awareness of the negative effects of producing cheap food. This, combined with scares about the safety of our food system, has people demanding to know the source of their food and how the animals they eat are treated. There is a renewed interest in organic, pasture-raised, regional, and seasonal foods. Groups like Slow Food International, which champions traditional foods and techniques, have helped create markets for small, local food artisans. There is a growth in sustainable farming and ethical animal husbandry and a renewed interest in raising heritage breeds. After a long decline in family and smallholder farming, young people are returning to the land and the numbers of small farms are growing. Helping make this smaller scale farming viable, there has been a growth in farmers' markets and community-supported agriculture. Skills that have been neglected—especially in North America—like charcuterie, cheese making, preserving, fermenting, braising, and the art of confit are all enjoying a resurgence of interest. These market channels and skills, along with the renaissance in cooking and eating odd bits, help make this kind of farming economically feasible.

Many chefs are doing their bit to help by sourcing their meat from small suppliers, and they often buy the whole animal to help reduce their food costs. This means they too have to find creative ways of using every part of the animal to make their investment worthwhile. As methods of cooking these tasty morsels are not well covered in culinary schools, they look to the past and comb other cultures for ideas. They must cook dishes that their customers will order and enjoy. And what is presented on restaurant menus filters into the home kitchen.

Animal anatomy is a mystery to most of us, including chefs, who rarely learn how to handle a whole animal in cooking school. Chefs are turning to butchers to understand how an animal is butchered, so that they can break down a carcass themselves. Some chefs have even left their stoves to work in the cold room, and butchery is becoming a newly "sexy" profession. However it must be remembered that butchery is a very highly skilled trade that takes a long time and much practice to master. It is time for a revalorization of the art of butchery, and I am glad to see more and more butcher shops opening, run by people who care about meat and about their craft.

> *However, the paradox with such animal parts is that there are actually less of them than there are of other parts of a carcass: while an animal has two rumps, and two forequarters, it has only one liver, one heart, two kidneys, one brain, and one tail. Yet, whereas scarcity usually renders things more precious and highly sought after, here there has become an increasing aversion to them.*
> CHERRY RIPE

Today one way we learn about food is by watching television personalities eat their way through foreign cultures. This is helping us become more adventurous eaters than we were in the 1960s. We are coming to realize that everyone in the world—from Scandinavia to the Middle East and from Asia to South America—eats and enjoys odd bits, according them a special place in their culinary traditions. We see that maybe we've been missing something. Once people discover how easy most odd bits are to cook, the demand for them will increase, and so will their availability. While I doubt odd bits will replace

hamburger, I'd be happy if they just became mainstream. Imagine spicy tripe in tomato sauce for sale alongside those beef and vegetable kebabs at the butcher's. Braised heart and cheeks a staple on winter menus. Liver stir-fry or devilled kidneys promoted as weeknight dinner fare in a food magazine. It's coming: there is an odd bits revival underway—and this is not a revolutionary movement, but rather a conservative one. It's a return to the past, and grandma would love it.

Why Trust Me?

Why me? Those of you who are familiar with my other books, *Bones* and *Fat*, know that I like to tackle unfashionable topics. And I believe that I am well qualified for this one. As a child I ate a lot of odd bits. There was corned beef: I can still taste the salty thick slices and the English mustard that I delighted in making, measuring out Keen's mustard powder with a tiny spoon into a small cut glass dish that held less than a tablespoon, adding water drop by drop until the right consistency was achieved. It was a powerful paste that balanced the spicing of the beef. There was tasty lamb neck stew with onions, sliced potatoes, and green peas and lamb's liver sautéed in butter. My mother made wonderful soups from bones and hocks, unctuous oxtail stew, and homemade meat pies filled with a palatable mixture of odd bits. I sucked the marrow from bones and ate ox tongue set in wobbly jelly every Christmas. These are all wonderful, tasty food memories, but no childhood is entirely golden, and there were odd bits that cast long, dark shadows over mine. The two main culprits were tripe in white sauce with onions, and crumbed lamb's brains. Eeergh! The mere thought of them still makes me queasy.

The tripe of my childhood was totally disgusting. Tripe with onions in a white sauce (we didn't know to call it béchamel) is a classic English dish. My mother's rendition of béchamel, as I remember it, was a thick, white sludge that blanketed the pieces of tripe, gluing them to the plate—not even the sprinkling of chopped parsley she added could help. I wasn't put off by any strong gutty odor or pungent flavor, but rather by the complete absence of both odor *and* flavor, and the odd, chewy, congealed texture of it all. Her lamb's brains were no better (although they came with crisp bacon slices, which were delicious). I developed a method for eating these dreaded brains. First I gobbled up the bacon, then I would carefully eat the bread crumb coating from each lump of brain, a skill perfected by much practice. That left only the naked cooked brains to deal with, and try as I might I could not swallow those soft, white, mushy lumps. Luckily for me, brains were always a Sunday night dinner. This was the only night I was allowed to eat in my pajamas, so I slipped those texture-less brains into my dressing gown pocket and waited for an opportune moment to dispose of them. These two culinary horrors were so deeply etched into my consciousness that I was well into my twenties before I tried brains or tripe again—and then only by chance.

Although I've had many culinary epiphanies in France, the one involving odd bits was accidental. I worked for a family in Paris, collecting their son from school and teaching him English. I had little money and less imagination, living on a diet of mackerel and mussels, two of the cheapest things I could buy and cook on a small, unreliable electric hot plate in my *chambre de bonne*. So whenever his parents asked me to dinner, I accepted and, being well brought up, I ate whatever they offered me. One evening I was served a dish that smelt strongly earthy, with pieces of something I couldn't identify; but its deep brown sauce studded with carrots and topped with fresh parsley looked wonderfully appetizing, so I dug in. The taste was rich, and the texture pleasantly chewy and slightly slippery. The sauce was flavorful and gelatinously lip smacking. I loved it. When I asked what it was, I was shocked to learn it was tripe (it's the same word in both languages). It bore no resemblance to the parsley-flecked, white, tasteless glue of my childhood. This positive experience with tripe liberated my natural curiosity and other dishes followed—headcheese, *andouillette* (a sausage of intestines), pig's feet, and blood sausage, which I could buy prepared and warm up on my hot plate. Not all my adventures with odd bits were pleasant experiences. I recall a game *civet*—a stew of hare thickened with blood— that made me physically ill. I'd been very sick for several weeks before eating it and the sauce was just too rich for my system. My second *civet* was a much better experience, and my sojourn in France taught me that I could eat almost anything, as long as it was cooked well and I was healthy.

> Ancestral memory is much like the stuff we keep in a trunk in the attic—we know it's there, but we don't open the lid till we need it, and when we do, all we find is the remnants left by rats.
> ELISABETH LUARD

France is not the only place I discovered delicious odd bits. I now have eaten ribs from all animals—not odd to you, perhaps, but it was a cut missing from my Scottish-Australian childhood. In southern Texas I tasted menudo for the first time. This fiery Mexican soup includes tripe, calf's feet, and hominy and supposedly cures a hangover; I can attest that it's delicious without one. In Asia many dishes, from duck's tongues to pho (a soup based on bones and garnished with blood cakes) thrilled my taste buds. Even the country of my ancestors, Scotland, introduced me to the delights of haggis and devilled kidneys.

My conversion to brains came later, in Toronto. My husband and I were enjoying a tasting menu at our favorite restaurant, when a course with a brain fritter arrived. I wasn't worried: it was only a garnish. I could set it aside or slip it into my serviette (after all I was experienced in spiriting away brains). But as the chef was a friend, I decided I should take the plunge and try it. All that I now remember of that whole tasting menu is just how wonderful that brain fritter was—a light crisp coating enclosing a rich, creamy center: the perfect ratio of soft filling to crunch. My conversion to odd bits was complete.

So, who better than me to lead you through the world of odd bits? I understand when people say, "I don't eat that!" I know they simply have yet to eat a tasty rendition of the dish. There are wonderful dishes to discover and rediscover, if you keep an open mind. Some are familiar, others new and challenging, and all are delicious. An animal carcass is more than prime cuts—there is so much more to enjoy. One of the most readily available odd bits, liver, comes in a range of tastes from chicken to beef, and it is fast food—quicker and easier to cook than a grilled cheese sandwich.

But odd bits is not a category exclusively concerned with offal; it covers cuts we've forgotten—from brisket to shank, neck to tail, cheeks to chuck. All of them will be championed in this book. Tasty and often cheap, odd bits can be cooked in a myriad of ways that allow the cook to be creative. Once you understand the basics of odd bits, they will be no more mysterious than a New York steak, and you will be cooking, eating, and enjoying them more often.

When many people still don't even know what a whole chicken looks like, can I make them care about its giblets? Perhaps not, but that is no reason not to assemble a guide for those who do care. I'll admit that not all odd bits are delectable, and some are more about texture than taste, but that doesn't

mean any of them should be thrown away. If you don't like them plain, improve them with a spice or a sauce, chop them into a farce, or add them to the stockpot. Every part of the animal deserves to be eaten, and I hope you will feel the same way after reading this book, if you don't already.

This book is a personal exploration of the world of odd bits. It is not the definitive book; there are some odd bits not mentioned here, rather, it reflects my choices and what I like to eat. I hope this book will inspire you to set off on your own culinary voyage of discovery.

Notes for the Cook

I'll offer just a brief explanation of how this book is organized, and why. It is important to know where in the animal the cut comes from, as this helps you understand how to cook it. So this book is broken down like an animal: into the head, the front, the middle, and the back end. Like any organizing scheme, it is not perfect, and some odd bits overlap or could be included in more than one section. But you'll understand the general idea.

It is important to note that cooking is an art, not an exact science, despite the beliefs of some chefs and the claims of some current trends. The ingredients and equipment one cook uses will never be exactly the same as those of another. While I have carefully tested all the recipes in this book, the cooking times may vary and the number of servings a recipe yields will depend on your personal preference for portion size. Approach these recipes as you should any recipe— with a good dose of common sense.

Although volume measures are provided in this book, cooking by weight is a more accurate method and how I cook, so I give those measures too, as often as it's appropriate. In several recipes where a specific amount of salt is required, only a weight measure is given. (Note that the recipes in this book use sea salt, because it has the best flavor and is free of additives.) I strongly advise buying a kitchen scale if you don't already own one.

It's always a good idea to think carefully about what you buy, cook, and eat, and to know where it comes from. Start with fresh, high-quality products, and you will be on the way to eating well in every sense of the word. This philosophy is of utmost importance when cooking with odd bits. Where your animal comes from, how it has been raised, and what it has eaten will all affect the quality of its meat, fat, and organs. Demand naturally raised animals from producers who care for their animals, because the health of the animals is of greatest importance when you are eating their organs—as is the proper handling of the organs and other odd bits after slaughter and before sale. Small farmers will often be very happy to sell you odd bits—they more than anyone know that their animals are not simply steaks and chops.

Some odd bits discussed in this book are not available in parts of North America, or are even banned for human consumption. Those odd bits I tested in France, with meat purchased in an inspected butcher shop, and I am still alive and healthy. It is right that the government should inspect and control our food system, but there are times when they are protecting us from something that will not harm us. The government might better spend some of our money educating us how to shop and use our common sense, rather than continuingly telling us what not to eat. Our senses of smell and touch and our eyes can tell us almost all we need to know about what's good for us, if we let them.

Take action: lobby for changes in regulations if misguided rules are making certain odd bits unavailable; ask your supplier, your butcher, or your farmer for these odd bits. Often availability is simply a question of demand. If nobody wants these cuts, then it is not worth the time to clean and prepare them for consumption. My wish is that all these cuts will become widely available again, and I encourage you to try making these dishes if you find yourself in a place where they are legally available.

We must educate ourselves, and we must educate our children—there is no point in their being computer literate and food illiterate. Food is a rich, sensual pleasure as important to a culture as poetry or music. Cooking and eating are the heart of a civilization: they shape and express us. We must take back the responsibility for what we cook and eat. Relax, enjoy, and celebrate food and—most importantly—*cook*.

Sourcing Odd Bits

It is not very helpful to list butchers or suppliers in certain towns or cities: that is way too specific for a book that I hope has no borders. Instead, I want to encourage you to find your own sources. I am adamant about seeking out local butchers. We need more quality butchers and the way to achieve that is by supporting them. If there are no butchers in your area, don't give up; there are other options. Visit local farmers' markets; their numbers are growing steadily everywhere, and there are now over 6,000 in the United States. Talk to the farmers and tell them what you are looking for. Don't be afraid to ask for odd bits: they will be more than happy to have a market for them. Order what you want in advance so they can arrange with the abattoir to put them aside for you. Perhaps if you live near an abattoir, you can call them and ask if they know where you can source odd bits. They probably will give you the names of local farmers. Talk to the chef at your favorite restaurant. Many chefs are now buying whole animals; perhaps they will sell the odd bits they can't put on their menu because they don't have enough, or they can connect you with their supplier. Join a group like Slow Food and just ask around. My friend Ray lives a couple of hours outside of Toronto, and his neighbor raises a few heritage breed pigs. Every year Ray buys a whole pig. The pigs are sent to the local abattoir, where they are killed and broken down, but Ray doesn't want the odd bits and is happy to give them to me (perhaps I'll send him a copy of this book). Be creative, ask, demand, and insist. The way odd bits will return to our markets and butcher shops is if we ask for them.

Guidelines for Choosing Odd Bits

How an animal is raised, slaughtered, butchered, and aged all are important factors in the final quality of its odd bits. Unfortunately, these are difficult parameters to judge by just looking. You need a butcher or supplier that you can trust and build a relationship with. How to tell? Well, there are several good clues. Do they handle their products with care and respect? Are they knowledgeable and willing to answer questions? Can they offer advice and suggest alternative cuts? Are they willing to source unusual odd bits for you? Do they slaughter the animals themselves, or have a good relationship with the abattoir, so that they can fulfill any special requests? For your part in the relationship, you must be flexible and willing to make substitutions when buying odd bits. Most of the recipes in this book can be made with several different cuts from the same animal; help your supplier out by buying cuts that others overlook.

Inform yourself and use common sense when shopping. Odd bits should smell clean and pleasantly meaty. They should have a good color and be moist but not wet and sticky, and they should not be drowning in pools of blood.

The final proof is in the eating. Was it flavorful? Demand more from suppliers and you'll be rewarded.

Linguistic Notes for Odd Bits Recipes

While we speak all English, in the kitchen we often have different words for the same thing.

Arugula = Rocket
Beet = Beetroot
Broiler = Grill
Corned beef = Salt beef
Fava beans = Broad beans
Ground meat = Minced meat
Headcheese = Brawn
Heavy cream = Double cream

Once you knock an animal on the head it is only polite to eat the whole animal.
FERGUS HENDERSON

ONE

Get a Head: Challenging

Have you ever noticed that in most diagrams depicting meat cuts the animals are headless? For most of us, the thought of staring down a decapitated animal head in our kitchen is unnerving, a too-tangible reminder that meat comes from a living, breathing animal. However, the head is one of the best parts of the animal. It is not simply an odd bit but a cornucopia of them. Here you find the eyes, ears, cheeks, brain, and tongue—all unique in flavor and texture.

Heads Up

There is no denying that an animal's head is a powerful symbol. It demonstrates man's mastery over beast—that's why the hunter hangs it over the fireplace. In medieval England, the boar's head took pride of place on royal tables, and in many cultures the head is offered to an honored guest or to the most revered member of the family. Today animal heads rarely make it into our kitchens, let alone onto our tables. However, cooking and eating it, either whole or in parts, represents not our mastery over the animal, but our respect for it.

I want to introduce you to the pleasures of the head by showing you how to cook it whole; later in the chapter we'll learn how to cook its parts. While cooking a whole animal head may seem off putting, it is easier than you think: just simmer it until the meat falls off the bone. Once the skull is discarded, the head is less intimidating, and easier to eat. You can enjoy it in a soup or a stew, or make headcheese (page 17). Even if you don't fancy eating the head, you will have a useful, rich, gelatinous stock. If you're adventurous, you can tackle roasted pig's head, with its crunchy skin and fatty, succulent meat (page 20); if you're not so bold, start with one of the head's parts—the cheeks, meaty muscles made for braising, are a good place to begin. From there, you can tackle tongue, brain, and ear, and then eventually a whole head, perhaps as headcheese, will make it to your table.

How to Choose

I've never been stared down by a whole cow's head, and only a few calf's heads have looked me in the eye. Both are more common as a collection of parts: cheeks, brains, and tongues. While in Europe boned and rolled calf's head already cooked and ready to eat is a common sight, the choice of whole heads on this side of the Atlantic is more limited. In North America, it is pig, sheep, goat, or one that is still attached when you buy a whole small animal, like a rabbit or squab. As whole heads can be difficult to source, this chapter will give plenty of recipes for the tasty parts that make up the head.

> . . . the fleshy parts of a head are exquisitely tender . . . the memory of its surpassing succulence remains with one just as the recollection of the bouquet, aroma and flavor of an exquisite wine stays with one through the years, stimulating the longing for a repetition of so perfect an experience in degustation.
>
> C. LOUIS LEIPOLDT

The most readily available head is a pig's head, so in this part of the chapter I have concentrated on it—no hardship, as it is one of the best to cook: meaty and delicious. But all cleaned heads can be cooked using the same methods, and you can make headcheese using the head of a sheep, goat, or rabbit, or you could mix the meats from different animals. Check Sourcing Odd Bits (page 10) for suggestions on where to buy a whole head.

It's important to understand how the head is processed. After killing, animals (with the exception of pigs and sometimes calves) are skinned, and this removes their ears and eyelids. The result is a fearsome expression with the eyes staring and often the teeth bared. Pigs keep their skin, and are scalded whole in a tub of boiling water and then scrubbed to remove their hair. So whole pig heads

ready for sale still have their ears and eyelids. This gives them a more benign expression, with eyes closed as if they were sleeping. Occasionally, pig's heads are skinned if the abattoir lacks a scalding tank big enough to process them. Avoid these heads, as two of the best parts of a pig's head are the skin and the ears.

Before you buy a head, decide how you are going to cook it, and check out the size of the pot or pan you intend to use. Heads come in all sizes, but it is often hard to judge if it will fit, so take a tape measure with you to the butcher's. The practical approach is to ask your butcher to split the head in half, making sure he removes the tongue in one piece first. Once the head is split, you can easily remove the brain (see page 40), but if you are squeamish, ask him to take it out for you. He can also remove the eyes if they bother you; I usually just leave them as for some they are a tasty treat (see page 63).

If you're poaching the head, it is often more practical to have your butcher cut it again, into quarters along its jaw line. Pigs often have long jaws, and you may discover that while half a head will fit in your pot the snout will be bobbing above the surface of the liquid.

How to Prepare and Cook

Cleaning the head is the most important step. No matter how well a pig's head is scalded and cleaned at the abattoir, there will be still be a few hairs, especially around the mouth, the chin and in the ears. The best way to remove them is by singeing or shaving, or a combination of the two. A propane torch is fairly standard kitchen equipment these days, but if you don't have one in the kitchen you'll probably have one in the garage. It's the perfect tool for burning off any hair. Simply singe the hair with the torch and then rub it off with a towel (the only downside of this method is the unpleasant smell of burnt hair). You could also hold the head over a gas flame to singe any stray hairs. To shave a pig, a razor is the best tool—just use a disposable one, as it will be full of pork skin when you finish. No shaving cream is required. Less pleasant is cleaning the pig's ears, but it must be done. Simply take a damp paper towel and wipe the ears out thoroughly.

As sheep's and goat's heads are skinned, they are usually devoid of hair and ears. Thus they are less work, but you should still check to make sure there are no stray hairs. Whatever animal you are using, give the head a very good rinse under cold running water, and pat dry. Soaking the head in salted water for several hours is also a good way to clean it and draw out any blood, but if you plan to brine the head, you can skip this step.

A pig's head with its fatty skin is perfect for roasting, but more commonly heads are poached and then made into head cheese.

Headcheese: Nothing Cheesy About It

While heads make great stock, a better way to appreciate their multitextured meat is in head-cheese. *Fromage de tête*, headcheese, *coppa di testa*, brawn, and *Presskopf* are all terms for cooked head meat pressed into a mold or formed into a sausage. It's usually made with a pig's head, but the head meat from cows, sheep, calves, or even rabbits can be used for headcheese.

But why do we call it headcheese? Your first thought might be that it is a sort of culinary duplicity intended to make this dish more acceptable. Well, I am not sure how appetizing the term headcheese is, and anyway you'd be wrong. To understand this strange name we must look to the French, who also call it headcheese, *fromage*

de tête. In the French language, the word *fromage* comes from the Latin *forma*, which does not signify cheese itself but rather how cheese is made. To make and shape cheese, the curds are pressed into a basket or a pierced wooden frame called a *forma*; the term *fromage* was applied to anything pressed into a mold. For example, in eighteenth-century France, *fromage glacé* was not cold cheese but molded ice cream. Perhaps to be clearer we should have adopted the German *Presskopf*, which means "pressed head," but we did not, and *headcheese* in all its oddity is now commonly used in English-speaking countries.

> If we are going to live on other inhabitants of this world we must not bind ourselves with illogical prejudices, but savor to the fullest the beasts we have killed. Why is it worse, in the end, to see an animal's head cooked and prepared for our pleasure than a thigh or a tail or a rib?
> M. F. K. FISHER

In England, however, the word often used is "brawn," and it has an even more complicated lineage. It is a German word, and it arrived in England with the Normans, who used it to describe a rich dish of wild boar meat. The meat wasn't set in jelly but packed into a pot and covered with verjuice (see page 19). Later, fat replaced the verjuice and the dish resembled rillettes or potted meat. As wild boar became scarce in England, pork was substituted, and by the eighteenth century, jelly had replaced the fat. Thus brawn became a mixture of pig's head meat set in jelly.

Today the term headcheese covers any cooked meat set in a mold with a jelly. It can be head meat, feet, or hocks. Craig Claiborne in his *New York Times Cookbook* has a recipe for "mock-headcheese," where pork hocks replace the head meat and, in Claiborne's opinion, create a more palatable experience. I don't agree.

Headcheese for the Unconvinced

This is a great way to begin cooking the whole head—it is straightforward to make; it just takes time. This recipe is for everyone who thinks they don't like head-cheese. There is no melting tongue, pieces of chewy skin, or crunchy ears; instead there are just pieces of meat and carrots set in a well-flavored jelly made from the cooking liquid. Try it: if you like it you may be ready for the next step, Advanced Headcheese (page 19).

The inspiration for this recipe was in Jane Grigson's *Charcuterie and French Pork Cookery*, a book many people unfortunately overlook when it comes to cooking piggy odd bits. This recipe makes one terrine, and unless you are running a restaurant, you probably don't want two terrines of headcheese (if you do, just double the recipe). Half a pig's head should yield enough to fill a six-cup / one and half-liter loaf pan, but it is hard to accurately estimate, as yield depends on the size of the head.

Treat this recipe as a satisfying project to spread over several days. Start by brining the head for at least two days, but preferably three; then take a day to cook and make the headcheese—though this, too, is better split up over two days. Then the cooking liquid can sit overnight in the refrigerator, making it easy to remove the excess fat. The brain and tongue can be used in other recipes but cook the ear along with the head as it adds extra gelatin. If you want to try the ear see page 23. Dijon mustard, cornichons, and crusty bread are classic accompaniments for headcheese. Some devotees eat it with just a drizzle of vinegar; I prefer verjuice and a peppery salad like watercress. You can also serve it with the Vinaigrette for Porky Bits or Salad (page 105).

1/2 pig's head, about 6 pounds / 2.75 kg, prepared (see page 14), brain and tongue removed

1 pig's trotter, prepared and split (see page 100)

1 gallon / 4 l All-Purpose Brine (page 22)

2 onions, quartered

6 cloves

2 carrots, peeled and cut in half crosswise

4 stalks celery, sliced

1 small fennel bulb, chopped

1 head garlic, unpeeled and halved crosswise

1 lemon, halved

2 fresh bay leaves

6 stems flat-leaf parsley

6 sprigs fresh thyme

1/4 teaspoon black peppercorns, crushed

6 juniper berries, crushed

1 1/2 teaspoons quatre épices (see page 28)

2 1/2 cups / 625 ml Bouillon Jelly (page 108)

1 1/2 teaspoons fine sea salt

3 tablespoons chopped chives

1 tablespoon chopped fresh tarragon

2 teaspoons red wine vinegar

Freshly ground black pepper

Cut off the ear and place it with the head and foot in the brine, making sure the meat is submerged, and refrigerate for at least 2 days and preferably 3 days.

Remove the head, ear and foot from the brine, rinse under cold running water, and place in a large stockpot. Cover with cold water and bring to a boil over medium heat. Drain, discard the water, and place all the pork bits in a clean pot. Insert a clove into 6 of the onion quarters and add to the pan with the remaining 2 onion quarters, carrots, celery, fennel, garlic, lemon, bay leaves, parsley, and thyme.

Tie up the peppercorns and juniper berries in a piece of muslin (or put them in a tea ball) and add to the pot. Pour in enough cold water to cover

continued

the head and bring slowly to a boil over medium heat. Skim the liquid and simmer, uncovered, skimming from time to time for about 3 hours or until the meat is very soft and falling off the bone; check the ear at 1 1/2 hours as it will cook quicker (see page 23). Once it is cooked, remove and set it aside for another recipe.

Remove the meat from the liquid and set aside to cool slightly. Strain the cooking liquid into a clean pan, setting aside the carrots but discarding the other vegetables, herbs, and spices (though don't forget to rescue your tea ball). Bring the liquid to a boil over medium heat and boil, skimming often, until it is reduced to 6 cups / 1.5 l.

While the cooking liquid is reducing, and as soon as the head is cool enough to handle, get to work separating the meat from the bones. First cut out the eyeball and either be adventurous or discard it. Remove and discard the skin. When it comes to the snout, you may want to discard the whole thing, but if you're up for a challenge, set it aside. You can serve it cold, thinly sliced with Vinaigrette for Porky Bits or Salad (page 105).

> *With just one hog's head, you'll find yourself standing in the middle of a playground of culinary opportunities.*
> RYAN ADAMS

Separate the meat from the bones, cartilage, and fat, removing any gristle or sinews as you go. When the meat has cooled, cut it into irregular pieces ranging from 1/4 to 3/4 inch / 6 mm to 2 cm. Measure the pieces—you'll want about 3 1/2 cups / 875 ml so there will be room for the carrots—and place them in a large bowl, add the *quatre épices* and toss together. Cut the carrots into about 1/2-inch / 1-cm pieces and place in another bowl; cover both bowls. Strain the reduced liquid into a measuring cup and leave to cool. Refrigerate the meat, carrots, and cooking liquid overnight.

The next morning, remove the bowls and the measuring cup from the refrigerator. Remove the fat from the top of the jellied liquid and set the fat aside for another use.

Now you have a choice—you can make the Bouillon Jelly or use the jellied liquid as is. (You have put this much time in so I suggest you take the extra step).

Pour the warm bouillon jelly into a measuring cup. Whisk in 1 teaspoon of the salt, chives, tarragon, vinegar, and pepper. Pour over the diced meat and stir to mix—you will probably need your hands to separate the cold meat. When it is well mixed, stir in the carrots, and taste the mixture; it must be well seasoned as the headcheese is eaten at room temperature. Add the remaining salt if necessary and taste again. It should taste a touch too salty. Place the meat mixture in the refrigerator for 30 minutes, or until the liquid just begins to thicken.

Meanwhile line a 6-cup / 1.5-l loaf pan with a double thickness of plastic wrap, letting the plastic overhang the pan on all sides.

Stir the mixture and check the seasoning again, and then spoon it into the prepared pan, pushing down on the meat pieces. Tap the pan hard on the counter to expel any air bubbles and refrigerate until set.

Pulling gently on the plastic wrap, ease the headcheese from the mold. Place it on a board and, using a bread knife, cut it into 3/4-inch / 2-cm slices. Headcheese is easier to slice when it is cold; however, it must be served at room temperature. Place the slices on serving plates, cover with squares of plastic wrap and leave at room temperature for about 30 minutes.

You can mold the headcheese in any container. I like to use a loaf pan because it yields even slices, but a bowl or cake pan will work too.

Advanced Headcheese

Now, if you are a true headcheese lover, you'll want some soft tongue, crunchy ears, and chewy skin in the mix. This is a variation of the main headcheese recipe, following the same method but adding in those other treasures found in the head. Ask your supplier to remove the whole tongue before cutting the head in half, and make sure the head comes with ears. (Sometimes they are missing—is there perhaps a passionate pig's ear lover in my local abattoir?) If they're missing, you can usually buy ears separately. When you include an ear, a tongue, and the skin, you'll end up with more meat, so make two molds or a large one. I don't add the carrots, and I pack in the meat, skin and cartilage and add less jelly, but it's your choice as to the mix.

Proceed as for Headcheese for the Unconvinced (page 17) but add the tongue to the brine. You can add the poached brain to the cooked head meat, but I prefer to keep it for another recipe. Check the ear and tongue from time to time as they cook quicker, removing the ear when the skin starts to come away from the cartilage and the tongue when a skewer pierces it easily, about 1¹/₂ to 2 hours. Remember to peel the tongue as soon as you can handle it (see page 50) and cut it into chunks. Slice the ear in half lengthwise, then slice it thinly crosswise. Set the ear and tongue aside to add to the cooked head meat mixture.

> *The boar's head was also a usual dish of feudal splendour. In Scotland it was sometimes surrounded with little banners, displaying the colors and the achievements of the baron at whose board it was served.*
> PINKERTON'S *HISTORY OF SCOTLAND*

When the rest of the head is cooked, proceed as in Headcheese for the Unconvinced, adding the diced tongue and sliced ear. Cut the snout, and some of the skin into small pieces and add them too. The amount of these tasty but challenging odd bits you add to the mix is up to you. The best headcheese is made from different-sized and different-textured pieces. However, it is good the first time to keep these more challenging pieces small.

VERJUICE AND CORNICHON

Verjuice and *cornichon* are two French words that have entered the Anglo-Saxon cooking lexicon. Verjuice, or "green juice," is usually made from unfermented sour grapes, but sometimes crabapples or unripe fruit are used instead. A common ingredient in European cooking during the Middle Ages, verjuice remained popular in France but fell out of favor elsewhere, its place taken by lemon juice and vinegar. While tart like lemon juice and acidic like vinegar, verjuice is subtler in flavor. A verjuice renaissance is underway, and this once hard-to-find ingredient is now available in fine food stores. While working on this book, I was given a bottle and discovered it is perfect to serve with headcheese; but you can always use a mild vinegar instead.

Cornichon is the French word for a small, tart, crunchy gherkin. They typically accompany charcuterie, cold meats, terrines, and pâtés, their acidity and crunch providing a perfect foil for the rich, fatty meat.

Roasted Pig's Head with Spiced Glaze

SERVES 2 OR 3

This is a dish for fat and skin lovers—and as close as I'll ever get to a roasted boar's head on my table. Although a head looks big, it will only serve two or three people, as there is a lot of bone, and it's best shared with a friend or two who are not afraid to eat with their fingers. The crispy skin, crunchy ear, delectable cheek, and sweet, juicy fat are all part of the joy of eating a pig's head. It makes a rich, delicious, and filling meal. Serve with small boiled new potatoes.

The hardest part of this recipe is finding a roasting pan big enough to fit the head snugly. There will be more than enough glaze, but it keeps for two months refrigerated and is delicious on the Glazed Grilled Pig's Ear (page 28) or roast pork belly.

1/2 pig's head, about 6 pounds / 2.75 kg, prepared (see page 14), brain and tongue removed

2 to 3 tablespoons lard

2 Vidalia or other sweet onions, halved and thickly sliced

6 cloves garlic

1 small bunch fresh thyme

4 large sprigs rosemary

4 juniper berries, crushed

4 cups / 1 l Court Bouillon (see opposite) or Poultry Stock (page 233)

4 cardamom pods

2 star anise, broken into pieces

1 tablespoon coriander seeds

1 small dried red chile

1/2 cup / 125 ml honey

2 tablespoons white wine vinegar or verjuice

Coarse sea salt and freshly ground black pepper

1 bunch watercress, trimmed

Pat the head dry and place on a baking sheet, uncovered, overnight in the refrigerator. This helps dry the skin so it will crisp up in the oven.

Remove the head from the refrigerator and preheat the oven to 350°F / 180°C.

Place a roasting pan over medium heat, add 2 tablespoons of the lard and cook the onions, stirring until the onions begin to color, adding more lard only if necessary.

Remove the pan from the heat and add the garlic, thyme, rosemary, and juniper. Place the head on the onions. Set 1/2 cup / 125 ml of the court bouillon aside and pour in enough of the remaining court bouillon so that it laps around the edges of the head—the amount of liquid you add will depend on your pan size. Cover the ear with a piece of aluminum foil, then cover the head with a piece of wet parchment paper and transfer to the oven. Cook for 2 1/2 hours, or until the skin and meat shrink from the bone and the internal temperature reaches 160°F / 71°C on an instant-read thermometer inserted in the cheek.

Meanwhile, make the glaze. In a small frying pan over medium heat, toast the cardamom, star anise, coriander, and chile until aromatic, about 1 minute. Crush the spices slightly using a mortar and pestle, then put them in a small saucepan, add the honey, and bring to a boil over medium heat. Boil hard for 3 to 5 minutes, until the froth turns dark and the honey begins to caramelize. Remove the pan from the heat and carefully pour in the reserved 1/2 cup / 125 ml of the court bouillon. The honey will spit and sputter. Stir to mix, then reheat gently, stirring to dissolve the honey, and simmer for 10 minutes. Let cool slightly and strain into a bowl, discarding the spices. The glaze can be made up to a week in advance, allow to cool and store in the refrigerator.

Increase the oven temperature to 400°F / 200°C. Remove and discard the parchment paper.

Brush the head with the honey glaze, and cook for another 20 minutes or until dark golden, basting 2 to 3 times with the glaze.

Preheat the broiler to high.

Transfer the head to a baking sheet; cut off the ear and place it next to the head. To make the sauce, strain the cooking liquid into a bowl and let stand for 5 minutes. Skim off the fat and set the fat aside for another use. Pour the liquid into a saucepan and bring to a boil over high heat, and continue to boil until reduced by half, then remove from the heat. Meanwhile broil the head and ear, watching carefully and removing them when the skin begins to puff and crackle. Place the head and ear on a carving board and cover loosely with aluminum foil to keep warm.

Add the vinegar to the sauce and season with salt and pepper. Taste the sauce and adjust it to your taste, add salt and a bit more vinegar to balance out the richness of the meat and the sweetness of the glaze if needed. Return the sauce to medium-low heat and stir in the watercress and cook just until it wilts.

For adventurous diners, you can place the whole head on a platter and serve the sauce separately: it's fun to attack the head with a knife and your fingers. Or you can remove the skin from the head and cut it into pieces. Then cut off the meat and slice it into chunks, removing as much or as little fat as you like. Slice the ear thinly. Place all the meat, fat, and ear slices on a warmed serving platter, pour over the sauce and watercress, and garnish with the pieces of skin.

Court Bouillon

MAKES 4 CUPS / 1 L

This liquid is very useful for cooking everything from delicate brains to gelatinous pig's feet. Simmering the bouillon for twenty minutes before adding the odd bits infuses the flavors into the water. This precooking is important when poaching brains and sweetbreads, but when cooking for pig's feet or ears there is no need to simmer it first.

This recipe is flexible; you can replace the lemon zest with lime to match the flavors in the final dish for Sumac Encrusted Lamb's Brains (page 41), or use orange for the Cheese and Just a Little Brain Fritters (page 42).

5 cups / 1.25 l water
1 carrot, peeled and sliced
1 shallot sliced
1 stalk celery
Large strip of lemon zest
2 tablespoons freshly squeezed lemon juice

2 star anise
One 5-inch / 13-cm cinnamon stick
1 large sprig thyme
1 fresh bay leaf
10 black peppercorns
4 cloves
Coarse sea salt (optional)

Place the water, carrot, shallot, celery, lemon zest and juice, star anise, cinnamon, thyme, and bay leaf in a saucepan. Bring to a boil over medium heat, skim, and add the peppercorns and cloves. Lower the heat, cover, and simmer for 20 minutes. Remove from the heat, let cool and strain, discarding the solids.

If using for an odd bit that hasn't been salted or brined, like brains, add about 1 teaspoon of coarse sea salt.

All-Purpose Brine

This recipe should make enough brine for half a pig's head weighing 6 pounds / 2.75 kg; half the recipe will be enough for a beef tongue weighing 3 pounds / 1.4 kg or the equivalent weight of pork or lamb tongues. If you want your cooked meat to have a rosy hue, add 3/4 ounce / 25 g of pink curing salt (see page 57) to this recipe.

8 ounces / 225 g coarse sea salt

1 cup / 61/4 ounces /180 g brown sugar

1 tablespoon toasted coriander seeds, crushed

1 tablespoon black peppercorns, crushed

1/2 teaspoon allspice berries, crushed

1/2 teaspoon juniper berries, crushed

4 cloves garlic, crushed

4 large sprigs fresh thyme

4 fresh bay leaves

1 gallon / 4 l water

Place the salt, sugar, coriander, peppercorns, allspice, juniper, garlic, thyme, and bay leaves in a saucepan. Add 8 cups / 2 l of the water, then place over medium heat and bring to a boil, stirring to dissolve the salt and sugar. Boil for 2 minutes, then remove from the heat. Pour into a glass container, add the remaining water and leave to cool completely.

Now the brine is ready to use. Thoroughly rinse the odd bit to be brined, pat dry, and place in the brine following the recipe instructions.

BRINING

Brining, or soaking food in heavily salted water, is a very old method for preserving and curing foods. The meat is submerged, for hours or days, depending on its weight, in a salt solution, and during this time osmosis occurs, increasing the amount of liquid inside the meat's cells. The result is a juicier, more flavorful piece of meat. While brine is simply a mixture of water and salt, most brines are balanced by the addition of sugar and enhanced with herbs and spices.

Use a nonreactive container for brining, such as a glass or stainless steel bowl or even a plastic bucket. The container must be large enough to submerge the odd bit completely in the brining solution, but small enough to fit in your refrigerator. Try to find one that is just wide enough to hold the meat—if the meat fits snugly in the container, you don't have to add as much brine. To estimate how much brine to make, place the odd bit you want to brine in the container and pour over enough cold water to cover. Remove the odd bit, then pour the water into a measuring jug. You can brine several odd bits in the same brine.

Your brining solution must be cold before you pour it over the meat, and you may have to weight down the meat with a plate and a weight so it's totally submerged. (I've found plastic containers filled with water or stones work well as weights). Cover the container with plastic and refrigerate for:

1/2 to 1 day for pork or lamb tongues

2 days for pig's ears and tails

2 to 3 days for calf's or beef tongue

2 to 3 days for split pig's head and feet

When you remove the meat from the brine, rinse the meat well under cold water and discard the brine.

Lend Me Your Ears

Ears deserve special consideration because of their amazing texture—and I am talking about pig's ears, because they're the only ears I've been able to buy, cook, and eat. What I love about my Paris market is that I can buy pig's ears fresh, salted, and, best of all, already cooked. My favorites are the ears that have been slowly cooked on the rotisserie, along with hocks and other assorted porky pieces. The juices drip leisurely onto the potatoes that sit in pans underneath, making them almost as tasty as the ears. The ears are crisp, burnt to just the right amount at the edges: all in all, the perfect take-out food.

While not the meatiest part of the pig (most of the meat is at the base of the ear where it joins the head), ears make up for their lack of flesh with their unique texture—a wonderful contrast between skin and cartilage. The skin is either crisp when roasted or softly chewy when poached, and either way it sandwiches the crunchy cartilage. You'll love it or hate it—there is no middle ground with pig's ears. If you fall into the cartilage-hating camp, please don't ignore ears altogether. Add them to a pork stew or a split pea soup, where they'll add flavor and body. If you love the contrast, your hardest decision will be whether to eat them soft or crisp.

How to Choose

Whether the ears come separately or with the head, try to buy ears that look clean, with little residual hair. Fresh ears should be light pink in color and feel lightly moist. They'll vary in size with the age of the pig.

Perhaps you cannot make a silk purse out of a sow's ear, but you can make some tasty hors d'oeuvres or a supper dish.
CALVIN SCHWABE

How to Prepare and Cook

If there are any hairs, either singe or shave them off and check that the ears are clean inside (see page 15). Ears can be brined for 2 days, but just a simple salting works well. I sprinkle each ear with about 2 teaspoons Spiced Seasoning Salt (page 28) and refrigerate them in a nonreactive dish for one to two days before poaching them in Court Bouillon (page 21). Simmer the ears until they are tender and the skin just starts to come away from the cartilage, about 1 1/2 to 2 hours.

de bouche à oreille: literally, "from the mouth to the ear"; by word of mouth

Let them cool a little in the bouillon, then transfer to a board. Make a small cut at the base of the ear, or if they are big, cut them in half lengthwise. Place them on a piece of parchment paper in a pie plate and cover with a second piece of parchment and another pie plate. Place a weight on top and refrigerate overnight. Flattening the ear will making it easier to cook on the grill. Reserve the cooking liquid to use in sauces or as a base for soup. Cooked ears can be refrigerated for several days or frozen for several months.

Poached ears can be added to salads and headcheese, or they can be cooked a second time, by roasting or grilling, to give them another layer of texture and crunch.

Cold Pig's Ear Salad

SERVES 3 OR 4

This is a simple salad of sliced cooked ear and vegetables. The only trick to making it is to spend the time finely dicing the celery and carrot. When the ears are cold, they are soft and chewy, with the cartilage and the raw vegetables adding crunch.

1 poached pig's ear (see page 23), thinly sliced

1/4 cup peeled and finely diced carrot

1/4 cup finely diced celery, including the leaves

2 tablespoons finely diced shallot

1 tablespoon small capers, rinsed

1 tablespoon red wine vinegar

1 tablespoon Dijon mustard

Coarse sea salt and freshly ground black pepper

1/4 cup / 60 ml extra virgin olive oil

Place the sliced ear in a salad bowl. Add the carrot, celery, shallot, and capers. Whisk together the vinegar and mustard and season well with salt and pepper. Slowly whisk in the oil, pour over the salad, and toss well. Serve at room temperature.

Twice-Cooked Pig's Ear Salad

SERVES 4 AS AN APPETIZER

I spent a lot of time trying to find a way to crisp up the pig's ears for this salad. The recipe is a variation of hot bacon or pancetta dressing, using pig's ears. There are two problems with cooking slices of pig's ear in a frying pan: they explode and pop with the heat; and, as you stir them, their gelatinous qualities cause the pieces to stick to each other and form a great sticky mess. Some recipes suggest deep-frying them. I tried it—scary and dangerous. The ears explode in the oil with a loud bang, usually just when you are looking in to see how they are going. So the answer I came up with is a twice-cooked ear and a splatter screen. If the ear has been poached and grilled, the pieces don't spit as much, and they are less likely to stick together. Even so, use a splatter screen to protect you and your kitchen, and try to keep the pieces from touching.

1 large poached pig's ear (page 23), grilled

2 tablespoons lard or duck fat

10 to 12 cups / 2.5 to 3 l mixed salad greens

2 tablespoons dry white wine

2 tablespoons sherry vinegar

3 tablespoons extra virgin olive oil

Coarse sea salt and freshly ground black pepper

Slice the ear in half lengthwise and then cut it into thin slices. Melt the fat in a large frying pan over medium-low heat; when hot, add the ear slices in a single layer and cook, turning from time to time, until they become crisp on all sides, about 10 minutes. Use tongs and don't be tempted to stir the slices or they will stick to each other.

Meanwhile trim, rinse, and dry the salad greens, and then place them in a large salad bowl.

Using tongs, transfer the pig's ear slices to the salad bowl. Pour the wine and vinegar into the pan and stir to deglaze. Add the olive oil and season with salt and pepper. When the oil is warm, remove the pan from the heat and pour the dressing over the salad. Toss well and serve immediately.

HEADS AROUND THE WORLD

In South Africa, whole animal heads are part of the culinary tradition. The early twentieth-century Afrikaans journalist and poet C. Louis Leipoldt wrote about his country's culinary culture. In one passage, he vividly describes a dinner where an entire ox head, with its horns still attached, adorned the table. The horns were so large they spanned the length of the long table, and the head stared at the guests with its glazed eyes. However, more disturbing to Leipoldt was the ox's expression. During cooking the flesh around the mouth shrinks away from the teeth and gives the ox a sinister leer that, as Leipoldt noted, "no living ox could ever manage." The sight of this huge, leering ox head was so horrifying that several of the foreign guests left the table.

In his cookbook, *Cape Cookery,* Leipoldt gives detailed instructions on how to clean and cook a whole ox head—with the horns, of course. He explains that it takes a good day and a half and that you'll need a very large bread oven. I doubt many ox heads are cooked in South Africa today, but roasted sheep's head is a very popular dish. In the townships, hawkers cheekily call them "smileys" because, like the ox, they acquire a gruesome grin when cooked. From Turkey to Afghanistan, *kallah pacheh* or *kaleh pache* (*kaleh* meaning "head" and *pache* meaning "feet") is enjoyed as a quick snack at railway stations, or is a breakfast choice for commuters. In this dish, the sheep's head and its feet are slowly simmered to make a stew or soup, and served with lemon and cinnamon. Further north, in Norway, *smalahove*—sheep's head cooked with cabbage and potato—is a traditional Christmas dish, washed down with plenty of aquavit. Across the North

> I am not yet Scotchman enough to relish their singed sheep head's head and haggis.
> TOBIAS SMOLLETT

Sea in Scotland, sheep's head was a Sunday dinner favorite among middle-class families. On Saturdays, the local butcher would give away a sheep's head to his best customers, who handed it over to their cook to make *powsowdie* (*pow* meaning "head" and *sowdie* meaning "boiled"). Many Scots also believed that eating the head had medicinal benefits, and it became so popular that during the eighteenth century special clubs serving only sheep's head opened. In her early nineteenth-century book, *Cook and Housewife's Manual,* Meg Dods explains how to prepare it:

Choose a large, fat, young head. When carefully singed by the blacksmith, soak it and the singed trotters for a night, if you please, in lukewarm water. Take out only the glassy part of the eye . . .

Not a recipe for today, that: finding a butcher is hard enough, let alone a blacksmith; and not even I want to try dissecting the animal's eyeball.

While not as dramatic as Leipoldt's ox, the entire boar's head has long graced the British table. The boar's head was often on the menu of dinners served at English kings' and queens' weddings and coronations. In 1170, King Henry II acknowledged his son as heir apparent with a feast that included boar's head. Why a boar? Well, since pagan times, the ferocious and dangerous boar has been a highly symbolic animal, its death

> . . . if you buy a calf's head that has been carefully boned and rolled up and tied with string, a process that takes a lot of time and care, you know you are being given something that has been prepared by someone who doesn't cut corners. And if you go into a restaurant where calf's head is on the menu, you know that the cook is someone who cares about sharing fantastic flavours—because it would be much easier to do a burger and chips.
>
> GIORGIO LOCATELLI

signifying man's mastery of nature (its flesh is tasty, too). Over time, the boar's head became a dish for special occasions, and a Christmas tradition. Chaucer mentions it in his *Canterbury Tales,* and at Queen's College, Oxford University, founded in 1340, the custom of presenting the boar's head on a silver platter at Christmas continues today. It is heralded with trumpets and accompanied by the "Boar's Head Carol":

The boar's head in hand bring I,
Bedeck'd with bays and rosemary.
I pray you, my masters, be merry
As many as are in the feast.
The boar's head, as I understand,
Is the rarest dish in all this land,
Which thus bedeck'd with a gay garland
Let us serve with a song.
Our steward hath provided this
In honor of the King of Bliss;
Which, on this day to be served is
In the Queen's hall.

This tradition has spread far beyond Oxford's walls, to Canada and the United States. Alas, today it's more a nostalgic tribute to the past than a dish to eat. Usually a pig's head stands in for a boar's, and often it is not even cooked, but simply decorated with aspic. The head has black pickled-walnut eyes outlined with cooked egg white and tusks fashioned from celery sticks—hardly a ferocious sight, or even an appetizing one.

> You sit together with a bottle of wine, the sheep's head and a pocket knife and you cut off, well, an ear for an ear and an eye for an eye. The ears are crispy and a bit gooey: very nice. My husband likes to pluck out the eyes with a knife and pop them into his mouth. I'm not so keen but they are not like jelly, as you might think, but firm and chewy and delicious if you don't look too closely. The tongue and cheeks are also lovely.
>
> DINE VAN ZYL

Spiced Seasoning Salt

MAKES ABOUT 1/4 CUP / 11/4 OUNCES / 35 G

I use this mixture to season pork from belly to feet and tails. I like to grind the sea salt with the *quatre épices* to make a finer salt. If you don't have a spice grinder, use a fine sea salt and mix well with the *quatre épices*. Please weigh the salt for the best mixture. *Quatre épices* is a French seasoning mixture that varies according to the whim of the producer. Commonly it is a combination of white pepper, nutmeg, cloves, and ginger, but cinnamon and allspice are often included. While it does not have the same flavor, ground allspice can be substituted.

Store the salt mixture in a glass jar and use it as a rub on pork roasts or in place of kosher salt in pork recipes.

> 11/4 ounces / 35 g coarse sea salt
> 1 teaspoon quatre épices or ground allspice

Place the salt and *quatre épices* in a grinder and blend until well mixed and the salt is finely ground. Store in a tightly sealed glass jar.

Glazed Grilled Pig's Ear

SERVES 1 TO 2 PER PIG'S EAR AS AN APPETIZER

This is as close as I can get to those rotisserie ears sold in my Paris market. Adding the glaze makes this sweet, sticky grilled pig's ear into great summer barbecue food. Serve them as an appetizer, or with grilled sausages, ribs, and other delicious porky bits for less adventurous guests. Both glazes are delicious, or you could simply use your favorite barbecue sauce.

> 1/2 to 1 poached pig's ear (see page 23) per person
> Spiced Glaze (page 20) or Tamarind Glaze
> (page 155)

Remove the cooked ears from the refrigerator and let them warm up to room temperature.

Preheat the grill to medium-high and lightly grease.

Brush glaze on the ears and grill for 3 to 4 minutes, then turn and glaze again and continue to grill for another 3 to 4 minutes, until crisp and hot. Cut into thick slices and serve with some extra glaze for dipping.

You can also bake on a lightly greased baking sheet in a 425°F / 220°C oven for 20 minutes, brushing with glaze from time to time. I cover them with a metal splatter screen, as I hate cleaning the oven afterwards.

> *Most people balk at the idea of eating ears, but I love the contrast between the crunchy cartilage and the gelatinous skin.*
> ANISSA HELOU

Cheek by Jowl

| *... [cheeks] yield rich, savoury juices, [and] are a good choice to include in stews, pies, and sausages.*
| ALAN DAVIDSON

While I agree with Alan Davidson that cheeks are rich and savory, they really are too tasty to lose in a sausage or even a pie: they deserve to shine in their own dish. The cheek is one of the meatiest parts of the head, and it has many uses. Pork cheeks are often cut to include the animal's jowls, making a sizable piece of meat with a good quantity of fat. This cut is cured like ham or bacon and, in England, becomes Bath chaps, while in Italy they use it to make *guanciale*, a type of pancetta (see page 34).

The recipes in this section use only the fresh nuggets of skinless meat that are the actual cheeks. The cheek gets a lot of work and is tough and sinewy, but it is full of flavor and when slowly braised it becomes meltingly tender. As beef, veal, and pork cheeks become more mainstream in restaurants, they are being rescued from the grinder and are finding their way into the butcher's case. Many recipe writers will tell you that lamb and goat cheeks aren't worth bothering with; well, that's not true. These cheeks, though small, are tasty. The only problem is that you may have to cut them from the head yourself, and you'll need several heads to make a meal.

How to Choose

Although cheeks are often labeled as offal, because they come from the head, this odd bit is muscle meat, so select the pieces as you would any other meat. The cheeks are thick, roughly oval pieces of meat and, depending on your butcher, they will be more or less trimmed. Ideally they should have only a thin layer of fat on the outside. The inside of the cheek should be free of fat and silverskin, revealing the meat with bands of sinew running through it.

Their size and weight varies depending on how well they are prepared, so use your judgment. Well-trimmed beef and veal cheeks range from 3/4 to 1 1/3 pounds / 350 to 600 g per cheek, pork cheeks will be around 3 1/2 ounces / 100 g each, and lamb and goat cheeks are about 1 3/4 ounces / 50 g.

How to Prepare and Cook

If necessary, trim the cheeks, removing any excess fat and any flaps of meat from the edges of the cheeks to leave a solid piece of meat. Turn the cheeks over and remove all the silverskin and fat from the inside of the cheeks. The veins of sinew running through the cheeks will melt during cooking.

| *Cheek, the muscle that works the mouth and face, is really just another cut of meat ...*
| HUGH FEARNLEY-WHITTINGSTALL

Removing the cheeks from a split head yourself is not that difficult. Place the head on a cutting board cut side down. Using a boning knife or other small sharp knife, make a cut under the eye to the bone. Keeping your knife on the bone, cut down and around the edge of the mouth to the jawbone to lift off the cheek meat in one piece.

Pork, lamb, and goat cheeks are best cooked whole. With beef and veal, you can leave them whole or cut them into smaller pieces. Most importantly, you want even-sized pieces of meat that will all cook in the same amount of time.

Veal Cheeks with Swiss Chard and Olives

SERVES 6

Alessandro Stratta, a protégé of Alain Ducasse, inspired this dish. His recipe was complicated, so I kept the same elements and simplified it. This is in part a make-ahead dish: the flavors improve, and this will leave you time to make the Potato Gnocchi (page 38), which are definitely worth the effort, to accompany the cheeks.

Veal cheeks have more collagen than beef cheeks, so instead of half a calf's foot I add a piece of pork skin. Again, size matters: in France, I used six cheeks; in Canada, three large ones that I cut in half. As for the Swiss chard, you may have to buy two bunches to get enough stems for the recipe.

$^1/_4$ cup / 1 ounce / 30 g flour

Coarse sea salt and freshly ground black pepper

3 pounds / 1.4 kg trimmed veal cheeks

$^1/_4$ cup / 60 ml olive oil

2 onions, chopped

1 carrot, peeled and chopped

2 stalks celery with leaves, sliced

6 large sprigs fresh thyme

4 cloves garlic, germ removed

2 fresh bay leaves

1 cup / 250 ml dry white wine

2 cups / 500 ml Veal Stock (page 233)

A piece of pork skin, a little smaller than the lid of the casserole.

1 large bunch Swiss chard

2 plum (Roma) tomatoes

24 good quality black olives

Preheat the oven to 300°F / 150°C.

Place the flour in a shallow dish and season well with salt and pepper. Dip the cheeks into the seasoned flour to coat then pat to remove the excess.

In a heavy flameproof casserole or Dutch oven over medium-high heat, heat 2 tablespoons of the olive oil. When the oil is hot, add the cheeks in batches and brown, transferring to a plate as they brown. Add extra oil as needed.

Once the cheeks are browned, lower the heat and add the onions, carrot, and celery to the pan. Cook over medium heat, stirring, until the vegetables begin to color. Add the thyme, garlic, and bay leaves and pour in the wine. Bring it to a boil and deglaze the pan, using a wooden spoon to scrape up the browned bits from the bottom.

Add the stock and the cheeks with any juices and return to a boil. Cover with the pork skin and the lid, transfer to the oven, and cook for 2 hours. Uncover and continue to cook until the cheeks are very tender, 30 minutes to 1 hour.

Discard the pork skin and transfer the cheeks to a plate. Strain the liquid through a sieve, pressing on the vegetables to extract all the juice. You should have about 3 cups / 750 ml of liquid. Discard the vegetables and herbs and let the cheeks and cooking liquid cool separately. Cover and refrigerate them overnight.

Remove the meat and cooking liquid from the refrigerator. The liquid should be a firm jelly. Remove any fat from the top of the jelly and set the fat aside for another use. You can skip this next step, which does not change the taste but is a more sophisticated presentation (I did keep a couple of Chef Stratta's complications). Tip the jelly onto a board. There will be 3 layers: a clear layer in the center and cloudy ones at the top and bottom. Using a knife, cut the jelly into the three layers. Place the clear jellied layer, about 1 cup / 250 ml with the cheeks in an ovenproof dish and set 1 cup / 250 ml of the cloudy layers aside to flavor the chard. (Keep any remaining jelly to flavor a soup or stew.)

Preheat the oven to 300°F / 150°C.

Rinse the chard, then cut the leaves from the stalks. Finely slice the leaves and set aside. Trim the stems, and remove any coarse "strings," and slice the stems into 1-inch / 2.5-cm pieces. Core the tomatoes and cut a shallow cross on the bottom of each one.

> *Some of the best dishes in the world are made with humble pieces of meat that are collectively known as variety meats or offal.*
> TERENCE AND CAROLINE CONRAN

Bring a saucepan of water to a boil, add the tomatoes, blanch for about 30 seconds, then use a slotted spoon to transfer them to a bowl of ice water. Add some salt and the chard stems to the pan and blanch for 2 minutes or until just tender. Using a slotted spoon, transfer the chard stems to a bowl of ice water. Bring the water in the pan back to a boil, add the sliced chard leaves, and stir until wilted. Drain and refresh the leaves under cold running water.

Drain the chard stems and place the stems and leaves in an ovenproof dish. Add the reserved 1 cup / 250 ml of (cloudy) jellied sauce, and set aside. Cover the cheeks and transfer to the oven until heated through, about 30 minutes. After 20 minutes, place the dish of chard, uncovered, in the oven for the remaining 10 minutes to heat through.

Meanwhile, drain the tomatoes, then peel and halve them and remove the seeds. Cut the tomatoes into small dice and set aside. Pit the olives and set aside.

To serve, place a portion of cheek on a plate, add the Swiss chard, spoon over the sauce, and garnish with the diced tomato and olives.

Alternatives: Veal shank; pieces of veal shoulder or breast

SWISS CHARD (SILVER BEET)

Swiss chard is a very underappreciated vegetable. In North America, its wonderful, fat, tasty stalks are trimmed off and discarded in favor of the leaves. In Europe, the stems are more popular than the leaves, and there are many dishes that use only the stems.

In Australia, where I grew up, Swiss chard is called silver beet, a name I prefer. After all, it is a relative of the sugar beet, and while it now appears in rainbow colors, the stems of the original are silvery green. Its name is odd: the word *chard* is from the Latin word for "thistle," but Swiss chard is neither a thistle nor a native of Switzerland. I think we should follow the Australians' example and rename it silver beet.

When buying chard, look for bunches that have more substantial stalks, or try to convince your supplier not to cut them all off. Their great, earthy flavor is a perfect match with veal cheeks.

Wine-Braised Beef Cheeks

SERVES 6

A simple beef stew that allows the cheeks to be the star. I always cook an extra cheek so I can make ravioli or Salad of Beef Cheeks (page 34). The sauce is velvety thanks to the calf's foot; but this is optional, so if you can't buy a calf's foot, don't let it stop you from making the recipe—it will still be good.

I add the diced cooked foot back into the dish for another layer of texture, but it's an optional step. Serve this with pureed potatoes and/or celery root (celeriac).

- 3 cups / 750 ml red wine
- 1 onion, halved and sliced
- 2 carrots, peeled and diced
- 2 stalks celery with leaves, sliced
- 4 cloves garlic, germ removed
- 2 fresh bay leaves
- 1 large sprig rosemary
- 1/4 teaspoon black peppercorns
- 2 to 3 beef cheeks, about 3 pounds / 1.4 kg total, trimmed (see page 29)
- Coarse sea salt and freshly ground black pepper
- 2 tablespoons beef dripping or lard
- 1/2 calf's foot, about 1 pound / 450 g, prepared (see page 100) (optional)
- 2 teaspoons red wine vinegar
- 1/4 cup chopped flat-leaf parsley

Pour the wine into a large saucepan and bring it to a boil. Reduce the heat so the wine bubbles gently. Tip the saucepan slightly away from you and, using a long match, light the wine. Once the flames die out, light it again, and keep lighting it until it no longer flames. Pour the wine into a large bowl (there should be about 2 1/2 cups / 625 ml). Add the onion, carrots, celery, garlic, bay leaves, rosemary, and peppercorns. Set aside to cool.

Cut the beef cheeks into 2 or 3 pieces so that all the pieces are the same size. Place in the marinade, cover, and refrigerate overnight, turning a couple of times if possible.

Remove the cheeks from the marinade, pat them dry, and season with salt and pepper. Strain the marinade, keeping the liquid and the solids separate.

Preheat the oven to 300°F / 150°C.

In a heavy flameproof casserole or Dutch oven, melt half the fat over medium-high heat. When the fat is hot, add the cheeks in batches and brown. Transfer the cheeks to a plate. Lower the heat, add the vegetables, herbs, and peppercorns from the marinade, and cook, stirring, for 5 minutes, or until they soften.

Pour in the reserved marinade liquid and bring to a boil. Return the cheeks with any juices to the pan, add the calf's foot, and return to a boil. Cover the meat with a piece of wet parchment paper and the lid, transfer to the oven, and cook for 3 to 4 hours, or until the cheeks are very tender.

Transfer the cheeks and the foot to a plate. Strain the cooking liquid through a sieve into a bowl, pressing on the vegetables to extract all the juice; discard the solids. Let the cooking liquid stand for 5 minutes, then skim off the fat and set the fat aside for another use.

Return the cooking liquid to the pan and bring to a boil. Continue to boil until the liquid coats the back of a spoon. Meanwhile, cut the meat and skin from the calf's foot into small dice; discard the bones. Return the cheeks and diced foot to the reduced sauce and reheat gently. Add the vinegar and taste, adding more salt, pepper, and/or vinegar if necessary. Sprinkle with the parsley and serve.

Alternatives: Oxtail, beef shoulder, or shank

Salad of Beef Cheeks

SERVES 4 TO 6

My friend Franck is a photographer in Paris and also a very good cook. Best of all, he loves to try new and different recipes, from jelly made with the rose hips in his garden to shoulder of the wild boar that he killed while driving to his country house. Over a meal of my Wine-Braised Beef Cheeks (page 33), he gave me his recipe for beef cheek salad. I was so disappointed I had no leftovers that I now always cook an extra cheek when making wine-braised cheeks. If you have any leftover sauce from the cheeks, use it here in place of part of the stock. I like to use salad greens that stand up to the strength of the cheeks: members of the chicory family, curly endive, escarole, or even radicchio are perfect.

1 pound / 450 g cooked beef cheeks
1 cup / 250 ml Beef Stock (page 232)
8 to 10 cups / 2 to 2.5 l salad greens
1 tablespoon red wine vinegar
1 teaspoon Dijon mustard
Coarse sea salt and freshly ground black pepper
1/4 cup / 60 ml extra virgin olive oil
2 tablespoons diced dry-cured sausage
2 tablespoons diced cornichons
2 tablespoons chopped fresh tarragon

Cut the cheeks into 3/8-inch / 9-mm slices. Place the slices in a frying pan and pour over the stock. Place the pan over low heat and reheat the meat gently, turning the slices several times.

Meanwhile, trim, rinse, and dry the salad greens, and then place them in a large salad bowl.

Whisk the vinegar and mustard together and season with salt and pepper, then slowly whisk in the olive oil. Toss the greens with the dressing in a bowl, then add the sausage, cornichons, and tarragon and toss again. Pour over hot cheeks and sauce, toss again, and serve on warm plates.

Alternatives: Veal cheeks, oxtail

BATH CHAPS AND GUANCIALE

Pigs store fat in their cheeks, making their jowls an ideal cut for curing. According to Dorothy Hartley, the British cookery writer and social historian, the English specialty Bath chaps traditionally included the tongue and a piece of the lower jawbone. Today there is no longer any tongue or bone, and it resembles a cone cut in half. Bath chaps can be brined or smoked, then cooked and eaten hot or cold like a ham. The word *chap* comes from "chop," which, in the sixteenth century, referred to the cheeks and jaws of an animal. The connection with the English spa town of Bath is less clear, although the area around the town is well known for raising pork using the whey from cheese production.

The Italian version of Bath chaps is *guanciale*. A specialty of the town of Lazio in central Italy, *guanciale* is more strongly flavored and fattier than pancetta. It is an essential ingredient in *bucatini all'amatriciana* and can be used like pancetta or bacon to flavor everything from vegetables to beans.

Al's Pork Cheeks

SERVES 4

What do you cook for a chef? People are nervous to cook for me despite my good manners and appreciation of anything cooked with love and care. When my friend, renowned Kiwi chef and cookbook author Al Brown, and his friend, business partner, and sommelier, Steve Logan, came for dinner, I was stressed not only about the food but also the wine. (Then I decided to devote all my attention to the food and let my husband agonize over the wine choices.) I made these pork cheeks and guess what? It was the first time Al had eaten pork cheeks. He liked them so much he put pork cheeks on the menu of his Wellington restaurant Logan Brown. What I love about pork cheeks is that they are a perfect size—about 3 1/2 ounces / 100 g each, so there is no need to cut them. The calf's foot is optional, but your sauce will have a much better texture if you add it. If you don't you should reduce the sauce slightly. Serve with a pureed root vegetable or noodles.

3 onions, halved

1 clove

3 cups / 750 ml Pinot Noir

3 carrots, peeled

One 1-inch / 2.5-cm piece fresh ginger, peeled and sliced

1 small star anise

1 fresh bay leaf

1 large sprig thyme

1 large clove garlic, crushed

1/4 teaspoon black peppercorns

1/2 calf's foot, about 1 pound / 450 g, prepared (see page 100) (optional)

8 trimmed pork cheeks, about 1 3/4 pounds / 800 g

Coarse sea salt and freshly ground black pepper

2 tablespoons lard

Insert the clove into one onion half; add it and another onion half to the wine in a saucepan. Slice 1 of the carrots and add to the pan with the ginger, star anise, bay leaf, thyme, garlic, and peppercorns, and the calf's foot. Bring to a boil, skim, and simmer uncovered for 1 hour. Strain the liquid through a sieve, keeping the calf's foot and liquid and discarding the vegetables and spices.

Preheat the oven to 300°F / 150°C.

Slice the remaining onion halves and 1 of the remaining carrots. Pat the pork cheeks dry and season with salt and pepper. In a heavy flameproof casserole or Dutch oven, melt the lard over medium-high heat. When the fat is hot, add the cheeks in batches and brown them. Transfer the cheeks to a plate, lower the heat to medium, and add the sliced onions and carrot. Stir and cook until lightly colored.

Pour in the strained wine sauce and stir to deglaze the pan, using a wooden spoon to scrape up any browned bits from the bottom. Add the cheeks and any juices along with the calf's foot. Bring to a boil, cover the cheeks with a piece of wet parchment paper and the lid, and transfer to the oven. Cook for 2 1/2 hours, or until very tender.

Meanwhile, dice the remaining carrot and cook in boiling salted water until tender. Drain and refresh under cold running water.

Remove the cooked cheeks and keep warm. Strain the cooking liquid and check the seasoning. Return the cheeks to the pan and pour over the strained liquid. Add the cooked diced carrot and reheat gently.

Alternatives: Slices of pork shank or neck; pieces of pork shoulder

Giselle's Navarin

This dish reminds me of my friends Ted and Giselle, sadly no longer with us. I first met them on a bus trip around Greece. My girlfriend and I ended up on a bus full of French tourists, and the only ones who would talk to us were Ted and Giselle. They even shared their wine, a local vino called Bull's Blood. They'd learnt their English while working for American companies in the 1940s, and it was so full of wonderful slang that every time we talked I felt like I was in a black and white movie. I visited them often at their home in the suburbs of Paris, and I remember Giselle cooking me lamb *navarin*. *Navarin* can be made in the winter with mutton or lamb and winter vegetables, but I always think of it as a spring dish, thanks to Giselle and her *navarin printanier*. The word *navarin* is a French term for stew, and probably comes from the French for turnip (*navet),* because small white turnips are a popular vegetable in braised dishes. Whatever the word's origin, it sounds much better than "stew." I make this with twelve good-sized lamb cheeks; if you can't find lamb cheeks use neck or pieces of shoulder. If you are shelling your peas fresh, about 1 pound / 450 g peas in the pod should yield enough shelled peas.

12 lamb cheeks, about 1¼ pounds / 570 g total

Coarse sea salt and freshly ground black pepper

1 to 2 tablespoons rendered lamb fat or lard

2 carrots, peeled

1 onion, chopped

2 cups / 500 ml Lamb Stock (page 234)

2 plum (Roma) tomatoes, peeled, seeded, and chopped

2 cloves garlic, germ removed

1 large sprig rosemary

1 large stem flat-leaf parsley

2 medium-small turnips or 6 baby turnips

16 pickling onions

12 small new potatoes

1 tablespoon unsalted butter

1 tablespoon sugar

1 cup / 4½ ounces / 130 g shelled peas

Preheat the oven to 300°F / 150°C.

Pat the lamb cheeks dry and season well with salt and pepper.

In a heavy flameproof casserole or Dutch oven, melt the fat over medium-high heat. Brown the cheeks in batches and transfer to a plate. Meanwhile, coarsely chop 1 of the carrots. Lower the heat to medium, add the onion and chopped carrot, stir, and cook until the onion is well colored. Pour in the stock and bring to a boil, scraping the bottom to deglaze the pan. Add the tomatoes, garlic, rosemary, and parsley. Cover with a piece of wet parchment paper and the lid, and transfer to the oven and cook for 1½ hours.

While the lamb is cooking, cut the remaining carrot into 12 equal pieces and scrub the potatoes. Peel the turnips; cut each of the medium ones into 6 pieces, or the small ones in half. Bring a saucepan of water to a boil, add a generous pinch of salt and the carrot and potatoes, and simmer, uncovered, for 10 minutes. Add the turnips and continue to cook until all the vegetables are just tender, about 5 minutes. Using a slotted spoon, transfer the vegetables to a bowl of ice water.

Add the pickling onions to the pan and cook for 3 minutes, then refresh under cold water. Peel the onions, leaving enough of the roots intact to keep the onions whole. Cut the potatoes in half, then set the vegetables aside.

In a small frying pan over medium heat, melt the butter. Add the sugar and stir to dissolve, add the onions, and cook until they are brown and caramelized. If the onions begin to stick, add a spoonful of water. Set aside.

When the lamb is tender, remove it from the oven, discard the parchment paper, and transfer the cheeks to a plate. Strain the sauce through a sieve into a bowl, pressing to extract all of the flavor and juice from the vegetables. Discard the vegetables and pour the strained sauce back into the pan. Place on the stove over high heat, bring to a boil, and boil the sauce to reduce to just over 1 1/3 cups / 325 ml.

Return the cheeks to the pan and add the potatoes, carrots, turnips, onions, and peas. Cook over low heat until the peas are cooked and the vegetables are heated through.

Alternatives: Lamb shoulder, neck, or shank

Eating with children is a way of vicariously retasting the spectacular strangeness and mystery of food. Flora wanted to eat a sheep's head—my favourite stall. We sat on a bench, crammed in with taxi-drivers and slipper-sellers. In front of us, a chef in a pinny the color of the last sultan's soul hooked heads out of a babbling vat and dumped them on a greasy chopping board, then, with hot dexterous fingers, pulled them to bits, cheek by jowl! Crenellated jaws were disengaged. Strong, dark tongues were peeled and sliced. A handful of chopped, glutinous baa-baa bits were piled on paper napkins in front of us. Flat bread was dipped into thin soup. We sprinkled a mixture of salt and cumin, and drank tooth-meltingly sweet mint teas.
A. A. GILL

PARCHMENT PAPER

Parchment paper is a great way to protect the meat and keep the moisture in a dish. I wet the paper first so it softens and sits down on the meat. This also means I can just tear off a piece and don't have to cut it precisely to fit my pan. When the dish is cooked, I leave the parchment on top of the cooling meat to prevent the surface from drying out.

Potato Gnocchi

MAKES ABOUT 48; SERVES 4 AS A MAIN COURSE OR 6 AS A SIDE DISH

Sure, you don't have to go to the trouble of making these, but they are easy, and so much better than anything you can buy. My gnocchi never have that perfect oval shape with the distinct grooves that I see in restaurants or packaged products, but their taste trumps my lack of expertise in shaping them. I am sure if I made them every day for a month, I would perfect my technique, but that would be a lot of gnocchi eating.

Potatoes vary in size, but the recipe is forgiving: only add as much flour as you need to make the dough workable. Prepare the gnocchi in the morning and cook them just before serving. The brilliance of gnocchi is that they take no time at all to cook. Resist the temptation to cook too many at once, as they need space to bob around in the simmering water. Serve them as a main course with ragu (page 71) or alongside Veal Cheeks with Swiss Chard and Olives (page 30).

> 2 large baking potatoes, about 1^1/$_2$ pounds / 700 g
>
> 2 tablespoons unsalted butter, diced, at room temperature
>
> 1 egg
>
> Coarse sea salt and freshly ground black pepper
>
> ^{1}/$_4$ cup / ^{1}/$_3$ ounce / 10 g freshly and finely grated Parmesan cheese
>
> About 1 cup / 4^1/$_2$ ounces / 125 g flour
>
> 2 tablespoons extra virgin olive oil

Preheat the oven to 400°F / 200°C.

Prick the potatoes with a fork and place on a baking sheet. Bake in the oven until very tender, about 1 hour.

Let the potatoes cool slightly, then cut them in half, scoop out the flesh, and discard the skins.

Pass the potato flesh through a ricer or food mill with the fine grill into a bowl. Add the butter, then beat the egg with salt and pepper and mix into the potatoes. Add the cheese and enough of the flour to make a soft but not sticky dough.

Let the dough cool enough to handle. Take half of the dough and, on a floured surface, roll it with your hands into a sausage ^{3}/$_4$ inch / 2 cm in diameter. Cut the sausage into ^{3}/$_4$-inch / 2-cm pieces. Form them into gnocchi by taking each piece and placing it on the ends of the tines of a fork and rolling it toward the handle, pressing it lightly into the tines Place the gnocchi on a parchment-lined baking sheet. Repeat with the remaining dough; you will have about 48 pieces. Cover with a towel and refrigerate until ready to cook.

> *Hogshead—a liquid or dry measure that varies depending on what is being measured. It is based on the capacity of a cask. In the past it was often used to measure liquids like wine and beer and is still used on the east coast of Canada to measure sardines.*

Bring a large saucepan of water to a boil, add some salt, and then lower the heat so the water just simmers. Add about a quarter of the gnocchi and stir. Once they rise to the top, cook them for another minute, then use a slotted spoon to transfer the gnocchi to a warm serving dish lightly coated with olive oil. Toss gently in olive oil. Repeat with the remaining gnocchi, and serve right away.

If I Only Had a Brain

Ahh, brains. There is no denying they have a serious image problem. Even I am an adult convert to brains—my excuse for avoiding them was how my mother cooked them. Unfortunately, too many adults react to brains in the same childish way.

Brains are an overlooked and undervalued odd bit with a checkered history. The Greek mathematician Pythagoras thought that consuming animal brains was the same as eating your parents' brains, which he no doubt believed was a bad precedent. Another Greek, Aristotle, listed numerous culinary preparations in his discussion of brain anatomy. More recently, during the 1990s, the consumption of brains was banned for fear that it would lead to Creutzfeldt-Jakob disease or CJD—the human equivalent of bovine spongiform encephalopathy (BSE) or, as the press named it, mad cow disease. Although the chance of getting the human variant of this disease is extremely slim—a million to one—the disease is fatal and gruesome. Thus the specter of mad cow gave us another reason to dislike brains. The practice of recycling the carcasses of cows and sheep into animal feed (and turning ruminants into cannibals) was a major cause of the outbreaks of BSE—a textbook example of the importance of being aware of how the meat we eat is raised.

> *Fried lambs brains . . . the result is like biting through crunch into a rich cloud.*
> FERGUS HENDERSON

Aside from the fear factor, brains require extra labor to extract them from the animal's skull, and they are very perishable. With low demand, they rarely leave the abattoirs intact; if they do, they are exported to countries where they are better appreciated. All this doesn't mean that they are impossible to get; they just need to be ordered in advance.

> *There is no reason, however, why people in good health should not enjoy brains. Their texture is smooth and indescribable, so that they afford our palates a sensation, which is rather tactile than one of taste. Since brains have no very pronounced flavor, one must season them with skill and a certain restraint . . . As to which kind of brains to buy, they are all equally good, though sheep's brains being smaller and therefore suitable for single portions, are more attractive.*
> EDOUARD DE POMIANE

If you've never had brains, you're probably wondering what they taste like. Well, brains don't taste strange or odd; in fact they really have little flavor at all. Like many odd bits, it's their texture that will win you over—they are rich and creamy, like thickly whipped cream. And while they are rich, they are very easy to digest. People commonly replace brains with sweetbreads in recipes and, while this works well enough, sweetbreads don't have that same uniquely soft, yielding texture.

How to Choose

Knowing your supplier and how the animal was raised is absolutely essential when it comes to buying brains. If you can, purchase the brains fresh and cook them within twenty-four hours. If frozen brains are your only choice, don't thaw until twenty-four hours before cooking them. Brains are sold in sets, or pairs, and the two lobes should be plump and symmetrical. The lobes are pink, covered with a shiny membrane that holds a web of blood vessels; this will be spotted with blood. While brains are soft, they should have some resistance and not be mushy.

There is often a third piece—part of the brain stem joined by white creamy spinal cord; these parts are edible too.

You can eat the brains of most animals, but lamb's, pig's, and calf's brains are the most readily available and can be interchanged in recipes. Three sets of lamb's or pig's brains are about equivalent to one set of calf's brains. Brains are rich, so depending on how they are served, count one set of lamb's or pig's brains per person or one set of calf's brains for three.

If you buy split lamb heads for cheeks or stock, you can extract the brains yourself. Turn the head cut side up, and you will see the brain sitting in a cavity at the top of the head. Using a spoon, gently scoop them out. As the head is split, the brain will already be separated into two lobes.

How to Prepare and Cook

Examine the brains carefully, as they may contain small skull fragments, especially between the two lobes. Soak the brains in cold salted water—about 1 teaspoon of coarse sea salt per cup / 250 ml of water—for 6 hours or overnight in the refrigerator to remove as much of the blood as possible, changing the water a couple of times and replacing the salt. After being refrigerated the brains will be cold, firmer, and a little easier to handle.

Remove the brains from the cold water and cut into two lobes if necessary. Turn each piece over, and with a small knife remove any remaining blood clots and peel off as much of the membrane as you can. Sometimes the membrane comes off easily, and other times it is practically impossible to remove. If you find that you are breaking the brain apart trying to remove it, leave it in place. For most recipes, the membrane can be left on: the reason for removing it is to give the brains a whiter, cleaner look, which is only important if you are going to present them whole and without any coating. Once the brains are poached, you can always have another attempt at peeling off the membrane.

> *I consider brains a delicacy. They are delicate in flavour, tender of texture and combine well with sharp flavors and crisp textures.*
> STEPHANIE ALEXANDER

As you will have discovered by this point, raw brains are extremely soft and delicate. They should be poached before using in a recipe. This firms them up, making them much easier to handle. Brains cook quickly, so simmer the Court Bouillon (page 21) ahead of time to extract the maximum flavor from the vegetables and seasonings. Strain the simmered court bouillon into a clean saucepan, then add the brains. Place the pan over medium-low heat and bring slowly to a simmer. Simmer very gently, until the brains have just a little resistance when pressed with your finger, five to fifteen minutes depending on the size of the brains. Using a slotted spoon, transfer the brains to a paper towel to drain. Poached brains can be kept refrigerated in the cooled court bouillon for up to 2 days.

Sumac Encrusted Lamb's Brains

SERVES 6 AS A SNACK WITH DRINKS

Breaded brains are a popular pub food in Australia—and they were my traumatizing Sunday night supper. This is an updated version of those brains my mother cooked. She would never have thought of adding chile or lime zest to her bread crumb mixture and I doubt that she has even heard of sumac. Sumac is a bush that grows wild in the Middle East and produces dark red-to-purple berries that are a popular cooking spice. They are used whole or ground, and are an ingredient in za'atar, a spice blend popular in Lebanon. Sumac's pleasantly tart flavor cuts the richness of the creamy brains.

> 3 sets poached lamb's brains (see opposite)
>
> 3 tablespoons flour
>
> 1 egg
>
> 1 tablespoon whole milk
>
> 1/2 teaspoon fine sea salt
>
> 1/2 cup / 1 3/4 ounces / 50 g dried bread crumbs
>
> Finely grated zest of 1 lime
>
> 2 teaspoons ground sumac
>
> 1 teaspoon chile powder
>
> About 1/2 cup / 3 1/2 ounces / 100 g lard

Preheat the oven to 200°F / 100°C. Place a baking sheet lined with paper towels in the oven.

Cut each brain lobe into 4 pieces. Place the flour in a shallow dish. Whisk the egg with the milk and salt and pour into another dish. Place the bread crumbs in a third dish and mix in the lime zest, sumac, and chile powder.

Coat the brain pieces lightly with flour, then dip them into the egg mixture, then coat with the bread crumbs.

In a frying pan over medium heat, melt the lard, you want about 1/4 inch / 6 mm of lard in the pan. When the lard is hot, drop a brain slice into the oil—it should sizzle. Add the coated brain slices in batches; don't crowd the pan, or the temperature of the lard will drop. Cook until the brain slices are crisp and golden brown, about 2 minutes per side. As they finish cooking, transfer them to the baking sheet in the oven to keep warm. Season the cooked brains with some fine sea salt and a squeeze of lime juice, then serve.

Alternatives: Pig's brains; calf's brain

BREAD CRUMBS

Making bread crumbs is easy—and who doesn't have the occasional slice of stale bread? To make fresh bread crumbs, allow bread to dry slightly at room temperature, then process it in a food processor to make fine crumbs. Fresh bread crumbs can be stored in the freezer for up to 6 months.

To make dry bread crumbs, either spread fresh bread crumbs on a baking sheet and toast in a 350°F / 180°C oven until dry and lightly golden (about 10 minutes), or place pieces of stale bread on a baking sheet and toast in the oven until golden, then transfer the toasted bread to a food processor to make fine crumbs. Store dried bread crumbs in an airtight container in the pantry for 3 months.

Cheese and Just a Little Brain Fritters

SERVES 6 AS A SNACK WITH DRINKS

Australian chefs and food writers Greg and Lucy Malouf are passionate about Middle Eastern food. Sheep's brains are very popular in that part of the world, and the Maloufs have several recipes for cooking them. This is my take on one of their recipes. I hope these fritters will tempt you to try brains—after all, it was a fritter that wooed me back to them. Frying and the addition of cheese often help persuade people to try something they think they don't like. I serve these as appetizers with drinks—that way guests only have to try one, but I'm pretty sure you won't have any left. The recipe is very straightforward; just make sure the cheeses are very finely grated, a microplane is the ideal tool.

3 eggs

^{1}/2 cup / ^{3}/4 ounce / 25 g very finely grated Gruyère, packed

^{1}/4 cup / ^{1}/3 ounce / 10 g very finely grated Parmesan, packed

2 tablespoons finely chopped chives

Finely grated zest of 1 orange

^{1}/2 teaspoon fine sea salt

Freshly ground black pepper

3 sets poached lamb's brains (see page 40)

1 tablespoon cornstarch

1 cup / 7 ounces / 200 g lard

Preheat the oven to 200°F / 100°C. Place a baking sheet lined with paper towels in the oven.

In a bowl, whisk the eggs, then slowly whisk in both the cheeses and the chives, orange zest, and salt, and season with pepper.

Slice each brain lobe into ^{1}/2-inch / 1-cm slices and toss them in the cornstarch to coat. Transfer them to the batter and stir to mix; you will have something resembling a lumpy pancake batter.

Melt the lard in a heavy frying pan over medium heat; you should have about ^{1}/2 inch / 1 cm of fat. When hot, drop a little batter into the oil, it should sizzle and rise to the surface. Now add a few spoonfuls of brain batter mixture to the fat; don't overcrowd the pan and adjust the heat so the fritters bubble gently. Cook the fritters about 3 minutes, or until set and golden on the underside. Using a slotted spoon, gently turn them over and cook for about another 3 minutes. As they finish cooking, transfer the fritters to the baking sheet in the oven to keep warm. Serve right away.

Alternatives: Pig's brains; calf's brain

> *I think if one were to hand round dishes of deep-fried pieces of brain as cocktail snacks at a drinks party, many people would proclaim, 'These are absolutely yummy, what are they?'*
> SIMON HOPKINSON

Pistachio Brain Soufflés

SERVES 6

Now don't let the combination of brains and soufflé in the recipe title frighten you off this recipe. You don't have to whisk any egg whites, and the brains add a rich creaminess to the soufflés' texture. No one will know what is making the soufflés so tender. This soufflé is so forgiving I turn it out onto the salad to serve; but you can serve the soufflés in their dishes—either hot or at room temperature—and the salad separately.

> 1/4 cup / 1 ounce / 30 g shelled pistachios
>
> Butter, at room temperature
>
> 1 tablespoon lard
>
> 1 shallot, finely chopped
>
> 1 set poached calf's brains (see page 40)
>
> 2 tablespoons dry vermouth
>
> 2 teaspoons chopped flat-leaf parsley
>
> 2 teaspoons chopped fresh tarragon
>
> Coarse sea salt and freshly ground black pepper
>
> 1/2 cup / 125 ml whipping (35%) cream
>
> 4 eggs, beaten
>
> 10 to 12 cups / 2.5 to 3 l salad greens
>
> 1 orange
>
> 1 tablespoon sherry vinegar
>
> 1/2 cup / 125 ml extra virgin olive oil

Preheat the oven to 350°F / 180°C.

Spread the pistachios on a baking sheet and place in the oven to toast for about 7 minutes. Transfer the warm nuts to a clean towel and rub to remove the skins. Discard the skins and coarsely chop the pistachios; set aside.

Butter six 3/4-cup / 175-ml ovenproof ramekins and place a disk of parchment paper in the bottom of each one; set aside.

In a frying pan over medium-low heat, melt the lard. Add the shallot and cook gently without coloring until soft. Meanwhile, cut the poached brains into 3/4-inch / 2-cm pieces.

Add the brains, vermouth, parsley, and tarragon to the pan and stir until the liquid evaporates. Remove from the heat and season with the salt and pepper. Place the brain mixture in a food processor and puree. Add the cream and blend, then add the eggs and blend again until mixed.

Stir in the pistachios and check the seasoning, then pour into the prepared ramekins. Place the ramekins on a baking sheet and bake for 20 minutes, or until the soufflés are puffed and lightly golden. The soufflés should remain slightly soft in the center.

While the soufflés are cooking, trim, rinse, and dry the salad greens and place in a bowl. Finely grate the zest from the orange and place in a small bowl. Squeeze 3 tablespoons of juice from the orange and add to the bowl along with the vinegar. Season with salt and pepper and then slowly whisk in the olive oil.

When the soufflés are cooked, run a knife between the soufflé and the dish to loosen. Pour the dressing over the salad and toss. Divide the salad among 6 plates, then turn out the soufflés onto the salad and serve.

Alternatives: Three sets of lamb's brains or pig's brains

> *Sir, I have seen brains on the butcher's counter equal to yours.*
> JULES RENARD

MOCK TURTLE SOUP

In the mid-eighteenth century, green turtles from the Caribbean became a favorite item on English menus. These gentle sea creatures, weighing from 60 to 100 pounds / 27 to 45 kg, were shipped live to London where popular taverns kept them alive in special tanks until they were cooked. Needless to say, they were an expensive meal: a serving cost about half a craftsman's weekly wage.

In a recipe from 1727, the turtle flesh is first soaked, then studded with cloves and roasted with wine and lemon juice. An even more popular dish was turtle soup, which came to the table in a turtle shell. According to the recipes of the day, to make this soup you first had to kill the turtle, and then the preparation—flavored with Madeira, cayenne, and anchovies—took over half a day to complete.

As with any expensive ingredient, there was a constant search for cheaper substitutes that could extend the turtle meat or even replace it. Hannah Glasse, in the sixth edition of *Art of Cookery* (1758), added calf's head to her turtle soup recipe because it had the same gelatinous texture. In later editions, she doesn't even bother to use turtle at all, replacing it with calf's head cooked in stock and flavored with Madeira. She does, however, maintain the pretense that it is real turtle soup by serving it in a shell. I guess the empty shells were cheaper than the meat.

Soon mock turtle soup was more common than the real thing, and some epicures even thought it was better. The popularity of mock turtle soup meant that calf's head as a dish in its own right virtually disappeared from the table. In the *Cook and the Housewife's Manual* (1826), Meg Dods refers to Mock Turtle or Calf's Head Soup, and by the time Dorothy Hartley was writing *Food in England* (1954), pig's ears were replacing the calf's head. According to Hartley, pig's ear gave ". . . a clear, strong, gelatinous soup, with almost transparent meat strips, and a great flavor of real turtle soup." Does Hartley assume that her readers are familiar enough with real turtle taste, or perhaps that they don't know the difference? Whatever her mock turtle soup tasted like, it wouldn't have had the distinctive greenish hue of the real thing, just its gelatinous texture. The soup was so popular that Lewis Carroll could create a character called the Mock Turtle in his book *Alice in Wonderland* and everyone knew what it was.

> 'Once,' said the Mock Turtle at last, with a deep sigh, 'I was a real Turtle.'
> LEWIS CARROLL

Sir John Tenniel, who brilliantly illustrated the book, reveals his familiarity with the soup in his drawing of the mock turtle standing on the beach. The turtle is perched on a rock; he has a turtle shell and turtle flippers, but his head and feet are those of a calf. He weeps, as he explains to Alice that he is no longer a turtle but only a mock turtle, and then he sings her this song:

Beautiful Soup, so rich and green,
Waiting in a hot tureen!
Who for such dainties would not stoop!
Soup of the evening, beautiful Soup!

Ravioli of Brains and Morels

SERVES 4 AS A MAIN COURSE OR 6 AS AN APPETIZER

This is my husband's favorite way to eat brains, and he is now an expert, having eaten his way through many brain recipes during the writing of this book. This recipe also converted a brain-fearing friend. You might think this is just a way to disguise the brains by hiding them in the ravioli, and I guess it is, but it also plays on their rich texture. Brains are wonderfully creamy and combined with the mushrooms they make a marvelous, delicate filling for pasta. If morels are not in season, use another mushroom with a good flavor, like *trompettes des morts*.

I use Chinese wonton wrappers rather than pasta sheets: they are lighter and thinner and, best of all, they're ready-made. This recipe makes about twenty, depending on the number of wrappers in the package (I usually have 40 to 44) so reckoning five ravioli per person as a main course or three per person as an appetizer, you'll have one or two extras if one of them bursts during cooking; and you also can freeze any extras before cooking. To cook frozen ravioli, drop them straight from the freezer into the boiling water.

While it is not necessary to cut the sealed wonton wrappers, it creates a better look and reduces the amount of pasta to filling. Use a fluted cutter if you have one.

Any leftover mixture can be spread on toast and placed under the broiler to warm through—it makes a great snack.

If the brain mixture is made with fresh brains, it can be frozen (without the chervil) for up to 2 weeks before using. Thaw it out in the refrigerator and then stir in the chopped chervil and make the ravioli.

4 ounces / 115 g fresh morels

2/3 cup / 5 1/4 ounces / 150 g unsalted butter

1 shallot, finely chopped

1/4 cup / 60 ml dry white wine

1 set poached calf's brains (see page 40), diced

Coarse sea salt and freshly ground black pepper

3 tablespoons chopped chervil

1 egg white

1 teaspoon water

One 8 3/4-ounce / 250-g package 3 1/4 inch / 8 cm square wonton wrappers

2 tablespoons chopped flat-leaf parsley

Rinse the mushrooms well and trim and discard the tough stems. Finely chop the mushrooms and set aside.

Place 2 tablespoons of the butter in a frying pan over medium heat. When it is foaming, add the shallot and cook gently until it is soft and just starting to caramelize. Stir in the chopped mushrooms and continue to cook until they are softened and all the moisture has evaporated. Add 2 tablespoons of the wine and bring to a boil, stirring to deglaze the pan. Add the diced brains, season with salt and pepper, and continue stirring until the brains soften slightly and the mixture resembles softly scrambled eggs, about 3 minutes. Remove the pan from the heat, stir in the chervil, and set aside to cool. You should have about 1 1/4 cups / 310 ml of mixture. If you're not filling the ravioli immediately, cover the mixture and refrigerate.

Whisk the egg white with the water. Place 1 wonton wrapper, floured side down, on the counter, and place a tablespoon of the brain mixture in the center. Brush the remaining surface of the wonton wrapper with egg white mixture, then top with a second wrapper, floured side up. Press well to expel all the air trapped in the ravioli and seal. Then using a 2 3/4-inch / 7-cm cookie cutter centered on the mound of filling, trim the ravioli into a round; press the edges again to make sure the ravioli is well sealed, and place on a parchment-lined baking sheet. Repeat with the remaining wrappers and mixture, and place, slightly overlapping on the baking sheet. Cover the ravioli with a clean dish towel and refrigerate until ready to cook, up to 4 hours.

Bring a large saucepan of water to a boil, add some salt, and drop in the ravioli in batches; don't crowd them. Simmer until the ravioli float to the surface of the water and the wonton wrappers become slightly transparent, about 3 minutes. Drain well.

While the ravioli are cooking, cut the remaining butter into small pieces and place in a frying pan over low heat. When the butter is melted, increase the heat to medium and cook until the milk solids just start to brown and you smell a nutty aroma. Remove the pan from the heat.

Pour in the remaining white wine; the butter will bubble and spit. Add the drained ravioli to the butter and turn them carefully to coat in the sauce. Sprinkle with parsley and serve immediately.

Alternatives: Three sets of lamb's or pig's brains

> *Our European friends—particularly in France, Italy, and Spain—have been enjoying brains for centuries. They are highly nutritious and have a wonderful, creamy texture and melting consistency. All I can say is, if you've never tasted them, then you don't know what you are missing.*
> SIMON HOPKINSON

Cooking in Tongues

> *Lucky indeed is a cook with a gift of tongues!*
> IRMA ROMBAUER

That simple phrase from Irma Rombauer in *The Joy of Cooking* reveals just how much tongue meat was once appreciated. Unfortunately, the appreciation is truly past tense. What is it about tongue that elicits such a negative response today? Many cooks are happy to tackle kidney or heart, but shy away from tongue. Perhaps it is that an animal's heart or kidneys are familiar, but only in an abstract way. But we are all intimately familiar with our tongue, there in our mouth and connecting us to our food. Is an animal's tongue just too much physical reality for some, with its bumpy and leathery skin, sometimes with spotty patches that we wouldn't want on our own tongue? Well, remember that the tongue is not an organ, or even a gland. It is a muscle just like tenderloin, but because it is in the animal's head, it is categorized as an odd bit and that scares people off.

I was lucky to grow up with tongue. Potted tongue set in jelly was a staple of our Christmas meal; this was always referred to as ox tongue, although I doubt it ever came from an ox. I'll admit right now it was not my favorite part of Christmas dinner. I think seeing the whole tongue entombed in jelly diminished its attraction—I preferred my jelly colored, sweet, and tongueless. I did eat it, though, and I've discovered tongue is tastier when liberated from its jelly and nestled in a sandwich with sharp mustard. I am happy to have tongue in my headcheese (see page 19) and I've recently discovered the amazing, soft, melting texture of hot, grilled tongue, so I want you all to give tongue a second chance.

But what does it taste like? Well, it tastes mildly like the animal that it comes from, but again it's the texture of tongue—tender, rich, smooth, and creamy—that will seduce you.

How to Choose

The world of tongues is vast. Duck tongues, popular in Asian cuisines, are tiny and have a small bone that makes them fiddly. In this section, I limit myself to beef, veal, lamb, and pork tongues; if you have access to game animals, don't hesitate to use their tongues in these recipes. The bigger the tongue, the coarser its texture, so I prefer tongues around 3 1/3 pounds / 1.5 kg or less, as their texture is finer. While veal tongues are the most prized, beef, lamb, and pork tongues are all worth eating.

> *. . . slices of cold boiled salted ox tongue, like little angels' wings . . .*
> FERGUS HENDERSON

Tongues can be bought fresh, frozen, brined, and sometimes smoked. Often your only choice will be a frozen one, especially with beef or veal tongue. The color of a tongue can vary from pink with a gray cast to almost all gray. Sometimes the skin of the tongue is quite mottled, often with odd dark spots. The color and the dark patches are no indication of quality; they are just a result of the animal's breed. Tongues have a thick, bumpy skin, and often there is fat and gristle still attached at the base of the tongue, none of which is very appealing and all of which is easily removed after the tongue is poached.

Besides availability, taste and size will influence your choice. Veal and lamb tongues are the mildest in taste, followed by beef and pork tongue. Pork tongue often comes with the head, and I prefer it in headcheese rather than by itself. Smaller lamb tongues take less time to cook, but it's more work to peel them. An average beef tongue weighs around 3 pounds / 1.4 kg; a veal tongue weighs from 3/4 to 1 1/2 pounds / 350 to 700 g; and lamb and pork tongues range from 3 to 8 ounces / 90 to 225 g. Tongue loses some of its weight during cooking, so count on about 7 to 8 3/4 ounces / 200 to 250 g uncooked weight per person.

How to Prepare and Cook

While brining improves the tongue's flavor, it is not essential, and you can make all of these recipes with fresh tongue. But whether fresh or brined, the tongue must be poached first. If your tongue is commercially brined, it will have a pinky hue (see page 57). I prefer to buy a tongue and brine it myself; that way I can control the saltiness better and eschew the pink curing salt.

> *Some recoil in horror when faced with the physical reality of a calf's, ox or lamb's tongue. There is absolutely no doubt what it is, whereas these cooks may not quite realise that a chop is in fact one of the ribs of a lamb! If you can get past this prejudice you will find that tongue is delicate in flavour, soft and melting of texture when served hot and smooth and creamy when cold.*
>
> STEPHANIE ALEXANDER

To brine a tongue, rinse it well under cold water, then brine it for half to one day for pork or lamb tongues and two to three days for veal or beef tongue (see page 22). Remove the tongue(s) from the brine and rinse well, then poach until tender (see opposite). If you're poaching a tongue that hasn't been brined, add a good pinch of some coarse sea salt to the poaching liquid.

Once cooked, a tongue must be skinned, or peeled, and this needs be done while it is still warm; otherwise the skin is very difficult, almost impossible to remove. Peeled tongues can be kept refrigerated for 4 days in their cooking liquid. Strain and keep the tongue cooking liquid, and if stock or water is required in the recipe, you can use it instead (remembering that it will be salty).

WHAT TO DO WITH COOKED TONGUE

The following recipes all start with cooked tongue. However you can ignore them all and just enjoy your tongue right now.

- Tongue sandwiches are a standard delicatessen menu item; use a good strong mustard. Try a hot tongue sandwich to appreciate the texture of warm tongue.
- Toss pieces of julienned tongue into a salad: tongue is one of the ingredients in a classic chef's salad.
- Use tongue instead of ham in a *croque monsieur* sandwich.
- Replace the corned beef in a Reuben sandwich with tongue.
- Add diced tongue to a beet or potato salad.

Poached Tongue

There are many recipes (and just as many cooks) that recommend blanching tongues for a few minutes and then peeling them before cooking. No less a figure than French chef Paul Bocuse is one. Well, I know I am not in the same league as M. Bocuse, but when I followed his blanching method, the only way I could remove the skin was by cutting it off with a knife. This removed a thick layer of the meat with the skin and left the tongue looking even less appetizing than before. I even tried his method with a French tongue (that is, one procured in Paris), with the same result.

Tongue must be poached until it is very tender, and you really can't overcook it.

2¹/₄ to 3¹/₃ pounds / 1 to 1.5 kg beef tongue or lamb tongues, brined (see page 22)

1 small onion, quartered

2 cloves

1 carrot, peeled and sliced

2 stalks celery, sliced

6 black peppercorns

6 allspice berries

3 stems flat-leaf parsley

1 clove garlic

1 large sprig thyme

1 fresh bay leaf

Place the tongue in a large saucepan. Insert the cloves in 2 of the onion quarters and add to the pan along with the remaining onion, carrot, and celery. Add enough cold water to cover the tongue by 2 inches / 5 cm, and place the pan over medium-low heat. Bring slowly to a boil and then skim any scum from the cooking liquid. Add the peppercorns, allspice, parsley, garlic, thyme, and bay leaf. Lower the heat and simmer, partially covered, until the tongue is very tender, 1¹/₂ to 2¹/₂ hours depending on the size of the tongue. To test, pierce the tongue with a skewer at the thick-

est part and the tip; it should be very tender in both places.

Transfer the tongue from the poaching liquid to a plate. Have a bowl of ice water at the ready to dip your fingers into. This makes handling the hot tongue easier. Or, you may want to follow my mother's method—she wisely puts on a pair of rubber gloves to peel her hot tongue. And don't believe any recipe that tells you to cool the tongue before peeling it: tackle it as soon as your fingers, rubber gloved or not, can handle it. Once it's cold you'll have to massacre the tongue to get the skin off.

Start at the back or throat end of the tongue and use a small knife to lift up the first piece of skin. Then, using your fingers, peel the skin off as though you were taking a glove off the tongue. Be careful when you reach the tip of the tongue that you don't tear it off. Discard the skin.

Even with the skin removed, you will notice there is still a bumpy impression, mainly at the back of the tongue. You can scrape off any bumps with the back of your knife. Now trim the fat and gristle from the base and underside of the tongue and discard it.

Everyone from Thomas Keller to my mother tells you to remove throat bones. When transcribing her recipe for me, my mother noted that in recent years there have been no bones with the tongues she's bought—nor, for that matter, she added wistfully, were there any sweetbreads. Apparently, there was a time when tongues were sold with the sweetbread attached. Needless to say, if you find any bones discard them, and if you discover a sweetbread, go back to that butcher.

Put the peeled tongue back into the strained cooking liquid and leave to cool. The tongue can be kept refrigerated for 3 to 4 days in the cooking liquid.

Liv's Tongue Hash

SERVES 2

Now while you probably don't need me to tell you how to make hash, this recipe is here to remind you just what a good way this is to use up leftover cooked meat. Corned beef is the classic ingredient, but I think tongue is better—I love the way its soft texture contrasts with the crisp potatoes. Topping it with an egg makes it a perfect breakfast dish.

> 3 tablespoons bacon fat or lard
> 1 large cooked potato, diced
> 5 1/4 ounces / 150 g poached tongue (page 51)
> 1 onion, halved and sliced
> Coarse sea salt and freshly ground black pepper
> 2 eggs

In a heavy frying pan, melt half the fat over medium heat. When hot, add the potato and cook until golden brown on all sides, about 7 minutes. Transfer to a plate. Meanwhile, julienne the tongue and set aside.

Add the remaining fat to the pan, and when it's hot, cook the onion, stirring until softened. Add the tongue and potatoes, season with salt and pepper, and stir until everything is heated through.

Lower the heat and break the eggs, one by one, into a small dish, and then slide them on top of the hash. Season the eggs with salt and pepper, cover, and cook until the whites are just set, about 4 minutes.

Alternatives: Leftover cooked corned beef or heart

> *There was never a time, it seems to me, when there were not some pickled lamb's tongues on the shelf in our family larder. They were used for a quick snack, for a cold supper, for sandwiches, or for picnics. And how tender and delicious they were. . . . I fear that lamb's tongues are lost to most people today, who won't take the trouble to prepare them and don't know what eating pleasure they are missing.*
> JAMES BEARD

Spicy Tongue Tacos

SERVES 6

This is a great way to eat cooked tongue—mixed with this complex, spicy tomato sauce, served in a warm tortilla. I guarantee it will convert even the most skeptical to the delights of tongue. If you have no cooked tongue, use any cooked meat—beef cheek for example, or check the alternatives at the end of the recipe for more daring suggestions. To stay authentic, the cheese should be *queso fresco*, but I like to use ricotta salata. Corn or flour tortillas: your choice. I sometimes just spoon the mixture over toast.

1¼ pounds / 570 g plum (Roma) tomatoes

2 serrano chiles

¼ cup / 1¼ ounces / 35 g whole blanched almonds

3 ancho chiles

2 cascabel chiles

1 cup / 250 ml boiling water

1 tablespoon lard

1 clove garlic, chopped

1½ teaspoons coarse sea salt

A generous pinch allspice

A generous pinch of ground cinnamon

12 ounces / 350 g poached tongue (page 51)

12 flour tortillas

1 cup / 2¾ ounces / 80 g coarsely grated ricotta salata or queso fresco

Shredded lettuce

Thinly sliced onion

Cilantro (coriander) sprigs

Lime wedges

Preheat the broiler or grill to high.

Remove the cores from the tomatoes and pierce each serrano chile with the point of a knife (if you don't, you risk the chiles exploding). Broil or grill the tomatoes and chiles until their skins split and they are lightly blackened. Transfer them to a bowl, cover with plastic wrap, and set aside.

In a small frying pan over medium heat, toast the almonds until they are lightly browned, and set aside.

Using scissors, cut the dried chiles into large pieces, discarding the stems and seeds. Toast the pieces in a frying pan, turning once, until fragrant, about 2 minutes. Tip the chile pieces into a bowl, pour over the boiling water, and let steep for 30 minutes.

Peel the tomatoes and chop coarsely. Remove the skin and stems from the serrano chiles, cut them in half, and scrape out and discard the seeds; set the chiles aside. Drain the dried chiles and discard their soaking liquid.

In a frying pan with a lid, melt the lard over medium-low heat. Add the garlic and cook until fragrant, then add the almonds, tomatoes, drained dried chiles, salt, allspice, and cinnamon. Cover and cook for 20 minutes, or until the chiles are soft (the cascabels will not soften as much as the anchos). Let the mixture cool slightly.

Place the serrano chiles in a blender, add the tomato-almond sauce, and blend until smooth. Then, using a spatula, press the mixture through a coarse sieve back into a frying pan and check the seasoning.

Cut the tongue into strips about ¼ inch by 2 inches / 6 mm by 5 cm and reheat them in the sauce, adding a couple of tablespoons of water to thin the sauce just a little.

Warm the tortillas, and serve the tongue mixture in a warmed dish with the tortillas and bowls of cheese, lettuce, onion, cilantro (coriander), and lime wedges, and allow diners to assemble their own tacos.

Alternatives: Cooked chitterlings or tripe

Tongue with Salsa Verde

This is a perfect dish for a hot summer night, with the soft, dense meat of the cooked tongue contrasting with the piquant salsa verde. Best of all, the bright green color of the sauce brightens up what, it must be admitted, is a dull-colored meat—especially when brined at home without pink salt (see page 57). The eggs make a tasty and colorful addition and may encourage guests to taste tongue—I've made quite a few converts with this recipe. If you're serving this dish as a main course, serve it with Potato and Radish Salad (page 56). While the tongue is easier to slice cold, make sure you bring it to room temperature before serving.

1 cup / 20 g arugula leaves, coarse stems removed

1 cup / 15 g flat-leaf parsley leaves

1 tablespoon capers, rinsed

3 cornichons, rinsed

2 anchovy fillets, rinsed

1 1/2 tablespoons chopped shallot

1 clove garlic, germ removed

2 teaspoons freshly squeezed lemon juice

3 tablespoons extra virgin olive oil

Coarse sea salt and freshly ground black pepper

1 Poached Beef Tongue (page 51)

4 hard-boiled eggs, halved (see below)

Place the arugula, parsley, capers, cornichons, anchovies, shallot, garlic, and lemon juice in a food processor and pulse until coarsely chopped. Add the olive oil and pulse to blend.

Tip the sauce into a bowl and season with salt and pepper. Cover by pressing plastic wrap directly onto the surface of the sauce (this keeps it green) and refrigerate. While this sauce can be made up to a day in advance, it is at its best fresh.

Slice the tongue thinly and place the slices overlapping on a platter. Arrange the eggs around the tongue and then spoon over some of the salsa verde.

Alternatives: Veal tongue

HARD-BOILING EGGS

The fashion in Canada is to call these eggs "hard-cooked," because you don't really boil them with this method; but for me they will always be hard-boiled eggs. If you start with your eggs at room temperature, they will be less likely to crack. Using a pushpin, make a small hole in the rounded end of each egg and place them in a small saucepan. Cover with cold water and bring to a boil, uncovered, over medium heat, turning the eggs often to center the yolks. As soon as the water begins to boil, remove the pan from the heat, cover, and leave for 6 minutes. I like my egg yolks to be soft, even runny in the center. If you like them firmer, leave the eggs for another 2 minutes. Rinse the eggs under cold running water to stop the cooking, then tap them gently on the counter to fracture the shell and peel. Older eggs are always the best to use, as they peel more easily than fresh ones.

Potato and Radish Salad

SERVES 4

While I have a weak spot for potato and fresh pea salad with mint, this combination works better with dense meats like liver and tongue, because the radish adds a peppery bite. The radishes I use are the big ones the size of a large apricot that are popular in Ontario. If your radishes are smaller, just use more.

> 1 pound / 450 g new potatoes, scrubbed
>
> 1 fresh bay leaf
>
> Coarse sea salt
>
> 2 or 3 large radishes, trimmed
>
> 3 tablespoons extra virgin olive oil
>
> 2 tablespoons chopped flat-leaf parsley
>
> 1 tablespoon red wine vinegar
>
> Freshly ground black pepper

Place the potatoes in a saucepan, cover with cold water, and add the bay leaf. Cover and bring to a boil over medium heat, add a generous pinch of salt, then reduce the heat and simmer, partially covered, for 10 to 15 minutes or until the potatoes are cooked.

Meanwhile, cut the radishes into thin slices. Drain the potatoes, cut them in half, and toss with the oil, parsley, and vinegar. Add the radishes, toss again, and then season with salt and pepper. Serve warm.

Barbecued (Grilled) Tongue

SERVES 4 AS A MAIN DISH

Barbecuing for me means grilling outside on a charcoal or gas grill. It was only when I came to North America that I discovered there was such a thing as slow-cooked Southern-style barbecue. Working on this book and dealing with odd bits that often need long cooking, I was interested to discover new ways of cooking them on an outdoor grill. The throat end or thickest part of tongue is the best for grilling, because it has a light marbling of fat and the slices are larger. I'm going to suggest that this recipe replace our traditional tongue-entombed-in-jelly the next time I am back in Australia for Christmas. Serve this with Potato and Radish Salad (see above). You can make more or less of this as you like; count on five to six slices per person.

> Twenty to twenty-four 1/4-inch / 6-mm slices poached tongue (page 51)
>
> Olive oil
>
> Mustard Seed Glaze (page 98) or Tamarind Glaze (page 155)

Preheat the grill to medium-high.

Brush the tongue slices on both sides with olive oil. Place on the hot grill and cook for about 2 minutes per side. Brush with glaze and serve.

IF YOU LIKE IT PINK: A SHORT EXPLANATION OF NITRATES AND NITRITES

Salt, or sodium chloride, has been used for thousands of years to preserve foods: remains of salted fish and birds have been found in Egyptian tombs. Salt works by drawing the moisture out of the flesh; it renders microbes inactive by dehydrating them. The impurities found in ancient sodium chloride (namely potassium nitrate, or saltpeter) were also very effective in killing bacteria. In the Middle Ages, saltpeter was used in the extraction of minerals and as an ingredient in gunpowder. Polish hunters preserved their game by rubbing the inside of the animal carcass with a mixture of salt and gunpowder. In the sixteenth century, it was realized that that saltpeter—potassium nitrate—and sodium nitrate added color and flavor to cured meats, but no one understood exactly how.

Not until the beginning of the twentieth century did German scientists discover the answer. The bacteria in the meat decompose some of the nitrate into nitrite during the curing process, and it is this nitrite—not the nitrate—that was the active ingredient in saltpeter. Nitrite turns the meat pink by reacting with the myoglobin in the muscle. With the arrival of refrigeration, which slows the activity of microbes, less nitrite was required to preserve meats. Today the amount of nitrates added to food is much less than in the past, and it is highly regulated. We also eat less preserved meat, so we consume smaller doses of nitrites than our ancestors did. Nitrites are not harmful to us in small amounts—they occur naturally in leafy greens and root vegetables—yet they remain controversial. Why?

As nitrates breakdown into nitrites during the curing process, they produce nitrosamines and these have been linked to a risk of cancer. But there is no direct evidence that small quantities are a health concern.

Curing salt or pink salt is a commercially manufactured salt that contains nitrate and is dyed pink to ensure it is only used for curing meat and not mistakenly as a culinary salt. Unlike saltpeter, it has a precise percentage of nitrate and so is more reliable. Do not confuse this pink culinary salt with salts from the Himalayas, Hawaii, or the Murray Darling Basin in Australia; these are naturally pink salts and are simply sodium chloride. Curing salt is an essential ingredient when making dry-cured sausages. It is often added to brines for tongue, corned beef, and headcheese to give them a pink color. (I don't use it and as a result my tongue and headcheese don't have that familiar pink tinge.)

BUFFALO TONGUES

It is estimated that there were over fifty million buffalo roaming freely across the Great Plains before the arrival of white settlers. They ranged over 70 percent of the continental United States and into the Canadian provinces of Alberta and Saskatchewan. The buffalo was an important resource for the Native Americans, providing them with food, clothing and shelter. The tongue of the buffalo was a particular delicacy—set aside for the medicine men and women, to ensure the success of the hunt.

Generally Native Americans treated the buffalo with respect, killing only what they needed, but the white man was less discriminate. As early as 1846, the Indians were complaining to the local authorities about the wasteful slaughter of buffalo. Thomas Harvey, superintendent of the Indian Affairs in St. Louis, wrote to his superiors:

Notwithstanding that the Indians kill great numbers of the buffalo, they do not kill them wastefully. . . . Not so with the white man; he kills for the sake of killing.

With the end of the Civil War and the construction of the railways, the migration westward escalated. This meant that new sources of food had to found, and the plentiful buffalo provided the answer. Back in the East, buffalo skins were popular for coats and blankets, in better restaurants in the larger cities buffalo tongues were a fashionable dish, and even buffalo bones were valuable as fertilizer. The hides sold for three dollars, and the tongues were worth twenty-five cents each, making buffalo hunting a lucrative full-time job, especially during the economic recession of the 1870s. A hunter armed with long-range rifle, could kill 250 buffalo a day. Former hunter Frank H. Mayer remembered:

The whole Western country went buffalo-wild. It was like a gold rush. . . . Men left jobs, businesses, wives and children and future prospects to get into buffalo running.

Commercial hunters were not the only threat, hunting buffalo for sport was a popular pastime. Sportsmen traveled on special buffalo trains that took them right to the animals so they could shoot the beasts without even leaving the comfort of their railway carriage. By the end of the nineteenth century, there were fewer than 2,000 buffalo remaining in all of the United States. The buffalo were saved by the work of the American Bison Society who created new buffalo reserves in the West, Native Americans who established herds on reservation lands, and government legislation making it illegal to kill buffalo on federal reserves.

The buffalo (more correctly bison) have prospered and today their meat is commercially available in restaurants and upscale butcher shops; however buffalo tongues have yet to regain their past popularity.

Warm Lamb Tongues in Ginger, Mustard, and Cream Sauce

SERVES 4

In one of my older cookbooks, there is a picture of braised lamb tongues. In the center of a large oval platter is a dubious, dark puree of some vegetable, and around it are arranged whole cooked lamb tongues. It was not at all appetizing even to someone who loves tongue. In this recipe the tongues are sliced, so they are more appetizing. Cooked with two of my favorite ingredients—bacon and ginger—this rich, creamy dish goes well with lentils but would be delicious on pasta too.

> 8 poached lamb tongues (page 51)
>
> Tongue cooking liquid, strained
>
> 1³/₄ ounces / 50 g side bacon, cut into small, thin strips
>
> 1 cup / 6¹/₄ ounces / 180 g lentils de Puy
>
> Coarse sea salt and freshly ground black pepper
>
> 1 tablespoon finely chopped shallot
>
> One 1¹/₂-inch / 4-cm piece fresh ginger, peeled
>
> 2 tablespoons crème fraîche
>
> 1 tablespoon Dijon mustard
>
> 1 tablespoon chopped flat-leaf parsley

Cut the cooked tongues, slightly on the diagonal, into ¹/₄-inch / 6-mm slices and set aside with 1 cup / 250 ml of the tongue cooking liquid.

In a large frying pan over low heat, cook the bacon gently so that it renders its fat. Using a slotted spoon, transfer the bacon to a plate lined with paper towels to drain. Leave the fat in the pan.

Rinse the lentils well and place them in a saucepan. Cover with cold water and bring to a boil over high heat, then strain through a sieve and refresh under cold running water. Discard the blanching water.

Place the blanched lentils in a clean saucepan. Pour the remaining tongue cooking water into a large glass measuring cup and add enough cold water to make 3 cups / 750 ml. Pour over the lentils and bring to a boil over medium heat. Reduce the heat to low and simmer, uncovered, until the lentils are just tender, 20 to 25 minutes. Check them regularly so you don't overcook them. When the lentils are cooked, drain, transfer them to a dish, season with salt and pepper, and keep warm.

Add the shallot to the bacon fat in the pan and cook until softened. Cut the ginger into julienne strips and add to the pan. Stir, and then pour in the reserved tongue cooking liquid. Bring to a boil and deglaze the pan, using a wooden spoon to scrape up the browned bits from the bottom. Continue to boil the liquid until it is reduced by half. Lower the heat, add the crème fraîche and mustard, stir in the tongue to coat with the sauce, and continue to cook until it is heated through. Stir in the reserved bacon, season with salt and pepper, then sprinkle with parsley and serve with the lentils.

Alternatives: Beef or calf's tongue

> *avoir la langue bien pendue: literally, "to have a hanging tongue"; someone who talks well and a lot*

Cockscombs

Cockscombs are the fleshy growth on the top of a chicken's head. Despite being called cockscombs, they grow on both adult cocks and hens, but the male's comb is larger. Most combs are red in color because they are full of blood. Cockscombs play a vital role in regulating the bird's body temperature: because birds don't sweat, they cool their blood by moving it through their comb and wattle, the fleshy part that hangs from their beak.

In the kitchen, cockscombs have been popular since Roman times, valued for their unique, decorative shape and gelatinous texture; they remain popular in Italy today. It was there that I saw them for the first time: a large metal container brimming with pink fleshy cockscombs in the window of a poultry store. La Varenne's cookbook *Le Cuisinier François* (1651) has a recipe using cockscombs: *potage à la Reyne,* or the queen's pottage. The queen in this case was Italian: Catherine de Médicis, wife of the French king François I. The recipe was a mixture of odd bits: kidneys, sweetbreads, artichokes, and cockscombs cooked in a mushroom and poultry stock, then thickened with almond milk and presented in a hollowed-out bread roll. It was one of Catherine's favorite dishes, and she allegedly made herself sick by eating too much of it at one infamous sitting. Cockscombs were sold by the pound and remained a fashionable garnish in France and Italy through the latter half of the seventeenth century and into the eighteenth century.

Today, in classic French cooking, the term *à la Reine* denotes a creamy sauce with a garnish of sweetbreads, chicken testicles, and cockscombs. This mixture is presented in a vol-au-vent (a buttery puff pastry case) instead of the bread of Catherine's dish. It still appears on restaurant menus, but often, pieces of chicken replace the odd bits. Cockscombs are also an ingredient in the French *financière* sauce, along with mushrooms and sweetbreads.

Cockscombs are not at all easy to find, but you might be able to talk your poultry supplier into selling you some, and they store well frozen. Raw cockscombs are pale pink and fleshy, with some darker spots that resemble bruises. Many recipes begin by telling you to prick the cockscombs with a needle and squeeze out the blood. Well, in my experience this is not necessary at all. Rather, the first step is to soak them in cold salted water—about 1 teaspoon of coarse sea salt per cup / 250 ml of water—for several hours to remove any excess blood, and then place them in cold water and bring to a boil, then drain. Once they are blanched, their rough surface can be removed; this is not skin but rather a gnarly membrane with some feathery residue. It rubs off with the aid of a towel, some coarse salt, and a lot of patience—it is a rather tedious job. Don't blanch too many at once unless you have a friend to help you, as the scraping must be done while the cockscombs are still warm. If you find the membrane is impossible to remove or they get cold drop them in boiling water for 30 seconds to a minute, then try again. Also make sure they are clean inside the cut edge, where they were attached to the head.

> *Fleshy excrescence, often voluminous, found on the heads of cocks and other gallinaceans. It is chiefly used as a garnish for entrées.*
> LAROUSSE GASTRONOMIQUE

Cockscombs vary wildly in size, and generally the smaller ones cook faster, but not always. Sort through your cockscombs and cook similar sized ones together. Their flavor is very mild, so cook them in a well-flavored stock with an additional mirepoix of vegetables (diced onion, carrot, and celery), black pepper, bay leaves, thyme, fennel seeds, and wine.

The wine can be red or white. If you are going to serve them with a cream sauce, use white; I prefer them with mushrooms, so I use red. Add a good amount of salt and bring everything to a boil, then lower the heat and simmer them until they are tender. This can take from 1 to 3 hours depending on their size and age. Remove the cooked cockscombs and cool them, separated, on a flat surface—like pig's ears and feet, they are very gelatinous and will stick to each other.

These have been used since the time of Apicius as a garnish for chicken dishes.
IRMA ROMBAUER

My friend Albert Ponzo, a chef in Toronto, finishes his cockscombs by sautéing them with wild mushrooms, then adding a red wine sauce with a touch of cardamom. I deglaze my pan with red wine and add a little of the cooking liquid. It is their soft and gelatinous texture that makes them unique, and endears them to lovers of pig's feet and oxtail.

Like *Larousse Gastronomique*, I always considered cockscombs a savory garnish until a dinner in Montréal where I discovered one on my dessert plate. Cockscombs are bland, taking on the flavor of their cooking liquid. The cockscomb decorating my plate had been simmered in blood orange juice and tasted a little like a sugar free orange jellybean. This started me thinking—why not candy cockscombs like orange and lemon peel? They would be a perfect garnish on many desserts especially my Chocolate Blood Ice cream (page 226).

Next time I get a quantity of cockscombs I'll put some aside to cook in an orange flavored sugar syrup. When they are cooked I'll toss them in some sugar, they'll probably make a great snack too.

COCKSCOMBS IN TRANSLATION

I read Tolstoy's *War and Peace* when I studied Russian literature at university. I remember finding it tedious and confusing; there was a huge cast of characters with complicated names and too many pages filled with detailed battle descriptions, so I skipped all the battle scenes. A couple of years ago, I heard about a new translation by Richard Pevear and Larissa Volokhonsky, so I decided to tackle the book again. I loved it—even the battle descriptions were fascinating and thrilling. Later, I stumbled across an essay by Richard Pevear discussing the translation process and how hard it is to stay true not only to the sense of the words but also the music of the language. The passage about cockscombs was the most interesting:

Here is a very different and rather amusing example of the search for fidelity. Count Ilya Andreich Rostov, Natasha's father, is giving a banquet in honor of General Bagration. Ordering the menu, he insists that "grebeshki" be put in the "tortue." I assumed that tortue was French turtle soup, but what about grebeshki? The Russian word can mean either "cock's-combs" or "scallops." Which would you put in a turtle soup? I did research into the uses of cock's-combs, but with rather unappealing results. I looked at previous translations: one has "scallops" and thinks the soup is a "pie crust"; another has "cock's-combs" but in a "pasty"; in a third the "cock's-combs" are in a "soup"; the fourth agrees about the soup, but puts "croutons" in it. Going by my own taste, I decided to put scallops in the turtle soup. This reading got as far as the first set of page proofs.

Just then we met by chance (at a dinner in Paris) a woman who used to run a cooking school. We asked her which it should be. She, too, was puzzled. A few days later we received a long email from her. She had become so intrigued by our question that she went to the French National Library the next day and looked up the history of the culinary use of cock's-combs. She was happy to inform us that they came into fashion precisely around the time of the Napoleonic wars and were a key ingredient in turtle sauce. Suddenly the whole passage made sense, because the chef replies to the old count's order: "Three cold sauces, then?" The other translations have "three cold dishes" or "entrees," with no relation to sauces at all. Thanks to Mme. Meunier, we were able to make the correction in the second set of proofs.

Other Heady Bits:
Palates and Eye Balls

Palates

Even I hadn't considered eating the roof of an animal's mouth, but apparently beef palates were a popular food in the past. Robert May, an English cook, gives recipes for ox palate in his book *The Accomplisht Cook* (1660). In one, he mixes cooked diced palates with small roasted birds, bacon, oysters, fried artichokes, pistachios, and a panoply of odd bits including lamb and poultry testicles, cockscombs, marrow, and sweetbreads. The English cook Dorothy Hartley writes that palates must be peeled like tongue and can be added to brawn (headcheese). She cites an eighteenth-century recipe for palates served in a rich egg yolk and cream sauce, then garnished with pickled grapes.

> *The palate is tougher meat than soft tongue, but of the same type.*
> DOROTHY HARTLEY

Palates were common in France too: *Larousse Gastronomique* lists five different preparations. Apparently they are also an ingredient in Asian cooking: occasionally, dried water buffalo palate is added to dishes in the Laotian kitchen. I am going to stick with tongue.

Eyeballs

There are recipes for cooking eyeballs but you'll find none here. When one recipe began with the instructions to remove the corneas, lenses, and irises, I didn't read any further. I am a cook, not a surgeon. Many cultures relish eyeballs, but usually as the choice piece from a cooked head, not a separate dish. Icelanders, who eat lots of strange foods, including fermented shark, apparently delight in sheep's eyes and include them in sheep headcheese. Sheep's eyeballs are popular throughout the Middle East and North Africa. My first eyeball experience was while eating a dish of sheep's head couscous. The split sheep's head was in a broth of vegetables and the host offered me the eyes. I ate one and then asked for the brain.

> *They have a nice chewy texture without being tough, a little like squid but without the slipperiness. The secret is to remove the inky, black middle bit without bursting it before you bite into the gelatinous eye socket.*
> ANISSA HELOU

There is no reason not to try eyeballs—they don't taste strong and you might enjoy the texture. They are not like jelly as you might imagine, but pleasantly chewy. If you cook sheep's or pig's head you will have eyeballs to taste. My advice is to cut them in half: then you can remove the black center, which makes them look less like eyeballs and slightly more appetizing. If you are trying them for the first time, let them cool first, the texture is better.

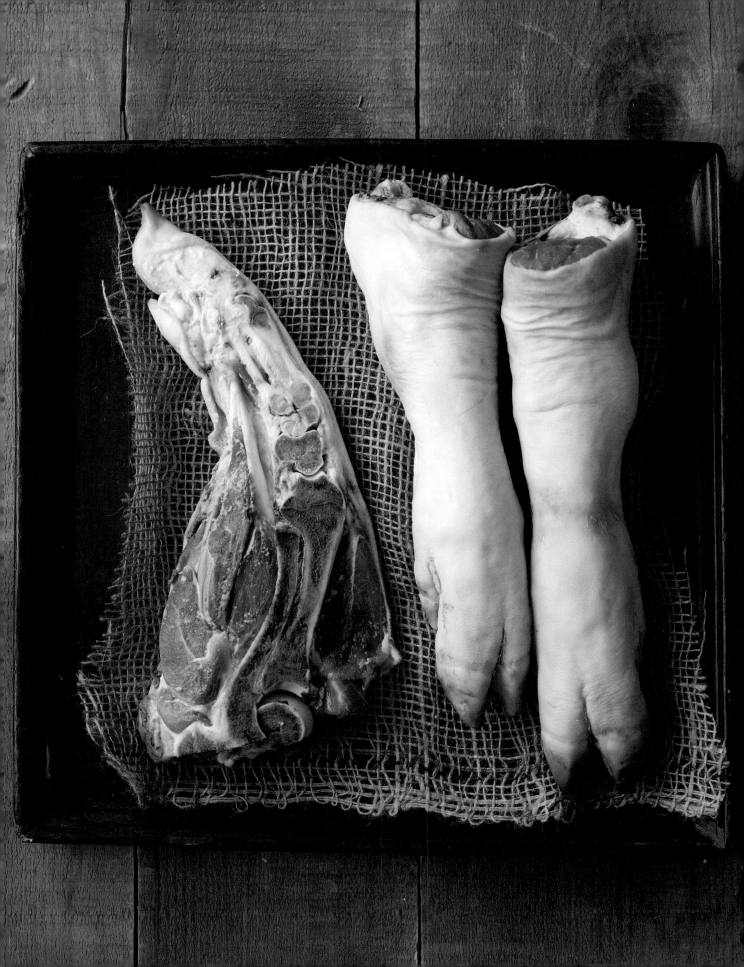

TWO

At the Front: Comfortingly Reassuring

This chapter covers some more familiar territory, so if you are still recoiling from the idea of eating eyeballs, you'll be much more comfortable here. I am sure you have all eaten shoulder, but at the front of the animal there is also the neck, the breast, and the feet. As many of these odd bits require long, slow cooking, they are often passed over in favor of quick-cooking cuts, or thought of as just not quite as good as the prime cuts. To suggest that they are inferior is a mistake. The front of the animal offers a lot of tasty choices that are well marbled and full of flavor—all good value.

However, the cuts can be confusing. The front legs of animals are called shoulders, and there are numerous names for the same cut depending on which animal it's from, including clod, scrag, blade, chuck butt, picnic breast, brisket, hock, and shank. I will explain all of them. This chapter also includes the most venerated of all odd bits—sweetbread. Probably the most prestigious odd bit, sweetbread has maintained its status throughout the history of cooking. Why? Scarcity—it is the only odd bit that disappears as the animal ages.

Necking

With names like "scrag end" and "clod," it is no wonder that neck is an overlooked cut. That's a shame, as its combination of bone and fat makes it a wonderful braising cut. I use lamb neck to make Irish stew, but I hadn't really considered cooking the necks of other animals. One day I asked my butcher for venison osso buco, and because he'd sold out of shanks he offered me neck instead; so I took the plunge. While not as meaty as shank, it was more economical, and ever since then I have been a fan of neck.

For anyone who cooks oxtail, neck will be familiar. Like the tail, it has vertebrae running down its center, and the amount of meat to bone increases as the neck gets closer to the body. The neck vertebrae are much bigger than those in the tail, so there is less meat and more bone. The age and sex of the animal influences the size of its neck too; for example, a ram's neck will be thicker and meatier than a ewe's. Lamb, venison, and goat neck can be ordered whole, or you can have your butcher cut it into thick slices. Larger necks like veal and beef are generally boned out and sold in pieces.

> When we buy lamb at Locanda, it is the whole animal, so we find ourselves with many different cuts, such as neck, which are perfect for stews.
> GIORGIO LOCATELLI

Poultry necks used to come attached to the bird or packed with the giblets (see page 147), but now birds are being sold without any of their tasty odd bits. In France, where the birds I buy still have their feet and heads attached, I am guaranteed the neck. More often, in North America necks are sold separately. While poultry necks don't make a dish on their own, they are worth asking for: the necks, especially from larger birds, have quite a bit of meat, and they make a great addition to stock. If you are lucky enough to buy birds with their neck skin intact and you like to make sausages, you're in for a treat. The skin of the neck, removed in one piece, makes an ideal sausage casing. Often in France it is stuffed with a mixture of finely chopped duck meat and pieces of foie gras, then cooked in fat. This delicious duck sausage is eaten hot or at room temperature with a salad. I have made it myself, but on this side of the Atlantic the neck skin is often split during processing, rendering it useless as a sausage casing.

How to Choose

When choosing neck, the same rules apply as with any meat or poultry (see page 11): it should have no strong smell and be moist to the touch, know your supplier and the source of your meat. With smaller animals, consider buying a whole neck: although the bone structure is complicated, once it's cooked, the meat falls off the bone. With neck slices, the amount of meat per piece varies greatly, so use your own judgment in deciding how many slices you will need. Ask your butcher to slice the neck for you. The slices closer to the animal's body will yield more meat. If you end up with a couple of pieces that are mostly bone, set them aside for your stockpot.

How to Prepare and Cook

Depending on the animal, the neck can be fatty. You can trim off excess amounts of fat, but leave on enough to baste and keep the meat moist during cooking, remembering that the fat can be skimmed off the cooked dish. There is a band of sinew encircling the neck that causes neck slices to curl as they cook, so before cooking them, make a couple of cuts through it to prevent this. If you are cooking a whole neck or boneless pieces, this step is not necessary.

Neck is a braising cut, so substitute it in any recipe you have for a slow-cooked braise or stew. While you can use boneless pieces, cooking it on the bone will add depth, flavor, and body to your dish.

You can make a stew from large poultry necks, but it is more practical to add them to stock or roast them with the bird to boost the flavor of the gravy. And if you love to gnaw on a bone, retrieve the neck from the pan—it is a very tasty odd bit to chew on.

Whole Lamb Neck with Lemons, Olives, and Mint

SERVES 4

I only cooked neck slices, until I saw a recipe for whole lamb neck calling for a 1¹/₂ pound / 700 g neck. Well, it must have been a baby lamb that I doubt would have even fed two people. My meaty ram neck weighed in at 4 pounds / 1.8 kg, and even then only yielded 1³/₄ pounds / 800 g of cooked meat (there is a ot of bone). As it was spring, I decided to use white wine, lemons, olives, and mint, all of which cut through the richness, and serve it with boiled new potatoes. The whole neck may seem intimidating, but once cooked, the meat and bones part company readily.

A whole large lamb neck, about 4 pounds / 1.8 kg

Coarse sea salt and freshly ground black pepper

2 tablespoons rendered lamb fat or lard

2 onions, chopped

2 carrots, peeled and chopped

2 stalks celery, sliced

2 lemons

1 bunch fresh mint

1 head garlic

1 fresh bay leaf

1 dried red chile

1 cup / 250 ml dry white wine

2 cups / 500 ml Lamb Stock (page 234)

1 cup / 5 ounces / 140 g green olives (about 30)

Remove the lamb neck from the refrigerator an hour before cooking.

Preheat the oven to 325°F / 160°C.

Pat the lamb dry and season well with salt and pepper. In a large, heavy flameproof casserole or Dutch oven, melt half of the fat over medium-high heat and brown the neck, then transfer to a plate.

Add the remaining fat with the onions, carrots, and celery to the pan, stir, and cook until the vegetables are slightly softened and beginning to stick to the pan.

Meanwhile, finely grate the zest from the lemons and set aside, and cut the lemons into thick slices, discarding the ends. Remove enough small leaves from the bunch of mint to make ¹/₂ cup / 5 g, then select 20 of the mint stems, setting the stems and leaves aside separately. Slice the top off the garlic head to expose the cloves. Add the lemon slices, mint stems, garlic, bay leaf, and chile to the pan. Pour in the wine and deglaze the pan, using a wooden spoon to scrape up the browned bits from the bottom.

Add the stock and bring to a boil. Return the neck to the pan, cover the lamb with a piece of wet parchment paper and the lid, transfer to the oven, and cook for 2¹/₂ hours. Uncover the pan and remove the parchment paper and continue to cook until the meat is almost falling off the bone, about 1 hour.

Meanwhile, crack the olives using the flat side of a heavy chef's knife. Remove and discard the pits, and set the olives aside.

Transfer the lamb neck to a carving board and loosely cover with aluminum foil to keep warm. Strain the cooking liquid through a sieve into a measuring cup, pressing on the vegetables to extract all the juice. Discard the vegetables. Let the liquid stand for 5 minutes—you should have about 2 cups / 500 ml—skim off the fat and set it aside for another use. Return the liquid to the pan, bring to a boil over medium heat, and boil until reduced to 1¹/₂ cups / 375 ml.

Using a fork, pull the lamb off the bone in large pieces. Cut the lamb meat into thick slices and place in a warm serving dish. Add the olives to the sauce, check the seasoning, and pour the sauce over the sliced lamb. Add the mint leaves and lemon zest and serve.

Lamb Neck with Quince and Turnip

SERVES 4

I share the title Queen of Quince with two other cookbook authors, Fran Gage and Barbara Ghazarian, who both live in California. We're planning to meet over a meal with quince in every course. To maintain my right to the crown, I never miss a chance to cook with quinces, and I'm happy to say they are now much easier to find. Quinces are delicious with meats, especially lamb, to which they add a wonderful aroma and depth. You must use hard green quinces for this recipe: the ripe yellow ones will cook into mush. If you can't find quinces or they are out of season, use two tart cooking apples instead, but don't add them until the last thirty minutes of cooking. Depending on the size of your lamb neck, you will need one or two slices per person. Serve this with pureed celery root (celeriac). As you need to soak the currants overnight, start this recipe the evening before you want to eat it.

1/3 cup / 1 3/4 ounces / 50 g currants

1 1/2 cups / 375 ml red wine

4 to 8 slices lamb neck, about 4 pounds / 1.8 kg (see page 66)

1 tablespoon coarse sea salt

1 tablespoon coriander seeds, toasted

12 cardamom pods, crushed and seeds removed

1 teaspoon black peppercorns

2 cloves

2 tablespoons rendered lamb fat or lard

1 large red onion, sliced

4 cloves garlic, finely chopped

2 quinces, peeled, quartered, and cored, then each quarter cut in half

4 white turnips, peeled and cut into eighths

1/4 cup chopped cilantro (coriander)

The night before you plan to cook the neck, place the currants in a bowl and pour over 1/2 cup / 125 ml of the wine, and leave to soak overnight.

Remove the lamb neck from the refrigerator 30 minutes before cooking. Preheat the oven to 300°F / 150°C.

Place the salt, coriander, and cardamom seeds, peppercorns, and cloves in a spice grinder and grind until powdery; set aside.

Pat the neck slices dry. In a large, heavy flameproof casserole or Dutch oven, melt half the fat over medium-high heat and brown the meat in batches, transferring the browned pieces to a plate.

Add the remaining fat and the onion to the pan and cook until the onion is soft. Then add the spice mix and garlic and cook until fragrant. Pour in the currants and any liquid, bring to a boil, and deglaze the pan, using a wooden spoon to scrape up the browned bits from the bottom.

Add the remaining wine, the browned lamb with any juices, and the quinces and turnips. Cover the lamb with a piece of wet parchment paper and the lid. Transfer to the oven and cook for 1 1/2 hours.

Turn the pieces of meat over, cover again with the parchment and the lid, and cook for another 1 1/2 hours. Uncover and remove the parchment paper and continue to cook until the lamb is almost falling off the bone, another 30 minutes to 1 hour. Stir in the cilantro (coriander) and serve.

Alternatives: Lamb shoulder or shank; pork neck, shank, or shoulder; venison neck or shank

WHAT'S IN A NAME?

It can be confusing shopping for odd bits, as the names for the same cuts of meat vary from animal to animal, place to place, and country to country. Also in many countries, the animal is butchered differently than it is in North America.

The word *chuck* is a general term describing beef shoulder. In the United States, it covers the neck, shoulder blades, and the first ribs, while in the United Kingdom it is a smaller cut centered on the shoulder blade. This name probably comes from an earlier meaning of *chuck*, a variation of *chock*, meaning a lump. But it didn't always refer to a lump of meat: in the nineteenth century, many foods like breads and hard tack were often called "chuck." The word *chunk* is likely related to both *chuck* and *chock*, but none of these words is very appetizing. In the western United States, *chuck* was used as a general term to denote food, and led to the term "chuck wagon".

> The 'Fifth Quarter' or 'il Quinto Quarto' as it is known in Italy, is, of course, a contradiction in terms. There is no such thing as a fifth quarter. Yet, this seemingly absurd term is the one used by both the French and Italian butchers to describe those parts of the animal—head, tail, feet and innards—that do not belong to the four quarters of the carcass.
> ANISSA HELOU

At the top of the front leg or shoulder of the animal is a wide flat bone called the blade bone. It is this bone that makes carving a shoulder challenging. With beef, a blade roast refers to the cut closest to the shoulder—although it rarely has the bone and you don't roast it. A blade roast of pork, which can be on the bone or boneless, is also cut from the shoulder; and in North America it has two other names: Boston shoulder and pork butt. The moniker of Boston comes from the popularity of this cut in that city, while butt refers to the barrels or casks that the pork was shipped in. The other section of the pork shoulder is called a picnic shoulder. Now, this may seem like an odd name until you look at how this cut was used. Hams are made with the pig's hind legs and are large and expensive. The lower section of the pig's front leg can be cured and smoked in the same way as a back leg, providing a smaller more economical "ham." In the early twentieth century, this affordable and easily transportable "ham" became a popular picnic food, and so it came to be called a picnic shoulder. The term stuck and is still used whether the cut is fresh or cured.

The name *brisket*, which describes the breast of beef and veal, is likely derived from Old Norse. It is not clear if it comes from the word *brjóst* meaning "breast," or a combination of two words: *brjósk*, meaning "cartilage," and *ket*, which refers to meat.

Clod is a British term for the cut of beef taken from the animal's neck. It was first recorded in *Queen Elizabeth's Household Book* (1601): "He hath for his fee two cloddes, one little rumpe, chine of beefe, of every oxe that is sent to the Queen's house."

So while the names can be confusing, they are easier to understand when you know the history behind them.

Ragu Masterplan

This is an excellent way to cook different odd bits. If you find yourself with a piece of shoulder, some slices of neck, a lamb's tongue, a piece of belly—none of which are substantial enough to make a dish on their own, combine them with other orphaned pieces to create a brilliant ragu. Ragu is a traditional Italian meat sauce, and it is infinitely variable. You can use the odd bits from one animal, or a mixture from different animals.

This recipe is for a lamb ragu, but no matter what meat I use, I always add some salty pork—I like the prosciutto odd bit: the shank end. I remove the skin and add the meat and fat to my ragu; bacon and pancetta are good substitutes. Use any combination of odd bits you like—just ensure that there is a good amount of fat. I grind everything except the tongues, which are cooked whole, then peeled and chopped (see page 50). For cooking beef, add a piece of orange zest, and more thyme and rosemary. For wild boar or other game, some crushed juniper berries are good, and for pork, add fresh sage leaves and replace the red wine with white wine. Take the time to cut the carrots and celery into a fine dice, as they add texture to the sauce.

About 3 1/3 pounds / 1.5 kg neck, shoulder, and prosciutto ends, ground

2 tablespoons rendered lamb fat or lard

2 onions, finely chopped

2 carrots, peeled and finely diced

1 stalk celery, finely diced

Coarse sea salt and freshly ground black pepper

2 cups / 500 ml red wine

2 lamb's tongues (optional)

One 28-ounce / 798-g can San Marzano tomatoes

3 large stems flat-leaf parsley

3 large sprigs rosemary

3 large sprigs thyme

2 cloves garlic

Preheat the oven to 300°F / 150°C.

Spread the ground meat on a paper towel–lined baking sheet and pat dry.

In a heavy flameproof casserole or Dutch oven, melt the fat over medium heat. When hot, add the onions, carrots, and celery and cook, stirring often, for about 10 minutes. You don't want the vegetables to color, but to cook until all the moisture has evaporated. When they begin to stick to the pan and are tender (try a piece of carrot to check for tenderness), add the ground meat to the pan and season with salt and pepper. Leave to cook without stirring for 5 minutes, then stir the meat and continue to cook for about 10 minutes, or until it begins to stick to the pan. Add the wine and bring to a boil. Stir and continue to boil until most of the wine disappears into the meat.

Now add the whole tongues, and the tomatoes, parsley, rosemary, thyme, garlic, and 2 teaspoons salt. Return to a boil, then transfer to the oven. Cook, uncovered, for 1 1/2 hours, stirring from time to time.

Check the tongues to see if they are cooked. If they are, remove them from the sauce and set them aside to cool slightly. If not, continue cooking until they are tender. Either way, return the sauce to the oven if it is not thick and clinging to the spoon; when it has thickened, remove the pan from the oven and discard the parsley, rosemary, and thyme. As soon as you can handle the tongues, peel (see page 51) and finely chop them and add them to the sauce. Check the seasoning and serve, or cool completely and freeze for up to 3 months.

A Shoulder to Lean On

The shoulder is a pretty straightforward cut. It is the front leg of the animal, which is smaller than the back leg because, like us, animals put on more weight on their back ends. It consists of several muscles and should be well marbled with fat, making it ideal for pot roasting and braising. Depending on the animal, the shank or hock is often removed and sold separately. With lamb and goat, chops are often cut from the shoulder, leaving a piece of meat that is roughly square in shape. On large animals, the shoulder is broken down into more manageable pieces that are sold both on and off the bone.

> It's a physical and sensory thrill to turn barely edible food—whether tripe or a well-worked muscle such as a shoulder, or even dried beans— into something that's great to eat, flavorful, and nourishing.
> THOMAS KELLER

How to Choose

The shoulder, with its mix of muscles, fat, and connective tissues, yields very flavorful meat. If you're buying a whole or half shoulder, your choice will be dictated by the size of your pan and the number of guests. If you are going to cook the shoulder in one piece, buy it on the bone, as the bones add flavor and texture to the sauce. For recipes using boneless pieces, it is always better to buy a whole piece and cut it into pieces yourself, as cut meat deteriorates more quickly. With pork, buy it with the skin if you can. Even if the recipe calls for skinless pork, skin is a very useful addition to many other dishes (see page 228).

How to Prepare and Cook

Generally shoulders, with their mix of muscles, are best braised until the meat falls off the bone. However, lamb shoulder is also excellent roasted; to make carving easier, ask your butcher to remove the blade bone. Keep the bone and add it to the pan when you roast the lamb or save it for your stockpot.

Whether roasting or braising, if the shank is still attached to the shoulder, make a cut around the bone end to release the tendons, so that the meat shrinks back from the bone as it cooks.

> Wrongly thought of as the poor man's leg, the [lamb] shoulder offers plenty of tender meat, albeit in a form that is not easy to carve.
> HUGH FEARNLEY-WHITTINGSTALL

To remove the skin from pork, simply make a cut at one end to free the skin from the fat. Peel the skin back using a knife. Try to leave as much of the fat as possible on the shoulder, and remove the skin in one or several large pieces.

Slow-Cooked Pork Shoulder with Cider and Rhubarb

SERVES 8

Whenever I see a recipe using rhubarb, I have to try it. I love rhubarb poached with crushed cardamom pods and stirred into thick, freshly whipped cream to make rhubarb fool—fabulous. I also like rhubarb paired with meat, especially pork. In this recipe, I combine all those tastes together—well, except the whipped cream. However, now that I think of it, I could add a little cream to the rhubarb sauce, but the rich pork really doesn't need it. The tangy rhubarb balances the sweet, fatty pork and adds a splash of color to the meat. This is a very forgiving dish, and you can easily scale it up or down, which makes it good dish for feeding a crowd. Serve it with spinach or asparagus. I like my rhubarb pieces to have a little texture, but even if they become very soft it doesn't change the flavor.

6 pounds / 2.75 kg bone-in, skin-on pork shoulder

Coarse sea salt and freshly ground black pepper

1 to 2 tablespoons lard

2 cups / 500 ml sweet apple cider

1 sweet apple, peeled, cored, and chopped

8 cardamom pods, lightly crushed

4 cloves garlic

2 dried chiles

2 fresh bay leaves

1 pound / 450 g rhubarb, trimmed

2 tablespoons honey

Remove the shoulder from the refrigerator about 1 hour before cooking. Using a sharp knife, remove the skin from the shoulder, preferably in one piece (see opposite).

Preheat the oven to 325°F / 160°C.

Pat the shoulder dry and season well with salt and pepper. In a heavy flameproof casserole or Dutch oven, heat 1 tablespoon of the lard over medium heat. When the fat is hot, brown the shoulder on all sides; 1 tablespoon of lard should be enough, as the shoulder will release fat, so add

extra lard only if necessary. Transfer the browned shoulder to a plate.

Tip any fat out of the pan and then pour the cider into the pan. Bring to a boil, stirring with a wooden spoon to deglaze the pan by scraping up the browned bits from the bottom. Remove the pan from the heat and add the apple, cardamom, garlic, chiles, and bay leaves. Return the shoulder to the pan along with any juices and place the pork skin over the top of the meat. If the piece of skin is not very big, cover the meat with a piece of wet parchment paper, too. Cover the pan with its lid, transfer to the oven, and cook for 2 hours.

Uncover the pan and remove the parchment paper. Push the skin off the meat but leave it in the pan, and continue to cook for another hour, or until the shoulder is very tender.

Meanwhile, cut the rhubarb into 1 1/2-inch / 4-cm pieces; set aside. Transfer the shoulder to a serving platter, cover loosely with aluminum foil, and keep warm.

Remove the skin from the pan and discard it. Strain the cooking liquid through a sieve into a large glass measuring cup and let stand for 5 minutes. You should have about 2 cups / 500 ml. Skim off the fat and set it aside for another use. Pour the cooking liquid back into the pan and place over high heat. Bring to a boil, and continue to boil until the sauce is reduced by about half. Stir in the honey, then lower the heat so the sauce barely simmers. Add the rhubarb and cook until just tender, 5 to 10 minutes. Remove the pan from the heat.

Carve the pork into thick slices, place on a warm serving platter, spoon over the rhubarb sauce and serve.

Alternatives: Fresh pork hocks, belly, or neck

Lamb Cobbler

Red wine, white wine, stock, and beer all work with lamb. It is a sweet meat, and parsnips, also called for in this recipe, are sweet too, so I like to balance them with the bitterness of beer. Although I am Australian, I'd much rather cook with beer than drink it, and my compatriots seem to be following suit: a recent survey revealed that wine is now Australians' favorite beverage.

The cooked lamb is turned into a simple pie by adding a cobbler or tea biscuit topping or, as my Aussie friends would say, a scone dough. You could make a more traditional pie using the Leaf Lard Pastry (page 87) for the top crust, or simply leave it as a stew with no topping at all. However, the biscuits are a great addition because they soak up some of the sauce as they bake. You can cook the lamb ahead of time, then reheat it and top with the biscuits. Serve this with a green vegetable.

3 pounds / 1.4 kg boneless lamb shoulder, cut into 2-inch / 5-cm pieces

Coarse sea salt and freshly ground black pepper

3 tablespoons rendered lamb fat or lard

2 onions, chopped

1 carrot, peeled and chopped

2 stalks celery with leaves, sliced

4 cloves garlic, germ removed, finely chopped

2 large sprigs rosemary

2 fresh bay leaves

3 cups / 750 ml dark beer

4 parsnips, peeled and cut into 1-inch / 2.5-cm pieces

Cobbler Dough

2 cups / 8³/4 ounces / 250 g flour

1 tablespoon baking powder

¹/2 teaspoon fine sea salt

1 tablespoon rosemary leaves, finely chopped

¹/2 cup / 4 ounces / 115 g cold unsalted butter, diced

1 egg, beaten

³/4 cup / 175 ml whole milk

Preheat the oven to 325°F / 160°C.

Pat the lamb pieces dry and season with salt and pepper.

In a heavy flameproof casserole or Dutch oven, heat 2 tablespoons of the fat over medium-high heat and brown the lamb pieces, adding more fat if necessary. As they brown, transfer the pieces to a plate. Add the onions, carrot, and celery to the pan, stirring well, and cook, stirring and scraping the bottom of the pan—the moisture from the vegetables will deglaze the pan. Continue to cook, stirring from time to time, until the moisture from the vegetables has evaporated and they begin to stick to the pan.

Add the garlic, rosemary sprigs, and bay leaves, then pour in the beer and bring to a boil, deglazing the pan again by scraping up the browned bits from the bottom. Continue to boil for 5 minutes, then return the lamb and any juices to the pan, and cover the lamb with a piece of wet parchment paper and the lid. Transfer to the oven and cook for 1 hour.

Uncover, remove the parchment paper, and stir in the parsnips. Return to the oven, and cook, uncovered, for another hour, or until the lamb is tender. Discard the rosemary sprigs and bay leaves and transfer the lamb, vegetables, and sauce into a 9 by 12-inch / 23 by 30-cm baking dish; check the seasoning.

At this point you can leave the lamb to cool completely, then refrigerate, covered, for up to 4 days before proceeding with the recipe. This way you can remove any excess fat off the lamb if you wish. Before continuing, reheat the lamb in a 325°F / 160°C oven until warm in the center.

continued

Increase the oven temperature to 425°F / 220°C.

Combine the flour, baking powder, fine salt, and rosemary leaves in a food processor. Add the cold butter and pulse until the mixture has coarse lumps of fat about the size of small peas. Transfer the mixture to a bowl. Set 2 teaspoons of the beaten egg aside and mix the remaining egg with the milk. Stir in enough of the milk and egg mixture into the bowl to make a soft, slightly sticky dough. Turn the dough onto a floured surface and knead gently just until the dough comes together.

Pat the dough into a disk $1/2$ inch / 1 cm thick and, using a floured $2^1/2$-inch / 6-cm biscuit cutter, cut out rounds. Knead any leftover dough together, pat into a disk again, and cut out additional biscuits until all the dough is used up.

Place the baking dish on a baking sheet and then arrange the biscuits on top of the lamb stew and brush the tops of the biscuits with the reserved 2 teaspoons of beaten egg. Bake in the oven until the biscuits are puffed and browned and the lamb is bubbling, about 25 minutes.

Alternatives: Beef or goat shoulder

Haralds's Chili

SERVES 6

Why do men like cooking chili? Is it really any different from any other stew? Is it the macho attitude to peppers and heat? My husband, Haralds, has perfected his technique, and he loves to make this dish for our French friends, to make them try something different. He is adamant that his chili comes with the beans on the side, never mixed in with the meat. I mix them together on my plate. At my Paris butcher's, I was debating whether to buy shoulder or shank for this recipe: my butcher advised shoulder (not that he knew the first thing about making chili), assuring me it was juicier. I'm sure you can make this chili with shank too, and remember you have to soak the beans ahead of time.

3 ancho chiles, stems removed

1 cup / 250 ml boiling water

4 red bell peppers

4 onions

2 serrano chiles

$2^1/4$ pounds / 1 kg boneless beef shoulder

Coarse sea salt and freshly ground black pepper

$1/3$ cup / $2^1/4$ ounces / 65 g beef dripping or lard

1 tablespoon ground cumin

1 tablespoon ground coriander

1 cup / 250 ml dark beer

$1^1/4$ cups / 8 ounces / 225 g black beans, soaked overnight in cold water

1 teaspoon dried epazote or dried savory leaves

Using scissors, cut the ancho chiles into large pieces, discarding the seeds. Toast the pieces in a frying pan over medium heat, turning once, until fragrant, about 2 minutes. Place the chile pieces in a bowl and pour over the boiling water; let steep for 30 minutes.

Remove and discard the stems and seeds from the red peppers and chop the peppers finely. Cut 3 of the onions in half and then slice them; set the peppers and onions aside. Remove the stem and seeds from 1 of the serrano chiles and discard. Finely dice the chile and set it aside. Remove the ancho chiles from the water and chop finely. Discard the soaking water.

Preheat the oven to 300°F /150°C.

Cut the shoulder into 3/4-inch / 2-cm cubes. Pat the meat dry and season with salt and pepper.

In a large, deep Dutch oven or flameproof casserole over medium-high heat, add 1 tablespoon of the dripping and brown the meat in batches, adding more fat as necessary. Transfer the browned meat to a plate.

Lower the heat, add the sliced onions to the pan, and stir to deglaze the pan slightly with the moisture from the onions. Once the onions have softened, add the anchos, red peppers, diced serrano chile, cumin, coriander, and 1 1/2 teaspoons salt and stir to mix. Continue to cook until most of the liquid from the vegetables has evaporated.

Pour in the beer and bring to a boil, stirring with a wooden spoon to deglaze the pan. Return the meat along with any juices to the pan and bring to a boil. Cover with the lid, then transfer to the oven and cook for 2 hours. Uncover and cook for another hour, or until the meat is very tender.

Meanwhile, dice the remaining onion. In a medium saucepan, melt the remaining fat over medium heat, add the diced onion and the remaining whole serrano chile and cook until the onion is slightly softened. Drain the beans and add them to the pan with the epazote, then pour in enough cold water to cover and bring to a boil over medium heat. Cover, transfer to the oven, and cook for 1 hour, then uncover and continue to cook for another hour or until the beans are tender. Remove the chile and stir in 1 teaspoon of salt. Serve the chili and beans together but not mixed.

Alternatives: Beef neck or shank

EPAZOTE

Epazote is a strongly flavored herb from Mexico; it is also called Mexican tea and worm weed, among other things. Sometimes you can find it fresh in Latin markets, but it is more commonly available dried. Adding a little epazote to beans is a good idea because it's a carminative—that means it relieves flatulence, which is always a benefit when eating beans.

West Indian Goat Stew

SERVES 4

Suddenly goat was popping up everywhere on my culinary radar. My friends Bruce Weinstein and Mark Scarbrough were working on a goat cookbook, radical for Americans. And then I was in a local butcher shop when a customer came in looking for goat. I told him that goat was available at the Saturday market where I buy pork blood. Then I thought, why haven't I tried it? This recipe remedied that. I thought about using shanks, but my supplier only had one shank left, so I bought shoulder chops; you can use whatever you like. While the meat from mature goats is tough and strongly flavored, the meat from young animals is mild and tender. Don't fancy goat? Check out the alternative meats at the end of the recipe. I also added two Scotch bonnet peppers, as I like heat, but just use one if you prefer it less spicy. There is often a high ratio of bone per chop with goat, so if that's the case, add an extra chop. Serve this with rice.

4 goat shoulder chops, about 2 1/2 pounds / 1.2 kg

Coarse sea salt and freshly ground black pepper

2 tablespoons rendered lamb fat or lard

2 onions, chopped

2 carrots, peeled and cut into 1/2-inch / 1-cm slices

2 stalks celery, sliced

One 1 1/2-inch / 4-cm piece fresh ginger, peeled and finely chopped

4 cloves garlic, finely chopped

6 large sprigs thyme

2 fresh bay leaves

2 teaspoons allspice berries, ground

2 Scotch bonnet, habanero, or Thai chiles

One 5-inch / 13-cm cinnamon stick

2 cups / 500 ml Lamb Stock (page 234)

1 large sweet potato, about 1 1/3 pounds / 600 g, peeled and cut into 2-inch / 5-cm chunks

4 green onions, cut into 1/2-inch / 1-cm pieces

3 tablespoons chopped cilantro (coriander)

1 lime

Preheat the oven to 325°F / 160°C.

Cut the chops in half, pat the meat dry, and season well with salt and pepper.

In a heavy flameproof casserole or Dutch oven, add half the fat and place over medium-high heat. When the fat is hot, add the chops in batches and brown, transferring the browned chops to a plate.

Lower the heat and add more fat only if necessary, then add the onions, carrots, and celery. Stir and cook until all the moisture evaporates from the vegetables and they begin to stick to the pan.

Add the ginger, garlic, thyme, bay leaves, allspice, whole chiles, and cinnamon, stirring until fragrant. Pour in the stock and bring to a boil, using a wooden spoon to scrape up the browned bits from the bottom of the pan. Return the chops with any juices to the pan and cover the meat with a piece of wet parchment paper and the lid. Transfer to the oven and cook for 1 1/2 hours.

Add the sweet potato and green onions, cover, and continue to cook for another hour or until the meat is very tender. Remove the thyme, bay leaves, chiles, and cinnamon stick and discard. Check the seasoning, sprinkle with the cilantro (coriander) and add a good squeeze of lime juice, and serve.

Alternatives: Shanks, neck, lamb shoulder chops, beef or pork shoulder, oxtail

Brisket or Breast—
It's All About the Fat

While all animals have heads and shoulders, when you start moving back along the animal, it becomes more difficult to compare them. Brisket is unique to beef and calf, and it is located between the neck and the front legs of the animal—its chest. With sheep and pigs, this part is included with the shoulder.

Depending on your cultural background, brisket conjures up different images: a large piece of meat served at Passover; slow-smoked Texas-style brisket; or, in my case, pinkish corned beef cooked with carrots and cabbage and served with mustard sauce. I didn't give much thought to where the piece of meat was on the animal: it was just corned beef.

> The transformation that happens to a tough, unappealing cut of meat as it cooks long and gently is to me a fundamental pleasure of cooking—it lies at the core of why cooking is such a soul-satisfying act.
> THOMAS KELLER

Brisket is the term generally applied to beef, while on calves the cut may also be called breast. A beef brisket is a large, boneless cut that can weigh anywhere up to 10 to 12 pounds / 4.5 to 5.5 kg, so it is often cut into two sections. The first cut or "flat cut," which is rectangular in shape, is flatter and leaner than the triangular or pointed second cut, also called the front-end, or point cut, which is thicker and comes with a good cap of fat. Because of the fat, the triangular cut is my favorite. While most people think of braising brisket, well-marbled brisket is an ideal odd bit for making burgers and meatloaf, because of its fat content. It delivers a rich beefy taste that more expensive cuts don't.

Veal brisket or breast is available on the bone and can weigh up to 9 pounds / 4 kg, but there is a lot of waste. It can be cut into riblets, but a boneless veal breast is a more practical cut. It has a similar shape to a chicken breast—thicker along the side where it was joined to the chest, and tapering away at the outside edges. It weighs about 5 pounds / 2.25 kg and can be cooked whole, stuffed and rolled, or cut into pieces for braising.

How to Choose

Remember that the animal carcass is split down the center, so there are two pieces of veal breast or beef brisket on each animal. As beef brisket is sold in boneless pieces, look for a well-marbled piece of meat; don't let the fat frighten you off, it gives brisket its flavor.

Err on buying too much, as long as the piece fits in your pan. Brisket shrinks dramatically, even when cooked very slowly, and you will discover that the piece you jammed into your pan will be swimming around in its cooking juices by the time it's ready. When you are buying veal breast, you are buying a breast half on or off the bone. It will have less fat than beef brisket, but it should still have a covering of fat with a good layer running through the front half of the breast meat.

> I really believe we should eat everything from an animal; it doesn't make sense to eat only fillets and steaks, which make up only a small percentage. In Italy, just as I feel salumi represents the traditional food of the people, so do the recipes for brains, kidneys, and feet . . .
> GIORGIO LOCATELLI

How to Prepare and Cook

If you want, you can remove a little of the fat cap but I prefer to leave it in place. If you need to trim your brisket to fit your pan, keep all the off-cuts for making burgers (see page 89). Brisket and breast, whether whole or in pieces, are best cooked slowly, either with liquid or smoked barbecue-style. When carving, always cut brisket across the grain, to ensure the meat will be tender.

When you grind brisket, you break down the fibers in the meat effectively tenderizing it. Ground brisket makes fabulous beefy flavored burgers and meatloaf.

If you are rolling the veal breast, it is a good idea to trim both ends to make a more uniform piece, then butterfly it.

BUTTERFLYING

Butterflying is a technique of cutting meat through the center but not completely in half. It is then opened up like a book, and to some eyes it resembles a butterfly—hence the name. The advantage of butterflying meat is that it cooks more quickly and uniformly and is easier to stuff and roll.

Lay the veal breast fat side down on a cutting board. You will see that one side of the breast is thicker than the other. You start from this thick side of the breast and work toward the thin side. Using a sharp, long knife, cut through the meat, keeping the knife parallel to the fat side and the board, down the length of the long thick side of the breast. Cut as though you were slicing a cake into layers, but stop before you cut through the other side of the breast. Now open up the meat like a book. If both sides of this meat book are not exactly the same thickness or perfectly even don't worry, it is going to be rolled up.

Fennel and Orange Braised Veal Breast

SERVES 6

This dish takes time, so plan to make it over two days. Not only will the flavor be better, but the veal is much easier to slice when it's cold. When your guests arrive, you'll only have to heat it up. I like to use blood oranges: their color is great and their flavor has a berry note lacking in regular oranges. That said, regular oranges will work just fine here. Orange and fennel are a great combination I find myself using them again and again. The veal breast is generally too thick to stuff and roll up, so it is butterflied first (see above). This is not difficult, but if you're hesitant, ask your butcher to do it, and watch him so you can do it yourself the next time. While the veal has lots of collagen, make sure you use Veal Stock to ensure a wonderful, rich, unctuous sauce. Serve with Potato Gnocchi (page 38) and spinach.

1 large head fennel with leafy tops
4 garlic cloves, germ removed, and finely chopped
4 blood oranges
1 large shallot, finely chopped
1 tablespoon fennel seeds, toasted and ground
3 tablespoons olive oil

1/2 boneless veal breast, about 2 1/2 pounds /
1.2 kg, butterflied (see opposite)

Coarse sea salt and freshly ground black pepper

1 onion, chopped

1 large carrot, peeled and chopped

2 stalks celery, chopped

1 cup / 250 ml dry white wine

2 cups / 500 ml Veal Stock (page 233)

2 fresh bay leaves

2 large sprigs thyme

Preheat the oven to 325°F / 160°C.

Remove the green feathery leaves from the fennel and chop them finely; you should have about 2 tablespoons. Cut the fennel bulb in half lengthways, remove and discard the central core, and chop the fennel bulb.

Place the chopped fennel leaves in a small bowl and add the garlic. Finely grate the zest from 3 of the oranges and set the oranges aside. Add the zest, shallot, and fennel seeds to the bowl and stir in 1 tablespoon of the olive oil, then mix well.

Lay the butterflied breast fat side down on the counter and open it up like a book. Spread the fennel and orange mixture over the meat. Season with salt and pepper and then, from the long, thinner side, roll the meat into a tight, thick roll. Tie it with butcher's string at 1 inch / 2.5 cm intervals and then season the rolled meat with salt and pepper.

In a heavy flameproof casserole or Dutch oven just big enough to hold the meat, add the remaining olive oil and place over medium-high heat. When the oil is hot, brown the meat on all sides, about 10 minutes, then transfer it to a plate.

Add the chopped fennel bulb, onion, carrot, and celery to the pan. Cook, stirring occasionally, until the vegetables soften, about 5 minutes. Pour in the wine and deglaze the pan, using a wooden spoon to scrape up the browned bits from the bottom. Add the stock and a large strip of zest from the remaining orange, then return the meat to the pan with any juices. Bring to a boil, cover

the veal with a piece of wet parchment paper and the lid and transfer to the oven.

Cook the veal for 1 hour, then turn the veal and cover again with the parchment paper and the lid and continue to cook for another hour. Uncover the pan and remove the paper and continue to cook, uncovered, for 1 hour longer, or until the meat is very tender, turning once.

Remove the pan from the oven and allow the veal to cool in the cooking liquid. Take the meat out of the pan and strain the cooking liquid into a glass measuring cup, pressing on the vegetables to extract all the juices. You should have about 2 to 2 1/2 cups / 500 to 625 ml. Discard the vegetables and cover and refrigerate the veal and the cooking liquid separately, overnight.

Preheat the oven to 325°F / 160°C.

To finish the cooking, remove the meat and liquid from the refrigerator. Remove the string from the veal and cut the veal into 1/2-inch / 1-cm thick slices. You should get about 12 good slices and some smaller, less attractive ones.

Remove any excess fat from the top of the jellied cooking liquid. The jelly should be set solid; tip it out of the measuring cup onto a board. Cut off the muddied jelly from the bottom and set aside; it can be frozen and added to a soup or stew.

Place the clear jelly in a saucepan, bring it to a boil over high heat, and boil until reduced to 1 cup / 250 ml. The sauce will be syrupy and sticky. Finely grate the remaining zest from the fourth orange, and squeeze the juice (you should have about 1/4 cup / 60 ml); set aside the zest and juice. Remove the pith from the other 3 oranges and cut them into segments, reserving any juice.

Place the veal slices in a baking dish in a single layer. Pour over the sauce and orange juice, cover with foil, and cook for 15 minutes. Uncover, turn the slices, and cook for another 15 minutes. Then add the orange zest, segments, and any juice, and serve.

Summer Corned Beef

For me, corned beef is a winter dish, with carrots and cabbage simmering away on top of the stove. However, my cousins in Australia introduced me to a new way of cooking it—on the barbecue. Now I can eat corned beef all year. This is not Texas-style smoked brisket; it is slow-cooked corned beef. It is denser than boiled corned beef and has a lightly caramelized taste. Serve it with a fresh cabbage slaw. Ask your butcher for a uniform piece of corned beef brisket that is not too thick and with a good layer of fat, and don't be surprised by how much it shrinks. If you happen to have any leftovers, try the Corned Beef Appetizers (see below).

> 2 1/2 pounds / 1.2 kg corned beef brisket
> Olive oil
> 2 cups / 500 ml pilsner beer
> Mustard

Rinse the corned beef, then place it in a bowl of cold water and soak for 6 hours or overnight to remove any excess salt.

Drain the meat and pat it dry. Rub the meat all over with olive oil.

Place a drip pan under the center of the grill rack to catch the fat and juices, add 1/2 cup / 125 ml water to the pan, and preheat the grill to indirect medium heat.

Place the corned beef fat side up on the grill over the pan, close the grill lid, and cook for 30 minutes. Baste the meat by pouring about 1/2 cup / 125 ml of beer over it. Cover and continue to cook for another 1 1/2 hours, basting again in 30 minutes, and then again 30 minutes later. After 2 hours, turn the corned beef fat side down, pour over the remaining beer, cover the grill, and cook for another 15 to 30 minutes, or until it is easily pierced with a skewer.

Remove the corned beef from the grill and let it stand for 5 minutes, loosely covered with aluminum foil. Slice thinly across the grain and serve with the mustard.

Corned Beef Appetizers

Now, this is just a way to use up any leftover corned beef. You could make corned beef hash following the tongue hash recipe (page 52), but this is something different. While corned beef might technically qualify for a place on a charcuterie platter, I am not sure it deserves to be there—but then I am biased toward good cured sausage, rillettes, and pâtés. In Toronto, a French-inspired restaurant does put corned beef on their platter, and they also serve an *amuse-bouche* of corned beef before the meal. I don't know why I had never considered serving corned beef this way.

> Thin slices of cooked corned beef
> Slices of toasted egg bread or brioche
> Grainy mustard
> Thinly sliced radishes

Spread the toast thickly with grainy mustard. Top with the corned beef slices, cut into fingers, garnish with the radish slices, and serve.

Too fussy for you? Just turn it all into a fabulous sandwich.

Brisket Braised with Caramelized Onions and Chile

SERVES 6

Chef Jean-Georges Vongerichten inspired this recipe. Eating at his Paris restaurant, Market, one can't but be amazed at how his cooking crosses cultures and cuisines. Originally from the Alsace region of France, Vongerichten has traveled the world and fallen in love with different flavors and spices, especially those from Asia. This is one of my favorite ways to cook brisket; the darkly caramelized topping of onions contrasts with the rich tender meat. Serve it with noodles or pureed potatoes.

3^1/$_2$ pounds / 1.6 kg beef brisket, with a good layer of fat

Coarse sea salt and freshly ground black pepper

2 serrano chiles

1 carrot, peeled and sliced

1 stalk celery, sliced

2 fresh bay leaves

1 large orange

3 tablespoons beef dripping or lard

3 onions, halved and sliced

2 to 3 cups / 500 to 750 ml Beef Stock (page 232)

Hot pepper sauce (optional)

Preheat the oven to 325°F / 160°C.

Remove the brisket from the refrigerator and season with salt and pepper. Place the brisket fat side up in a Dutch oven or casserole where it fits very snugly, and add the chiles, carrot, celery, and bay leaves. Remove the zest from the orange in large strips and add to the pan; set the orange aside.

In a frying pan over medium heat, melt the dripping, add the onions, and cook, stirring until the onions are golden brown. Place the onions on top of the brisket.

Pour 2 cups / 500 ml of the stock into the frying pan, bring to a boil, and deglaze the pan, using a wooden spoon to scrape up the browned pieces from the bottom. Remove the pan from the heat and carefully pour the liquid around the brisket. The liquid should come about three-quarters up the sides of the meat; add more stock if necessary. Cover, transfer to the oven, and cook for 2 hours.

Uncover and cook for another hour, or until the meat is very tender when pierced with a skewer. Transfer the brisket with its onion crust to a plate and loosely cover with aluminum foil to keep warm.

Strain the cooking liquid through a sieve into a measuring cup (you should have 1^1/$_2$ to 2 cups / 375 to 500 ml), and let it stand for 5 minutes. Meanwhile, squeeze the juice from the orange into a saucepan. Skim the fat off the cooking liquid and set the fat aside for another use, and add the liquid to the saucepan. Bring to a boil over medium heat and boil until reduced to about 1 cup / 250 ml. Taste, season with salt and pepper, and add a little hot pepper sauce if desired. Carve the brisket into thick slices and serve with the sauce.

Wine-Braised Veal

My mother sends me clippings from Australian news-papers to help me keep in touch with "home." Many of them are food related, and these are the ones I find the most interesting. She sent me a clipping about Maris, a restaurant close to her house where we had enjoyed a delicious summer lunch. My interest was piqued by the chef's use of star anise, a favorite spice of mine, in his braised veal breast. This is my version of chef and owner Patrick Craig's recipe—veal is cooked in a rich, sweet wine sauce balanced with vinegar. This recipe is flexible, so if your veal breast is smaller or bigger than the one I call for, don't worry. This is also a good recipe to make ahead: the fat is easier to skim from a cold sauce, and the flavors improve with reheating. Serve this with potatoes or pasta.

1/2 boneless veal breast, about 2 1/2 pounds / 1.2 kg

Coarse sea salt and freshly ground black pepper

1/4 cup / 1 3/4 ounces / 50 g beef dripping or lard

2 onions, halved and sliced

2 carrots, peeled and sliced

2 stalks celery, sliced

2 tablespoons tomato paste

3/4 cup / 4 3/4 ounces / 135 g brown sugar

8 cloves garlic

4 fresh bay leaves

4 star anise

1/2 teaspoon fennel seeds, toasted

1/2 teaspoon coriander seeds, toasted

2 cups / 500 ml red wine

2 tablespoons balsamic vinegar

Preheat the oven to 300°F / 150°C.

Cut the veal crosswise into 1-inch / 2.5-cm slices; you should have about 12. Pat the slices dry and season well with salt and pepper.

In a heavy flameproof casserole or Dutch oven, melt 1 tablespoon of the dripping over medium-high heat. When the fat is hot, brown the meat in batches, adding more dripping if necessary, and transfer the browned pieces to a plate.

When all the meat is browned, lower the heat to medium and add the onions, carrots, and celery, and cook, stirring and adding the remaining fat if necessary, until the onion begins to brown. Stir in the tomato paste and cook, stirring, for 3 more minutes. Add the sugar, garlic, bay leaves, star anise, fennel, and coriander. Pour in the wine and deglaze the pan, using a wooden spoon to scrape up the browned bits from the bottom. Return the veal slices and any juices to the pan. Cover the meat with a piece of wet parchment paper and the lid, transfer to the oven, and cook for 1 hour. Uncover the pan and remove the paper and continue to cook, uncovered, for another 30 minutes, or until the veal is very tender.

Transfer the veal to a warm serving dish and keep warm. Strain the liquid through a sieve, pressing against the vegetables to extract all the juice. Discard the vegetables. Let the liquid stand for 5 minutes, then skim off the fat and set it aside for another use. Return the cooking liquid to the pan, place over high heat, bring to a boil, and continue to boil until the sauce is reduced to about 1 cup / 250 ml. Add the vinegar, return the sauce to a boil, check the seasoning, then pour over the veal and serve.

Alternatives: Large pieces of veal shoulder or neck, veal cheeks

Beef and Vegetable Pie

SERVES 6

I like making savory pies, especially when the weather turns cooler. The meat and vegetables all cook together and the pastry supplies the starch: it is a complete meal in one package. This is a real double-crust pie, where the filling is baked in the pastry. As you may have noticed, I've developed a passion for brisket, but beef shoulder would be a good choice here too. Of course you can make this pie using any meat, and you can vary the vegetables.

Leaf Lard Pastry (see opposite)

1 1/4 pounds / 570 g beef brisket, cut into 3/4-inch / 2-cm pieces

2 carrots, peeled and cut into 1/2-inch / 1-cm pieces

2 parsnips, peeled and cut into 1/2-inch / 1-cm pieces

1 onion, chopped

1 stalk celery, cut into 1/2-inch / 1-cm pieces

3 tablespoons chopped flat-leaf parsley

2 teaspoons fresh thyme leaves

1 tablespoon flour

1 1/2 teaspoons coarse sea salt

Freshly ground black pepper

Beef dripping or lard for greasing

1 tablespoon port

1 teaspoon mustard powder

1 tablespoon whole milk

Preheat the oven to 400°F / 200°C and place a rimmed baking sheet on the lowest rack of the oven. Remove the pastry from the refrigerator.

In a large bowl, toss together the meat, carrots, parsnips, onion, celery, parsley, thyme, and flour. Add the salt and season well with the pepper; set aside.

Lightly grease a 9 1/2-inch / 24-cm pie plate.

On a floured surface, roll 1 pastry disk into an 11-inch / 28-cm circle and line the pie dish with it. Fill the pie with the meat mixture, mounding it in the center. Nestle a pie bird into the center of the pie. In a measuring cup, whisk together the port and mustard powder, then add enough water to make 1 cup / 250 ml of liquid, and pour into the pie. Brush the edges of the piecrust with a little of the milk.

Roll out the second pastry disk into an 11-inch / 28-cm circle and cover the pie, cutting a slit in the center to expose the pie bird. Trim and seal the edges well. Brush the top of the pie with the remaining milk, and place the pie in the oven on the baking sheet.

Bake the pie for 30 minutes, then reduce the oven temperature to 325°F / 160°C and continue to bake for another 1 1/2 hours. If the pastry starts to brown too much, cover the top of the pie with a piece of aluminum foil.

Remove the pie from the oven and let stand in a warm place for 10 minutes before cutting.

Alternatives: Shoulder or boned shank from beef, veal, lamb, goat, or venison

Leaf Lard Pastry

MAKES ENOUGH FOR TWO 9¹/₂-INCH / 24-CM PIE CRUSTS; OR TO TOP A 9 BY 12-INCH / 23 BY 30-CM BAKING DISH

Leaf lard is the fat from around a pig's kidneys. It is ideal for pastry making because of its brittle, crystalline structure. You can use lard rendered from back fat if no leaf lard is available.

- 2 cups / 8³/₄ ounces / 250 g flour
- ³/₄ teaspoon baking powder
- ¹/₂ teaspoon fine sea salt
- ²/₃ cup / 4¹/₂ ounces / 125 g chilled rendered leaf lard, diced
- About ¹/₃ cup / 75 ml ice-cold water

Combine the flour, baking powder, and salt in a food processor and pulse to mix. Add the lard and pulse until the lard is reduced to pea-sized pieces, about 15 seconds. Turn the mixture into a bowl.

Pour the water over the flour and lard mixture and mix with a fork. Squeeze a bit of the mixture between your fingers. If it holds together, transfer the dough to a lightly floured surface; if not, add another couple of teaspoons of ice water and test again. Gently knead the dough into a ball.

If you are making a double-crust pie, divide the pastry in half and flatten into 2 disks. If you are covering a larger dish, leave the pastry in one piece. Wrap the pastry in plastic wrap and refrigerate for at least 30 minutes before using. This pastry freezes well.

Brisket Burgers

As with meatloaf, fat will make your burger tasty—
brisket is the perfect cut for making burgers. Grinding
your own meat is worth the effort: it assures the quality
of your meat, and you can grind it twice. The second pass
through the meat grinder helps develop a protein called
myosin, which makes the meat sticky. This will keep the
hamburger together and eliminate any need to overwork
the meat when forming the patties. This is a very simple
recipe, with only salt and pepper added to the meat. Of
course you can add whatever you want, but often I just
want my burgers to taste of beef and nothing else. For a
more complex taste, try Heart Burgers (page 122).

I use an electric meat grinder that fits on my stand
mixer, but a hand grinder works just as well, and builds
up your biceps.

When all the meat is ground, place a piece of bread
in the meat grinder: this will push the last pieces of meat
through the machine. Stop the machine when you see
the bread coming out.

Keep the burgers 1 inch / 2.5 cm thick so they can
cook through without burning, and don't make them
wider than your spatula for easy turning.

1²/₃ pounds / 750 g fatty brisket

1¹/₄ teaspoons coarse sea salt

Freshly ground black pepper

A little beef dripping or olive oil

2 tablespoons melted butter

4 buns, halved

Toppings: lettuce leaves, tomatoes, mustard, bacon,
mayonnaise, dill pickles

Cut the brisket into pieces that will easily fit into
your meat grinder. Place the pieces in a bowl and
add the salt and season with the pepper. Toss
together, then refrigerate along with your meat
grinder.

Using the larger grinder die (¹/₄ inch / 6 mm),
grind the meat mixture into a bowl, then pass the
ground meat through the grinder a second time.

Mix the ground meat gently and divide the
mixture into 4. With wet hands, form each portion
into a patty 1 inch / 2.5 cm thick and 4 inches /
10 cm in diameter. Place the patties on a plate,
cover, and refrigerate until ready to cook.

Preheat an outdoor grill or grill pan to high.
Lightly grease the grill and then add the patties;
season again with salt and pepper. Lower the heat
to medium-high and cook for 5 minutes, then
turn and cook for another 4 minutes for medium.

Meanwhile, brush the cut surfaces of the buns
with the melted butter and place cut side down
on the grill. Toast the buns lightly for 1 minute,
turning once.

Serve the burgers with the buns and your
choice of toppings.

*Alternatives: Veal brisket makes a delicious
burger; add some chopped tarragon to it. Any
fatty cut will do: try pork belly or lamb shoulder,
or mix different meats. Just make sure that you
have a good portion of fat, about 30 percent, for
juicy flavorful burgers.*

Argentinean-Style Meatloaf with Chimichurri

SERVES 6

Argentineans are known for their passion for beef, and they love to grill it outdoors. They often serve grilled meats with a thick parsley sauce called *chimichurri*. My meatloaf is baked, but *chimichurri* is still a good match. Grinding your own meat means you know exactly what cut you are using: you can control the fat percentage and guarantee the freshness. Unlike for the burgers (page 89), the meat for this meatloaf is only ground once. What to serve with this? Mashed potatoes of course; otherwise it's going against the natural order. The meatloaf is also delicious cold or in a sandwich.

2 tablespoons beef dripping or lard

1 large onion, chopped

1 pound / 450 g spinach, stemmed, washed, and coarsely chopped

2^1/$_4$ pounds / 1 kg ground brisket

^{3}/$_4$ cup / 2 ounces / 60 g fine fresh bread crumbs

1 egg

Coarse sea salt

Chile powder

Freshly ground black pepper

3 cups / 45 g flat-leaf parsley leaves

1 shallot, finely chopped

1 clove garlic, germ removed

^{1}/$_3$ cup / 75 ml extra virgin olive oil

1 tablespoon red wine vinegar

^{1}/$_2$ teaspoon dried oregano

In a large frying pan over medium heat, add the dripping; when the fat is hot, add the onion and cook until softened, about 5 minutes. Increase the heat to medium-high, add the spinach, and continue to cook, stirring, until the spinach wilts and all the water from the spinach has evaporated. Set aside to cool.

Preheat the oven to 350°F / 180°C.

In a large bowl, mix the brisket, bread crumbs, and cooled spinach mixture. Whisk the egg with 2 teaspoons of salt and 1 teaspoon of chile powder and season with pepper; add to the beef and mix well. Take a spoonful of the mixture and flatten into a patty. Cook the patty in a frying pan to verify the seasoning.

Pack the meat mixture into a 6-cup / 1.5-l loaf pan, mounding it in the center. Place the loaf pan on a rimmed baking sheet and bake for 55 minutes, or until the meatloaf shrinks from the sides of the pan and the juices from the center of the loaf are just tinged with pink.

Meanwhile, place the parsley leaves, shallot, and garlic in a food processor and process until finely chopped. Add the olive oil, vinegar, oregano, and a pinch of salt and chile powder and process until well mixed. Transfer the *chimichurri* to a small bowl.

Remove the meatloaf from the oven and let it rest for 10 minutes. Carefully remove the meatloaf from the pan, slice and serve with the *chimichurri* sauce.

Alternatives: Boned beef shoulder or shank

Sweetbreads: Neither Sweet nor Bready

This odd bit has a very strange name: it is a gland that is neither sweet nor breadlike. The word's origins go back to the sixteenth century; "sweet" was a reference to the odd bit's reputation as a prized delicacy. The "bread" part of the name is not related to bread as we think of it, but comes from the Old English word *broed,* meaning "flesh."

> Chef Daniel used to say that they should have the feel of a firm, young breast.
> SUSAN SPICER

There is also a lot of confusion as to just exactly what they are, and while researching this book I discovered many different opinions. Some people still believe that "sweetbreads" is a pseudonym for testicles. It's not: those odd bits have more than enough euphemistic names (see page 213). At chef school, I learned that sweetbreads are the thymus glands of young animals, calf and sometimes lamb. This is why they are so special, expensive, and limited in supply; however some people, including butchers, have expanded the term to include the inferior pancreas. Julia Child described them this way:

> A whole sweetbread, which is the thymus gland of a calf and usually weighs around 1 pound, consists of 2 lobes connected by a soft, white tube, the cornet. The smoother, rounder, and more solid of the two lobes is the kernel, heart, or noix, and the choicest piece. The second lobe, called the throat sweetbread or gorge, is more uneven in shape . . .

She neglects to mention lamb sweetbreads, which are equally tasty. As Child points out, the thymus gland consists of two parts, which is why they are often referred to in the plural. Sweetbreads are made up of a thin, knobby lobe, the "throat" sweetbread, and its rounder, firmer twin, often called the "heart" sweetbread. Heart refers to its shape, not its location. The heart sweetbread is generally preferred because it is more compact than the throat one and slices more evenly. The thymus gland atrophies as the animal ages, so sweetbreads are only found in young animals. The pancreas, also a gland, is located near the animal's stomach and, unlike true sweetbreads, it does not disappear as the animal ages. This accounts for its substitution for and confusion with sweetbreads. It is not a sweetbread, but is often given the moniker of "stomach sweetbread."

In France, I had a long dinner conversation with a food writer and a cooking teacher. When I discussed eating the pancreas, I was met with a look of horror—and the French are not squeamish when it comes to eating organs and glands. They considered the idea of eating pancreas disgusting, let alone substituting it for sweetbreads. Despite the French reaction, the pancreas is edible; it has a coarser texture and less fine flavor than sweetbreads and, of course, is cheaper.

How to Choose

With the confusion over sweetbreads even among butchers, it is very important that you buy them from a source you can trust. Price is usually a good clue that you have the real thing: remember there are two types: the rounder, smoother heart sweet bread and the longer less compact throat sweetbread. Both sweetbreads are not a solid piece of flesh, but are a collection of nodules held together by a membrane, which will help indicate that you have the real thing. The membrane should be intact and shiny. As with all fragile odd bits, freshness is of utmost importance, so choose sweetbreads that are plump, moist, and white to pale pink in color with no discoloration. Calf sweetbreads, especially from milk-fed animals, are the most highly prized and have the mildest flavor. However, if you find lamb sweetbreads, they are equally good, though they're smaller. Pork sweetbreads are sometimes available; they have a more distinct flavor and their texture is less refined.

Sweetbreads are rich, so about 5 to 6 ounces / 140 to 170 g per person is enough. Sweetbreads can be frozen.

How to Prepare and Cook

Sweetbreads must be prepared as soon as possible after purchase. The first step is to soak them in salted cold water—about 1 teaspoon of coarse sea salt per cup / 250 ml of water—for 4 to 6 hours, changing several times, to remove any blood. Sweetbreads can be braised or even grilled (page 98) without any advance preparation, but for most recipes they must be poached first.

Tender and creamy, with a delicate flavor, they have long been popular with restaurant chefs, less so with home cooks.
HUGH FEARNLEY-WHITTINGSTALL

Drain the sweetbreads and place them in a saucepan, noting their soft, wobbly texture. Cover the sweetbreads with the cooled Court Bouillon (page 21) and bring them slowly to a simmer over medium-low heat. If you have no court bouillon, you can cover them with cold water and add a teaspoon of sea salt and a lemon wedge. Check the sweetbreads from time to time; depending on their size, they may be ready even before the water simmers. While they cook, fill a bowl with cold water and add some ice cubes. The sweet-

breads are ready when they are just firm to the touch but still have some springiness to them (they are only partially cooked).

Slide them into ice water to stop the cooking, then drain them and place them on a board. Remove any fat and gristly, sinewy bits or blood vessels, and then peel off as much of the membrane as you can using a knife. This is much easier to do while the sweetbreads are still warm. Don't worry if the sweetbreads (especially the throat one) separates into smaller pieces.

Line a pie plate with a clean dish towel and place the peeled sweetbreads on top. Fold the cloth over the sweetbreads and top with another pie plate. Place a weight, like 2 cans of beans, on the second pie plate and refrigerate for 3 to 4 hours, or until the sweetbreads are firm. Now the sweetbreads are ready to use; they can be kept covered in the refrigerator for up to 2 days. You will notice that a little pink liquid will seep out of the sweetbreads; this is normal.

Often your cooked sweetbreads will naturally fall into small pieces, and other times you will be able to cut them into slices. It really doesn't matter how they are cut; more important is that they are in equal-sized pieces so they cook evenly.

While sweetbreads are often added to creamy sauces, I like them with a coating of flour or bread crumbs—this provides a crisp exterior to contrast with the creamy, soft, rich interior. So even if I am serving them in a classic mushroom cream sauce, I dust them in seasoned flour and fry them in clarified butter before adding them to the sauce. You can use calf or lamb sweetbreads in any of the following recipes. There is no real alternative for sweetbreads, though brains work well in all these preparations. But while sweetbreads are creamy like brains, they have much more substance, body, and flavor. Sweetbreads contain gelatin and albumin, both of which firm up with cooking, giving sweetbreads their unique texture.

Sweetbreads with Orange and Cumin

SERVES 2

The orange and cumin here add a layer of flavor to the sweetbreads, and the juice makes a simple orange butter sauce to serve with them. You can just serve them with the sauce, or serve them over some lettuce leaves, to contrast with the richness of the sweetbreads. To make 1/2 cup / 125 ml of clarified butter, start with 3/4 cup / 6 ounces / 170 g unsalted butter and follow the instructions below.

> 1 orange
>
> 1 egg
>
> 2 teaspoons cumin seed, toasted and ground
>
> 2 tablespoons flour
>
> 3/4 cup / 2 ounces / 60 g fine fresh bread crumbs
>
> 11 1/2 ounces / 325 g sweetbreads, prepared (see page 92)
>
> Coarse sea salt and freshly ground black pepper
>
> 1/2 cup / 125 ml clarified butter
>
> Boston or Bibb lettuce leaves (optional)

Preheat the oven to 200°F / 100° C. Place a baking sheet lined with paper towels in the oven.

Finely grate the zest from the orange and then squeeze the juice. Whisk the egg with the orange zest, 1 tablespoon of the juice, and the cumin, then pour into a shallow dish. Place the flour in another shallow dish and the bread crumbs in a third shallow dish.

Cut the sweetbreads into 1/2-inch / 1-cm slices. Season the slices with salt and pepper, then dip them into the flour to coat, shaking off the excess. Next, dip the sweetbreads into the egg mixture and then into the bread crumbs.

Place the clarified butter in a large frying pan over medium heat. When the butter is hot, add the bread-crumbed sweetbreads in batches, if necessary, and fry until brown, about 10 minutes, turning once. Transfer the sweetbreads to the paper towel–lined baking sheet and keep warm.

Carefully pour the remaining orange juice into the pan—it will splutter—and stir with a wooden spoon to deglaze the pan.

Transfer the cooked sweetbreads to warmed plates, add 3 or 4 small lettuce leaves, and pour over the pan juices. Serve immediately.

Alternatives: Brains

CLARIFYING BUTTER

Cut unsalted butter into small pieces and place them in a small, heavy saucepan over very low heat. Once the butter has melted, skim any foam from the surface.

Remove the pan from the heat and let the melted butter stand for 5 minutes. The butter should separate into a clear golden liquid and white milk solids, which will fall to the bottom of the pan.

Carefully strain the golden liquid through a fine-mesh sieve lined with a double layer of cheesecloth into a clean glass jar, leaving the milk solids behind. When cool, cover the container and store the clarified butter in the refrigerator.

Sweetbreads Prune Style

SERVES 2

My Paris friend Bénédict told me I should go to Prune, a restaurant in New York, and order the sweetbreads. Well, I did, and I could see why he liked the restaurant so much. This tiny restaurant feels very much like Paris, with everyone happily sitting cheek by jowl—it's an atmosphere that breeds camaraderie, and you end up chatting with your fellow diners. The chef is a woman, Gabrielle Hamilton, and she cooks European-inspired food and, as Bénédict promised, the sweetbreads were superb. This is my take on Gabrielle's recipe.

2 slices double-smoked bacon

2 tablespoons flour

1 egg, beaten

3/4 cup / 2 ounces / 60 g fresh breadcrumbs

11 1/2 ounces / 325 g sweetbreads, prepared (see page 92)

Coarse sea salt and freshly ground black pepper

Lard

1/3 cup / 75 ml dry vermouth

2 teaspoons finely chopped shallot

1 teaspoon white wine vinegar

1 teaspoon whipping (35%) cream

1/4 cup / 2 ounces / 60 g cold unsalted butter, cut into cubes

1 teaspoon small capers, rinsed

Freshly squeezed lemon juice

Preheat the oven to 200°F / 100° C.

Place a baking sheet lined with paper towels in the oven.

Place the bacon slices in a small frying pan over very low heat and cook gently so they render their fat and turn crisp. Transfer the cooked bacon slices to the baking sheet and keep warm. Reserve the fat in the frying pan.

Place the flour in a shallow dish, pour the egg into another shallow dish, and place the bread crumbs in a third shallow dish.

Cut the sweetbreads into equal-sized pieces. Season the pieces with salt and pepper, then dip them into the flour to coat, shaking off the excess. Next dip the sweetbread pieces into the egg and then the bread crumbs.

Add enough lard to the pan with the bacon fat so the fat is 1/4 inch / 6 mm deep in the pan. Place the pan over medium heat and, when hot, add the bread-crumbed sweetbreads in batches. Fry the sweetbread pieces until golden, about 10 minutes, turning once. As they finish cooking, transfer them to the baking sheet in the oven to keep warm.

Combine the vermouth, shallot, and vinegar in a small saucepan and place over medium-high heat. Bring to a boil, then reduce the heat and boil gently until the mixture is reduced to about 1 tablespoon. Stir in the cream and season with salt and pepper.

Place the pan over very low heat and slowly whisk in the butter pieces, thoroughly incorporating each piece before adding the next. While you're whisking, keep the sauce warm but not hot, so that the mixture emulsifies. When all the butter is incorporated, taste and adjust the seasoning, add the capers and a squeeze of lemon juice, and remove from the heat.

Divide the sweetbreads between 2 warm plates, spoon over the butter-caper sauce, garnish with a bacon slice, and serve.

Alternatives: Brains

Sweetbreads with Morels and Fresh Fava Beans

SERVES 2 AS A MAIN COURSE OR 4 AS AN APPETIZER

Morels and favas are a classic spring combination and two of my favorite foods to eat. They also match well with rich, creamy sweetbreads. You could use fresh peas if favas are unavailable. And dried morels or even regular brown mushrooms would be fine. I like to keep my sweetbreads in larger pieces for this recipe. Use the liquid from poaching the sweetbreads if you don't have any stock; just remember to use a lighter hand with the salt. As a rough guide about $11^1/2$ ounces / 325 g of favas in the pod will yield enough shelled beans for this recipe.

> Coarse sea salt
>
> $3^1/2$ ounces / 100 g shelled favas
>
> $11^1/2$ ounces / 325 g sweetbreads, prepared (see page 92)
>
> Freshly ground black pepper
>
> 2 tablespoons flour
>
> $1/3$ cup / $2^1/2$ ounces / 75 g unsalted butter
>
> 1 shallot, finely diced
>
> $6^1/4$ ounces / 175 g fresh morels, trimmed
>
> 1 tablespoon dry white wine or vermouth
>
> 2 tablespoons olive oil
>
> 1 cup / 250 ml Poultry Stock (page 233) or sweetbreads cooking liquid

Bring a small saucepan of water to a boil over high heat. Add some salt and the favas and cook until just tender, about 2 minutes. Drain and refresh the favas under cold running water. Now slip the beans out of their outer skins by pinching and squeezing. Place the favas in a small bowl of cold water and set aside; discard the bitter skins.

Cut the sweetbreads into equal-sized pieces and season well with salt and pepper. Next, toss them in the flour to coat, shaking off any excess; set aside the floured sweetbread pieces.

In a frying pan over medium heat, add 1 tablespoon of the butter. When the butter is foaming, add the shallot and cook gently until soft. Add the mushrooms, turn up the heat, and cook them quickly until just tender. Add the white wine and stir, then transfer the shallot and mushroom mixture to a bowl.

Wipe out the pan and add the remaining butter and the olive oil and place over medium heat. When the fat is hot, add the sweetbreads, in batches if necessary, and cook until they are golden and crispy on all sides, about 10 minutes. Transfer to a plate lined with paper towels. Tip out any remaining fat from the pan and discard.

Pour in the stock and bring to a boil, then deglaze the pan, using a wooden spoon to scrape up the browned bits from the bottom. Boil until the liquid is reduced by half, then reduce the heat and add the mushroom and fava mixture and sweetbreads to the pan. Cook gently until heated through. Check the seasoning and serve.

Alternatives: Brains

Grilled Sweetbreads with Mustard Seed Glaze

SERVES 2

This glaze was inspired by talented Australian chef Teage Ezard, whose cooking I've really enjoyed. One of my great food memories is eating his Jerusalem artichoke crème brulée. Yes, it was dessert, and it was fabulous—he has a talent for successfully combining unusual ingredients. This is a wonderful glaze for sweetbreads, and you will have more than enough; it keeps well refrigerated, so use it also on grilled tongue (page 56). The unusual element in this recipe is that the sweetbreads are not cooked first but are simply soaked. I was skeptical at first, but on the grill this works well. You need to start this recipe the day before, as both the mustard seeds and the sweetbreads need to be soaked. There are three types of mustard seeds: white (or yellow), brown, and black. White mustard seeds are the mildest; they are the main ingredient in American mustard and are used for pickling.

> 1 teaspoon white mustard seeds
>
> 1/2 cup / 3 1/2 ounces / 100 g sugar
>
> 6 tablespoons / 90 ml white wine vinegar
>
> 2 tablespoons water
>
> 2 teaspoons grainy mustard
>
> 11 1/2 ounces / 325 g soaked veal sweetbreads (see page 92)
>
> Coarse sea salt and freshly ground black pepper
>
> 2 tablespoons olive oil

Place the mustard seeds in a small bowl, cover with warm water, and leave to soak for 8 hours or overnight. (This can be done while you are soaking the sweetbreads.) Drain and set aside.

Place the sugar, vinegar, and water in a small saucepan over medium-low heat. Stir to dissolve the sugar, then increase the heat and bring the liquid to a boil. Cook without stirring until the liquid is reduced and a very light caramel color, 8 to 10 minutes. As the liquid reduces, brush the sides of the pan with a pastry brush dipped in cold water to prevent any crystals forming on the sides of the pan.

Remove the pan from the heat and pour the liquid into a small bowl; stir in the drained mustard seeds and the grainy mustard. You should have about 1/3 cup / 75 ml.

Trim the sweetbreads of fat and blood vessels and carefully remove the membrane. Place them flat on a cutting board and butterfly them (see page 80). Open up the sweetbreads like a book, pat dry, season well with salt and pepper, and brush with olive oil.

Preheat the grill to medium-high and place the sweetbreads cut side down on the grill and close the grill lid. Cook for 6 to 8 minutes, turn the sweetbreads over, brush with mustard glaze, and cook for another 6 to 8 minutes, until they are browned and their juices run clear. Brush again with the glaze and serve.

Hot to Trot—Feet

I admit to having mixed feelings about animal feet. It's not that I don't eat them; after all the foot, like the ear or the shank, is just another part of the animal. No, it is not a prejudice against feet per se; it's just that not all feet are created equal. Most animal feet are edible, and they come in all sizes from elephant to chicken. While elephant's feet were popular with travelers in Africa in the past, today only cow's, calf's, sheep's, lamb's, pig's, and poultry feet make their way into kitchens—and even then not all of them are worth the trouble. Previously I've encouraged people to eat chicken feet, which are popular in Asian cuisine, as are duck feet; and while I'll still eat them in restaurants, I can honestly say the best part of the dish is the sauce. They are lot of work to prepare for not a great deal to eat.

But even if you're not interested in *eating* animal feet, don't overlook *cooking* with them. They are all excellent additions to stock, adding both body and flavor. Feet are mainly bones, skin, and cartilage, with varying amounts of meat, and they yield lots of gelatin, which enriches stocks and sauces.

Lamb's feet are popular in many countries, but depending on the breed there is not a lot of meat on them. In her book *Food in England*, Dorothy Hartley explains:

> *Sheep's trotters are the ceremonial part of the Bolton Wanderer's football team dinners. Only the heavy types of mountain sheep, such as the Pennine Range sheep, can make this dish well. (I don't think a sparrow could make a meal off a Welsh trotter, but in the larger breeds of sheep, the trotters are almost as meaty as a pig's.)*

I cook a lot with calf's feet and cow's feet; they are full of collagen and add a rich, unctuous quality to my sauces, and they are essential in dishes like Calvados Tripe (page 141). But rarely do they make the leap from the pan to my plate. Occasionally, I dice the meat from the cooked foot and add it back into a stew, but usually once it has done its work I toss it away. The prince of feet, if there can be such a thing, and the ones I cook just to eat, are pig's feet: rich and fatty, they have enough delicious meat to make them worth eating.

My love of pig's feet has developed slowly, and I'm still not a big fan of the French classic *pied de porc pané*, a whole pig's foot cooked, then covered in bread crumbs and cooked again. Several chefs have made their reputations with variations of this dish. Pierre Koffman boned out pig's feet and then stuffed them with sweetbreads and morels, while French-Canadian chef Martin Picard primed them with foie gras. The Italians make *zampone*, a boned-out trotter stuffed with chopped pork and pork odd bits and slowly braised; it's a specialty from the town of Modena. The word *zampone* is a derivative of *zampa*, meaning leg, foot, or hoof. These are all delicious but time-consuming, cheffy creations, and they are the reason you go out to eat. I prefer to cook my pig's feet in simpler recipes.

> *These are one of the most gastronomically useful extremities. If your butcher has pork, there must be a trotter lurking somewhere.*
> FERGUS HENDERSON

How to Choose

When buying feet, you have a choice of front and back feet. The back feet are bigger, heavier, and meatier. The feet usually include the animal's ankles, except with lamb; their ankles are left on the carcass after slaughter to prevent the meat from shrinking up the bone and to provide a handy hook to suspend it. Pig's feet can also include part of the shank, which makes them very large, I prefer them without it.

Lamb's, cow's, and calf's feet are all creamy white in color with pinkish coloring around the toes, while pig's feet are completely pink. All feet should all be smooth, slightly moist, and plump.

Three-clawed chicken feet are usually pink or yellow in color, but depending on the breed can be blue, black, or even green. Usually the outer scaly skin has been removed and the feet are sold separately from the bird. If you are lucky enough to buy a bird that still has its feet, just cut them off at the ankle and keep them for stock.

How to Prepare and Cook

For chicken feet, use a pair of kitchen scissors to cut off the nails. If there are any hard or rough pieces of scaly outer skin, hold them over a gas flame or use a propane torch to blister and loosen the pieces and then rub them off with a towel.

A cow's foot is big, so ask your butcher to cut it into sections using his band saw. While they are usually clean when you buy them, give them a rinse and check to make sure there are no tufts of hair. If you find any, singe it with a propane torch (see page 14).

> Crubeens is the Irish term for pig's trotters, and up until the mid-twentieth century they were a popular pub food. They are cooked pig's feet, liberally sprinkled with salt, and were the perfect accompaniment to a glass or two of stout. Publicans provided them free, to encourage their patrons to order another drink.

A calf's foot should also be clean when you buy it. Rinse it and check between the toes for any stray hairs and singe them off. Before using a calf's foot, the large bone should be removed.

Place the foot on a board and make a cut, starting between the toes, along the length of the foot and through to the bone. Cut the skin and tendons away from the bone but leave them attached to the skin and the toes. Turn the foot over and repeat on the other side. Sever the tendons that connect the large bone to the toes, then twist and remove the bone and set it aside for stock. You can now split the foot into two pieces by cutting between the toes. You can also ask your butcher to do this for you.

Place pieces of cow's foot or split calf's foot in a saucepan and cover with cold water. Bring the water to a boil over medium heat, then remove the foot and discard the water. The foot is now ready to use.

> Trotters—an English term for animal feet, usually pig's

Pig's feet simply need to be rinsed and inspected for any stray hairs. If you want to serve pig's feet whole, you must bind them to make sure they hold their shape during cooking. To do this, place two feet together and wrap them with long strips of cotton sheet or muslin, tying to secure them. This will prevent them from twisting out of shape as they cook.

All the recipes in this chapter use diced pig's feet, so no binding is necessary. Ask your butcher to split the pig's feet lengthwise so they will cook more quickly; he can do this quickly with a band saw. As with all porky extremities, pig's feet are improved by brining (see page 22) or marinating in Spiced Seasoning Salt (page 28) for a day or two before you plan to cook them.

Poached Pig's Feet

MAKES ABOUT 1¾ POUNDS / 800 G

    4 pig's feet, split prepared (see opposite)
    4 tablespoons Spiced Seasoning Salt (page 28)
    8 cups / 2 l Court Bouillon (page 21)

Place the feet in a single layer in a glass container and sprinkle with the spiced salt, turning to coat. Cover and refrigerate for a day or two, turning them occasionally.

Preheat the oven to 275°F / 140°C.

Rinse the pig's feet under cold running water and place them in a deep Dutch oven or flame-proof casserole big enough to hold them snugly in a single layer. Pour in enough court bouillon to cover the feet. Cover with a piece of wet parchment paper, then the lid, and transfer to the oven.

At 1½ hours, check to make sure that the feet are still submerged; if not, add a little water. After 3 hours, test the feet by inserting a skewer into the meat. The meat must be very tender and practically falling off the bone; this can take up to 4 hours.

Remove the pan from the oven, uncover, and leave until just cool enough to handle. Remove the feet from the liquid; if you leave them too long the liquid will set. Strain the cooking liquid through a sieve, discarding the solids. Pour into a clean saucepan and bring to a boil over medium heat and boil, skimming often, until it is reduced to 6 cups / 1.5 l. Set the liquid aside to cool, then use it to make Bouillon Jelly (page 108) or to flavor soups and sauces.

Meanwhile, remove and discard all the bones from the meat, keeping the meat, skin, and tendons.

Terrine of Pig's Feet

MAKES ONE 3-CUP / 750-ML MOLD

Our local Paris restaurant serves a terrine of pig's feet and, as I prefer my pig's feet off the bone, this dish is one of my favorites. This recipe replaces some of the diced feet with apple and onion, so it is more approachable and the texture is interesting. If you're a pig's feet lover, you can add more feet to the mix. To slice the terrine thinly, use a bread knife and slice it when it is very cold.

    2 Poached Pig's Feet (above)
    2 tablespoons lard
    1 onion, diced
    1 apple, peeled, cored, and diced
    1 stalk celery, finely diced

    3 tablespoons dry sherry
    2 tablespoons chopped flat-leaf parsley
    12 large mint leaves, halved and sliced
    1 tablespoon Dijon mustard
    1 tablespoon salt-packed capers, rinsed and chopped
    Freshly squeezed lemon juice
    Coarse sea salt and freshly ground black pepper
    ½ to ¾ cup / 125 to 175 ml Bouillon Jelly (page 108)
    Vinaigrette for Porky Bits or Salad (page 105)

continued

Cut the meat, skin, and tendons from the pig's feet into dice ranging from $^1/_2$ to $^3/_4$ inch / 1 to 2 cm.

In a large frying pan, melt the lard over medium-low heat, add the onion, and cook, stirring, until soft. Add the apple and celery and continue to cook until the onion just begins to color. Increase the heat and add the pig's feet. Stir continuously until the meat heats though and begins to stick, then add the sherry and deglaze the pan by scraping up the browned bits from the bottom.

Remove the pan from the heat and add the parsley, mint, mustard, and capers. Mix well and season with the lemon juice, salt, and freshly ground pepper. In a small saucepan, heat the bouillon jelly until it liquefies.

Line a 3-cup / 750-ml loaf mold with a double layer of plastic wrap, making sure the wrap overhangs on all sides, and pour in a spoonful of the melted jelly. Spoon in the pig's feet mixture, and then pour in enough jelly to almost cover the mixture. Tap the mold on the counter to expel any air.

Refrigerate the terrine until almost firm, then add enough of the remaining liquid so that the mixture is covered by a thin glaze of jelly. Refrigerate until set. Pulling gently on the plastic wrap, ease the terrine out of the mold. Serve thinly sliced with the vinaigrette.

Toasty Pig's Feet

MAKES 4 TOASTS

This is a very good introduction to pig's feet. My friend François made this for lunch in Paris: pig's foot bruschetta that you can serve with a salad or as an appetizer. You can decide just exactly how much chopped foot you want on each toast.

2 Poached Pig's Feet (page 101), finely chopped

Coarse sea salt and freshly ground black pepper

4 slices country-style bread

2 tablespoons Dijon mustard

2 tablespoons chopped flat-leaf parsley

2 tablespoons dried bread crumbs

6 cups / 1.5 l salad greens

Vinaigrette for Porky Bits or Salad (page 105)

Place the chopped meat in a frying pan over low heat to warm through, and season with salt and pepper.

Heat the broiler to high.

Place the bread slices on a baking sheet and toast well on one side and lightly on the other. Spread the lightly toasted side of each slice with mustard.

Add the parsley to the warm pig's feet in the pan and mix well. Divide the mixture among the toasts, spreading to cover. Return the toasts to the broiler and cook until the topping is hot, bubbly, and golden, about 2 minutes, then sprinkle with bread crumbs.

Meanwhile trim, rinse, and dry the salad greens. Place them in a salad bowl and toss with enough vinaigrette to coat. Serve the toasts with the salad.

CHICKEN FEET WARS

The relationship between the United States and China is often fraught with tension that extends through all levels of government and society. Various subjects cause this tension: the Chinese tacit support of North Korea; the pegging of the Chinese yuan to the US dollar; substandard and dangerous products of Chinese manufacture; mistreatment of workers; American support for the Dalai Lama; and arms sales to Taiwan. To gain the upper hand in these disputes, both countries threaten to restrict trade or block imports from each other. Well, China has now threatened the United States with chicken feet.

Yes, chicken feet: a part of the chicken most Americans don't give a second thought to. For the Chinese, chicken feet are a delicacy, especially in the southern regions of the country, and the feet from America are very highly prized. Why? Americans prefer white chicken meat, and this has created a demand for big-breasted chickens. The bigger the bird, the bigger feet it needs to support its weight. The United States is the leading supplier of supersized chicken feet to China, and China is the US poultry industry's biggest and fastest growing market for chicken feet.

> The foot of an animal is far more wholesome than the chemicals, additives, and processed fats many people consume regularly, most of the time without knowing it.
> GIORGIO LOCATELLI

Worth only a few cents a pound (450 g) in the United States, chicken feet sell for up to eighty cents a pound in China. This can mean the difference between a profit and a loss for American producers, especially in tough economic times. Friction over chickens between the United States and China is not new; the outbreak of bird flu in 2004 resulted in both countries banning imports from the other. The United States resumed imports of processed chicken from China, but again in 2010 there were problems when the Chinese imposed duties of over 100 percent on US poultry imports, primarily feet and wings, as a countermove to the US tariffs on Chinese-made tires.

American poultry producers are pleading their case to United States trade officials and hope that the quality of their jumbo feet and the Chinese love of these chewy odd bits will prevail over China's protectionist trade policies.

Salad of Pig's Feet and Vegetables

SERVES 4 TO 6

An Italian recipe *insalati di nervi* from my friend Francesco Tripoli inspired this recipe. Francesco sent me emails from Italy describing everything he was eating, especially the odd bits; it made me very envious. This is a good recipe to introduce people to pig's feet: I served it to a friend who doesn't eat pork except in Chinese dumplings, and even she liked it.

Make this salad while the pig's feet are still warm, so that the dressing coats them well and ensures that they don't stick together. If you make this salad ahead; just remember to bring it to room temperature and toss it again before serving. Lupini beans have a crunchy texture even from a can and are a popular snack around the Mediterranean region. They are, strictly speaking, a seed from various species of lupines, a member of the pea family, which are more commonly grown for their flowers. Raw lupini seeds are bitter and toxic so must be treated to make them edible. If you can't find them, substitute cooked dried beans.

1 cup / 6¹/₄ ounces / 175 g diced cooked pig's feet (page 101), about 2 feet

1 cup / 5¹/₂ ounces / 155 g canned lupini beans, rinsed

¹/₂ cup / 3 ounces / 70 g green olives, rinsed

2 canned artichoke hearts, rinsed

1 carrot, peeled

2 inside celery stalks with leaves

1 small fresh chile, stem removed

Vinaigrette for Porky Bits or Salad (see below), made without the cornichons

Freshly ground black pepper

Place the diced pig's feet in a salad bowl with the beans.

Crack the olives and discard their pits, then coarsely chop them and add them to the bowl. Cut the artichokes into ¹/₂-inch / 1-cm pieces and add them to the bowl. Finely dice the carrot and celery stalks. Cut the chile in half lengthwise, remove the seeds and discard. Dice the chile very finely. Add the carrot, celery, and chile to the bowl and then toss the salad with the vinaigrette until well coated. Season with the pepper; because of the canned ingredients you shouldn't need any salt.

Alternatives: Pig's cheek, tongue, hock, or ear

Vinaigrette for Porky Bits or Salad

MAKES ABOUT ¹/₂ CUP / 125 ML

This is a sharp vinaigrette that is perfect for gelatinous, rich porky parts or to dress the salad that accompanies them, or to serve with a pork terrine.

1 teaspoon Dijon mustard

1 tablespoon white wine vinegar

Coarse sea salt and lots of freshly ground pepper

¹/₃ cup / 75 ml extra virgin olive oil

3 tablespoons chopped flat-leaf parsley

2 tablespoons finely diced shallot

1 tablespoon finely diced cornichons

Whisk together the mustard and vinegar and season well with salt and pepper. Slowly whisk in the olive oil and then stir in the parsley, shallot, and cornichons.

ARTISTIC ODD BITS

Odd bits as art? Well, beauty is in the eye of the beholder. I think a pig's head, an oxtail, and even innards are beautiful, but I know they repulse others. I realized this when I posted on my blog a photograph of intestines with the mesentery attached soaking in water. When I looked at them, I saw a beautiful sea creature, but others were disgusted. While I think odd bits are beautiful, I didn't imagine that they would inspire an artist; but it seems they've inspired many works, including some unusual creations by women artists.

Victoria Reynolds, an American artist based in Los Angles, is fascinated by meat and flesh. She began by painting slices of luncheon meats, then pieces of meat, and now she paints odd bits: oxtail, tripe, pig's uterus, fat, and intestines. Her images concentrate on the texture of the odd bits and are quite abstract; they are often placed in very ornate decorative frames. So on seeing the paintings for the first time, you are struck by the beauty of the image before realizing what it is: the viewer mistakes tripe for draped fabric, the intestines for flowers or sea creatures, and has a positive reaction to the images. However, the artist notes that when viewers realize the paintings depict odd bits, they recoil in horror, revealing the deep-seated prejudice we have against these parts of the animal. Reynolds sees even more than flowers and fabric in her paintings of animal viscera; she points out images of the devil, Saint Luke, a satyr, and other religious symbols.

Her images are stunning (many of them can be seen on the Internet), and they reveal that there is beauty in all parts of the animal. Unfortunately, Reynolds admitted in an interview that she doesn't know how to cook many of the odd bits she paints, and they usually end up as cat food.

Pinar Yolaçan, a young Turkish-born photographer, is based in New York City. She studied design and fashion before becoming fascinated with odd bits. She has drawn on her fashion and design sense to create a series of photographs called *Perishables*. These photographs depict elderly women clothed in dresses, sweaters, collars, and shirts made from odd bits. In one image, a woman sports a chicken head collar; another has a belt of chicken feet; a tall, thin woman wears a simple, elegant intestine scarf, and another has a beautiful ruffle of book tripe on her dress. One of my favorite photographs is of a woman wearing a sweater with arresting honeycomb tripe sleeves. I'd love that sweater. Many of the "clothes" in these images are beautiful and elegant at first glance, and it is only on closer inspection that you realize what they are made from. In other images Yolaçan's odd bit models are deliberately ugly and their clothing ungainly, exploiting one's feelings about both odd bits and older women. Yolaçan is playing with ideas that flesh, both animal and human, will wither and die, and that fashion can turn women into pieces of meat. She doesn't stop there; in another series of photographs, Yolaçan shows women wearing jewelry she has designed—no diamonds or rubies here, just more odd bits. One woman wears a plain lamb's heart pendant, another sports a large flashy choker of six beef kidneys, and a very refined older woman has an elegant necklace of testicles that match her dress—all very striking images.

Born in Germany, Julia Lohmann makes her home in London, England. As a child, this young designer dreamed of being a vet, and her work is inspired by animal welfare. She has designed couches in the shape of headless, reclining cows—covered in leather, of course. Unlike other traditionally shaped leather sofas, they force you to realize where the leather came from. What I like best in her work are her lamps. One, called "Flock," is a ceiling of fifty lights, each light encased in a preserved sheep's stomach. Even more beautiful is her *Ruminant Blooms* series of lights and lamps using pieces of cow's stomach. They are exquisite, especially those made with honeycomb tripe. Animal parts aren't Lohmann's only inspiration; seaweed and even bacteria become art objects in her hands.

Other artists don't paint odd bits or create clothes, jewelry, or furniture with them: they simply cook them. In his book *The Bauhaus Group*, Nicholas Fox Weber chronicles the artist Paul Klee's culinary expertise. This Swiss-born artist was interested in dreams and myth, and mixed surrealism, cubism, and primitivism in his art. After World War I, he settled in Munich and taught at the Bauhaus school, where he wrote about the science of design, and cooked. Weber describes how Klee's approach to cooking mimicked his approach to art. He illustrates this with some of Klee's recipes, including one for pork kidneys: a mixture of onions, leeks, celery, apples, beets, and garlic are cooked together and then diced pork kidneys are added at the end. In another, cooked veal shanks are garnished with yellow beets, celery, and leeks served with potatoes in their skins. Weber also reveals what he calls Klee's "most remarkable culinary invention," a lung ragout that he cooked one Tuesday in January:

> . . . *a ragout of lungs spiced with blond spices. Recipe—Start at 1/2 past 11—boil a little water with some salt, add the whole lungs, 12 o'clock remove the lungs and slice finely on a board, 5 past 12 return the lungs to the pot. Ingredients added immediately: a chopped onion, some garlic, a strip of lemon peel, some horseradish, two carrots, butter and pepper. Ingredients at 1/4 to 1: Flour dissolved in cold water, some vinegar, a lot of chopped parsley, a little nutmeg. Serve at 1 o'clock.*

Lungs, it seems are a popular German dish (see page 161), and I love Klee's way of writing a recipe, with the timing included so that everything is ready for his one o'clock lunch.

Fried Pig's Feet Terrine Severo Style

SERVES 4 AS AN APPETIZER

Pig's feet terrine has a completely different texture when it is hot, and some people prefer it. This recipe is a take on the one served in my local Paris restaurant, Le Severo, and I add a bread crumb coating to add crunch. It is important to use dried bread crumbs, because if you cook the slices too long, the jelly holding them together will melt and the slices will fall apart. I am not a big fan of nonstick pans, but this is one time when one is very useful. Serve with a spoonful of Vinaigrette for Porky Bits or Salad (page 105) or with a green salad dressed with the same vinaigrette.

1/4 cup / 1 ounce / 30 g flour

1 egg, beaten

Coarse sea salt and freshly ground black pepper

1/2 cup / 50 g dried bread crumbs

Four 2/3-inch / 1.5-cm slices Terrine of Pig's Feet (page 101)

1 tablespoon lard

Preheat the oven to 325°F / 160°C. Place a baking sheet in the oven.

Place the flour in a shallow dish. Whisk the egg with salt and pepper and pour into another shallow dish; place the bread crumbs in a third shallow dish.

Coat the terrine slices in flour, shaking off the excess, then dip them into the egg mixture to coat. Place them in the bread crumbs, turning to make sure they are well coated.

In a nonstick frying pan, large enough to hold the 4 slices, melt the lard over medium heat. When the fat is hot, fry the terrine until golden, about 1 1/2 minutes on each side. Transfer the slices to the baking sheet and bake in the oven for about 5 minutes, or until soft to the touch.

Bouillon Jelly

MAKES 5 CUPS / 1.25 L

If you clarify the court bouillon after cooking pig's feet, you will have a liquid with enough natural gelatin to set. I get a kick out of making aspic, a savory jelly, without any commercial gelatin. I use this jelly to set my head-cheese (page 17) and pig's feet terrine (page 101). If you have a cheffy moment, you could also use it to coat a pâté or suspend a poached egg in jelly, or, once it's cold and set, it can be diced into cubes and used as a garnish. It can also be used like stock to flavor soups, sauces, and braises, but remember it is salty.

6 cups / 1.5 l court bouillon that has been used to cook pig's feet (page 101)

1 small carrot, peeled and diced

1 stalk celery, diced

3 stems flat-leaf parsley

2 egg whites

2 tablespoons water

Fine sea salt

Remove the bouillon from the refrigerator and remove the fat. Set the fat aside for another use. Tip the jellied bouillon into a saucepan and place over low heat just until it liquefies.

Meanwhile, place the carrot, celery, and parsley in a food processor and process until finely chopped. Add the egg whites and water and pulse to blend well.

Stir this mixture into the liquefied but not hot bouillon. Increase the heat to medium-high and bring to a boil, stirring constantly with a wooden spoon and scraping the bottom of the pan to prevent the egg white from sticking. As the liquid approaches a boil, it will appear to curdle; don't panic, this is what you want. As soon as the bouillon begins to boil, stop stirring and reduce the heat to very low.

The egg whites will form a congealed mass on the surface. Let the liquid simmer very gently for 15 minutes; you want to see small bubbles break through the egg white mass. Remove the saucepan from the heat and let it stand for 5 minutes.

Line a sieve with a double thickness of damp cheesecloth or a thin cotton dish towel, and place over a bowl. Ladle the egg white and bouillon into the sieve and allow it to drip slowly through the cloth. Don't press on the egg whites, as it will cloud the liquid. Taste it: it should be well flavored, add more salt only if necessary. Discard the debris in the sieve and allow the bouillon to cool. Refrigerate or freeze.

Old-Fashioned Jelly

MAKES ABOUT 5 CUPS / 1.25 L CLEAR JELLY

With readily available commercial gelatin, why would I want to make jelly from scratch? Turning animal feet into clear, flavorless jelly is a challenge, and a very satisfying if somewhat long process. Not only is it another way to use the whole animal, it also guarantees that you know exactly what parts of what animal went into your jelly. In France, I use calf's feet because they are readily available; in Toronto it's a cow's foot because they are easier to find. As they have little to no meat, they are neutral in flavor, unlike pig's feet. The jelly can be refrigerated for a week or frozen for up to 3 months.

2 calf's feet or 1 cow's foot, about 4 pounds / 1.8 kg, prepared (see page 100) but not blanched

Coarse sea salt

1 orange

1 lemon

1 cup / 7 ounces / 200 g sugar

3 egg whites

Rinse the feet well and place them in a large bowl. Cover with cold water, add 2 tablespoons of salt, and refrigerate for 8 hours or overnight.

Preheat the oven to 250°F / 120°C.

Drain the feet and place them in a saucepan. Cover with cold water and bring to a boil over medium heat. Reduce the heat and simmer for 10 minutes. Drain the feet and rinse well; discard the water. Place the feet in a clean, deep ovenproof saucepan, and pour over enough cold water to almost cover them.

Place the pan over medium heat and bring to a boil; skim well and transfer to the oven and cook for 7 hours, partially covered. You can place the pan over very low heat on top of the stove if you can keep the heat so low that it barely simmers. Check the pan every hour or so, skimming each time; if the water level has dropped, top it up with a little boiling water.

Remove the pan from the oven and let cool slightly, then strain the liquid through a fine-mesh sieve into a large measuring cup: you should have about 6 cups / 1.5 l; if you have more, boil the liquid to reduce it. Discard the feet. Let the liquid cool and refrigerate overnight.

continued

Next morning, carefully remove all the fat, which will be quite soft, from the surface of the jelly. Set the fat aside for another use. Wipe the surface of the jelly with a damp paper towel to remove any remaining traces of fat, then tip the jelly into a large saucepan and place over low heat.

Using a vegetable peeler, remove the zest from the orange and lemon, leaving behind the bitter pith. Add the zests and the sugar to the pan. Squeeze the juice from the zested orange and lemon and whisk together with the egg whites until frothy.

Once the jelly has melted, stir in the egg white mixture and bring to a boil over medium-high heat, stirring constantly with a wooden spoon and scraping the bottom of the pan to prevent the egg white from sticking. As the liquid approaches a boil, it will appear to curdle; don't panic—this is what you want. As soon as the jelly begins to boil, stop stirring and reduce the heat to very low.

The egg whites will form a congealed mass on the surface. Simmer gently for 15 minutes; you want to see small bubbles break through the egg white mass. Remove the saucepan from the heat and let it stand for 5 minutes.

Line a sieve with a double thickness of damp cheesecloth or a thin cotton dish towel, and place over a bowl. Ladle the egg white and liquid into the sieve and allow it to drip slowly through the cloth. As the liquid drips, don't press on the egg whites, as that will cloud the liquid. Discard the debris in the sieve.

Blood Orange Jelly

MAKES ONE 4-CUP / 1-L JELLY MOLD; SERVES 6

This is a simple orange jelly—blood oranges are my choice when they are available; otherwise use regular oranges. Does it taste better than a jelly made from a package? Absolutely yes. Better than an orange jelly made with fresh juice and gelatin? Yes again, but then I'm probably prejudiced because I've made it from scratch. It does taste different in a way I can't describe—and don't think it will taste meaty, because it doesn't.

To make unmolding the jelly easier, rinse the mold with cold water before pouring in the jelly, and make sure you fill the mold to the top. Before unmolding, loosen the edges of the jelly with a knife, then dip the mold into hot water for a few seconds. Place a damp, cold plate on top of the mold and then flip it over. Give it all a good shake and hopefully it will plop out. The damp plate allows you to move the jelly on the plate. If the jelly is being stubborn, wrap a hot damp cloth around the mold for a few seconds and try again. To cut jelly, use a thin wet knife.

5 blood oranges

1 lemon

2 cups / 500 ml Old-Fashioned Jelly (page 109)

1/2 cup / 3 1/2 ounces / 100 g sugar

Squeeze the juice from the oranges and lemon and strain into a measuring cup; you should have about 2 cups / 500 ml.

Strain the juice a second time through a fine-mesh sieve set over a bowl and lined with a double thickness of damp cheesecloth or a thin cotton dish towel. Discard the solids. You should now have about 1 1/2 cups / 375 ml.

Pour the jelly into a saucepan, add the sugar, and place over low heat, stirring until the sugar dissolves. Remove from the heat and pour in the strained juice and stir to mix. Rinse a 4-cup / 1-l jelly mold with cold water and then pour the jelly mixture into the mold. Refrigerate until set. Turn the jelly onto a plate and serve.

GELATIN

We are all familiar with the clear, sparkling, brilliantly colored, wobbling jelly held together by the magic of gelatin, but do you know that gelatin is in everything from ice cream to canned meats? It is also in your shampoo, skin moisturizer, the coating of capsules in your medicine cabinet, and of course jelly babies and gummy bears. But just exactly what is gelatin?

Gelatin is a protein derived from the skin, bones, and connective tissue of animals. Bones and skin are cleaned and degreased, then boiled in water. The resulting liquid is concentrated, dried, and then milled into gelatin. Gelatin has a long history. Ancient man used animal skins for protection from the cold and shelter from the elements. In the British Museum, there is a 4,000-year-old Egyptian granite carving that depicts the boiling of animal hides. Early man quickly discovered that the liquid left after the skins were removed was sticky and could be used as glue. Another carving in the town of Thebes shows just that: workers veneering wood with glue extracted from animal hides. The Greeks knew about gelatin; Homer describes the processing of an ox-hide in the *Iliad*:

> *. . . a huge ox-hide drunken with slippery lard*
> *Gives to be stretched, his servants all around*
> *Disposed, just intervals between, the task*
> *Ply strenuous, and while many straining hard*
> *Extend it equal on all sides, it sweats*
> *The moisture out and drinks the unction in*

And the Roman naturalist Pliny wrote that "glue is cooked from the hides of bulls."

However, while it was understood that skin and bones yielded gelatin, there was no commercial production until the late seventeenth century, in Holland, and then, at the turn of the eighteenth century, in England. The first mention of an edible gelatin is in a patent deposed in 1846 for a powdered gelatin "for forming compositions from which may be prepared jellies, and blanc-manges; also, when mixed with farina, or starch vegetable flour, for thickening soups, gravies, etc."

The word *gelatin* comes from the Latin *gelare*, meaning "to congeal." Gelatin is a hydrocolloid, which means it loves water; it can absorb up to ten times its own weight in water. It has two unique qualities that make it a valuable commodity in the kitchen, beloved by molecular cooks and essential to the food industry: its ability to form a reversible jelly (a jelly that can be turned back into a liquid again) and its low melting point—below body temperature. These qualities make it an excellent medium for delivering delicate flavors to our taste buds and give it a good mouthfeel.

More than 600 million pounds / 300,000 tons of gelatin are produced a year, and over 60 percent goes to the food industry, making gelatin a ubiquitous and widely consumed food protein. It stabilizes dairy products like cream and yogurt and is added to ices and ice creams to prevent crystallization. Gelatin holds canned meat together and thickens packaged soups and sauces. Low-fat and fat-free products couldn't exist without gelatin: it delivers the mouthfeel of the missing fat and makes reduced-fat foods almost palatable. Confectionary makers use gelatin in Turkish delight and marshmallows, as an emulsifier in caramel, and for the glue to stick the layers of licorice all-sorts together. Gelatin is also used to clarify wine and beer. Other commercial applications of gelatin include making hard and soft capsules and various cosmetic preparations in the pharmaceutical industry; for printing; and as the coating of photographic plates. Fans of television forensic crime shows will know that firearms are often discharged into blocks of gelatin because they simulate muscle tissue.

Gelatin contains between 84 and 90 percent protein, so not only is gelatin useful, it is good for you too. It contains many of the essential amino acids and, besides strengthening your hair and nails, it promotes the health of your joints. Several studies have shown that consuming gelatin helps combat arthritis and osteoporosis.

Commercial gelatin is simple to use. It is important to soak the gelatin in cold liquid first so that it softens and swells; this helps it to dissolve completely when heated. Heat destroys gelatin's ability to set a liquid, so only heat it enough to dissolve it in the liquid you are jelling. Fresh pineapple, papaya, and kiwifruit contain enzymes that destroy gelatin's ability to set a liquid, and these must be cooked before adding them to a jelly.

Gelatin has an indefinite shelf life, but the formaldehyde found in the adhesives used in the manufacture of kitchen cabinets can react with gelatin, rendering it insoluble in water, so always store gelatin in a sealed container.

Jelly

Jelly has a long illustrious history. As it took time to prepare, jelly was special food appearing only on the tables of the rich. The English king Richard II, who preferred to spend his wealth on lavish feasts rather than foreign wars, often served jelly colored with mulberries, indigo, and saffron, and filled with cooked meats or whole fish.

In the late sixteenth century, Italian cook Maestro Martino discovered the technique of clarifying jelly with beaten egg whites. This sparkling jelly was set in special glass dishes to show off its clarity. Cooks continued to look for new ways to display jelly; different colored jellies were set into the same dish, white and yellow jelly-filled eggshells to resemble real eggs and hollowed out lemons and oranges were filled with jelly and quartered to garnish platters of food.

The queen of jelly was Elizabeth Raffald. In her book *Experienced English Housekeeper* (1769), she explained how to make jelly flavored with orange, lemon and Madeira and colored with violets, cochineal, spinach, and saffron. Her most spectacular creations were molded jellies with a tableau in a dome of clear jelly that resembled giant glass paperweights: there were swimming fish, a hen's nest of lemon zest straw with eggs, a selection of fruit complete with vine leaves, and even the moon and stars to form a celestial jelly hemisphere.

A True Snout to Tail Meal

The Whole Pig

While working on this book my friend Rob invited my husband and me, along with many others, to dinner. Now, this wasn't just any dinner—Rob had been dreaming about it for months and planning it for weeks. I like to think that I inspired him. Rob wanted to do a pig roast—a big brazier of charcoal in his backyard where he could slowly roast a whole pig on a spit. He was planning a serious snout to tail dinner.

This was how we all cooked once. Our ancestors ate raw meat until they discovered fire. Then they realized how tasty cooked meat was. The discovery of fire, according to author Richard Wrangham in his book *Catching Fire*, was the key to our development from animal to man. When we began eating cooked food, our brains grew and our intestines shrank. "Cooking made us human," writes Wrangham.

Perhaps that is why we like to cook outdoors: it's some ancient genetic imprint. Standing around a fire watching the meat cook, then sharing it with friends, is certainly a pleasant way to pass the time. However, who among us cooks a whole animal anymore? We no longer have large open fireplaces equipped with spits big enough to roast whole animals. Few animals come into our kitchens whole—aside from seafood or birds, and usually the latter are missing their heads and feet.

> *Roast suckling pig is one of the world's great festive dishes—a lavish centerpiece at banquets and celebrations in almost every country where pork is eaten.*
> RICHARD OLNEY

Suckling pig is an animal that anyone with a good-sized oven can cook. Eating it is a true nose-to-tail experience, and the perfect way to celebrate odd bits.

How to Choose

While the first suckling pig I cooked was a spur-of-the-moment buy, my supplier Wayne had too many on his hands and was offering a deal, suckling pig must usually be ordered in advance. The best sources are your butcher, pork supplier, and ethnic markets.

Try to buy a fresh piglet; it is easier to check that it is intact—ears, tail and feet. Use the same criteria for judging as with other pork odd bits; it should smell clean and be moist to the touch but not tacky. The piglet will be split along its belly. If the pig's organs are not inside, make sure that your supplier gives you at least the kidneys.

> bon pied, bon oeil—literally, "good foot, good eye": in good health for your age

Be familiar with the capacity of your oven and make sure you have a pan big enough to hold the pig. Suckling pig ranges from 12 to 15 pounds / 5.5 to 6.8 kg. The pig is roasted in a crouching (sphinx-like) position, not lying down, so it takes up a little less space lengthwise but occupies more height. My oven wasn't the problem—it's plenty big enough. It was the pan. My big turkey roasting pan was too small, so I ended up with two large rimmed baking sheets stacked on top of each other and the piglet squeezed in on the diagonal.

How to Prepare and Cook

Remove the kidneys from the piglet and set aside. If your piglet comes with its liver and heart, set them aside for another use. Check the body for any stray hairs, especially on the chin, in the ears, and between the toes and remove them and clean the ears (see page 15). Rinse the pig and pat dry.

To improve the flavor and help the skin crackle as it cooks, rub the pig inside and out with Spiced Seasoning Salt (page 28) and place on a rack on a baking sheet, uncovered, in the refrigerator, overnight. Remove the pig from the refrigerator an hour before roasting, add stuffing if using, and close the belly and place it in a large roasting pan. Try to make the piglet sit upright, like a sphinx, by splaying its front and back legs. Make sure the piglet won't topple over while cooking; if necessary a piece of scrunched up foil makes a good support. If you don't have a pan big enough, you can cook it on a large heavy rimmed baking sheet.

When cooking the pig on a baking sheet, making the sauce is difficult, but with the aid of half the wine and a rubber spatula you can scrape the juices and browned bits into a saucepan.

Some books suggest roasting the piglet with a piece of wood or a ball of foil in its mouth—why? So the pig's mouth stays open and you can insert a small apple for presentation. I never bother with this.

> faire des pieds de nez—literally, "to make feet of the nose": to thumb your nose at someone

How to Carve

Use a sharp knife or scissors to cut through the skin; If the skin isn't crispy enough, place the pieces under the broiler to crisp before serving. Remove the legs and cut off the trotters at the knee, and slice the thigh meat into chunks. Repeat with the front legs, slicing behind the shoulder blades to remove them. Cut down the length of the backbone, then cut down behind the ear. Make a cut from the front parallel to the board to separate the loin from the belly. Lift the loin off by cutting between the meat and the ribs and slice into chunks. Cut off the ears and cut out the cheek meat from the head.

Roast Suckling Pig

SERVES 12

Even without an apple stuffed in its mouth, trumpets to bring it to the table, or a carol to sing, this pig makes an impressive entrance. Serve with braised bitter greens like broccoli rabe.

> 1 suckling pig, about 14^1/$_2$ pounds / 6.5 kg, kidneys reserved
>
> ^{1}/$_4$ cup / 1^1/$_4$ ounces / 35 g Spiced Seasoning Salt (page 28)
>
> 2 tablespoons lard or duck fat
>
> 2 large red onions, halved and sliced
>
> 20 large sage leaves
>
> 2 cups / 500 ml red wine
>
> 4^1/$_2$ ounces / 125 g day-old bread, cut into ^{1}/$_4$-inch / 6-mm dice
>
> 2 cloves garlic, chopped
>
> Coarse sea salt and freshly ground black pepper
>
> 2 to 3 tablespoons olive oil
>
> ^{1}/$_2$ cup / 125 ml Court Bouillon (page 21) or Poultry Stock (page 233)

The day before roasting, prepare the pig (see opposite) using the seasoning salt.

In a large frying pan with a lid, melt the fat over medium heat and add the onions and 8 of the sage leaves. Cook, stirring, for 5 minutes, then reduce the heat to low and cover. Continue to cook until the onions are soft, then uncover and pour in 1^1/$_2$ cups / 375 ml of the wine, increase the heat and bring to a boil, and continue to boil until the wine is reduced to a couple of tablespoons.

Remove the pan from the heat, stir in the bread, garlic and season with salt and pepper, and leave to cool. Dice the kidneys and finely shred the remaining sage leaves and mix into the cooled bread mixture.

Preheat the oven to 325°F / 160°C.

Place the pig on its back and place the stuffing loosely in its belly; remember the stuffing

will swell during cooking. Close the belly using trussing skewers about 1 inch / 2.5 cm apart and at least ^{1}/$_2$ inch / 1 cm in from cut the edge of the belly so they don't tear the skin. Take a piece of kitchen string and loop it around the skewers in a figure-eight pattern to pull them together so the edges of the belly are touching, then tie and secure. Transfer the piglet to a lightly oiled roasting pan and set it back in the sphinx position. Rub the skin all over with olive oil, then cover the ears and tail with aluminum foil to prevent them from burning.

Place the pig in the oven for 30 minutes, then baste with cooking juices. Continue to cook the pig for 2^1/$_2$ hours or until the temperature reaches 160°F / 71°C, in the thickest part of the thigh away from the bone, continuing to baste it from time to time. If the juices are burning on the pan, add a couple of spoonfuls of water. Turn off the oven, transfer the pig to an ovenproof platter, and let it rest in the oven, with the door ajar, for 30 minutes or longer.

Meanwhile, add the remaining ^{1}/$_2$ cup / 125 ml wine to the roasting pan, bring to a boil, and deglaze the pan, using a wooden spoon to scrape up the browned bits from the bottom. Add the court bouillon and bring to a boil over medium heat.

Check the seasoning, and then strain through a sieve into a sauceboat and keep warm.

Take the pig from the oven and remove the foil, string, and skewers, spoon the stuffing into a bowl, carve and serve with the sauce.

THREE

Stuck in the Middle: Familiar and Exotic

The middle of the animal is familiar territory. It's where most of the meat we eat comes from—chops, loins, ribs, steaks, and roasts—but this isn't even half of what is available. Pork spare ribs, for example, are a very popular everyday cut, but pork belly has been, until recently, an overlooked odd bit. As for what's inside the animal—well, it is just way too foreign for most of us to even consider.

In every animal, there is an exotic treasure trove of heart, liver, spleen, kidneys, stomach, intestines, and caul fat: this chapter will introduce you to these odd bits except caul fat, which is covered in chapter 4, The Back End. While I am passionate about eating the whole animal, the truth is that some parts, while tasty, have very challenging textures. Many of the odd bits in this section fall into this category: tripe, for example. I've introduced many friends to this much-maligned odd bit. Some of them just can't get past its slippery texture—but that texture is precisely what tripe lovers delight in. So I don't expect to convert you to eating every odd bit here, but I do want you to give them all another chance, especially the ones you think you don't like. Before you begin, you must leave your preconceived ideas at the kitchen door, because much of our dislike of these odd bits is between our ears and not on our palates. You should also forget about any badly cooked dishes you've eaten. Start with a beginner recipe; then if you still don't like an odd bit, it's okay, but don't discard it. There are many ways to use odd bits,

> To see the expressions on their faces after a few bites of rabbit kidney or sweetbread was a beautiful thing. A moment of recognition, a calming, reassuring wave of satisfaction, the dawning of knowledge that yes, this can be good. I like it. I love it. I want it again.
> ANTHONY BOURDAIN

such as stuffings and sausage mixtures, where their texture won't be overwhelming.

> *From butchers' shops in the south [of England], or most of them, you might think that the animals we eat get through life without a number of vital organs, and unmentionable parts. In the north, things are different, attitudes—if not display, which is thoroughly English and brutal—are decidedly European. Why waste good things, why send the best parts to the pet food factory?*
> JANE GRIGSON

This chapter, like the whole book, reflects my taste. It is just an introduction to what you can cook from the middle of the animal and is not meant to be exhaustive. As well as the exotic, there is the familiar, with recipes for pork belly and one for beef short ribs, both of which are quickly losing their status as odd bits. This is to show you that what is thought of as odd at one time can become everyday, whether it's a rib, a belly, or a heart.

Have a Heart

Many ancient cultures believed the heart embodied the strength and courage of the animal, so it was a favorite food of warriors and hunters. Others thought it held the animal's soul, so they didn't eat it, but sacrificed it to the gods. I just didn't think about it all. I wasn't prejudiced against cooking heart; I simply hadn't considered eating it, which is shocking when you think how long I have been cooking. The only hearts I saw were birds' hearts that came with the giblets (see page 147), and I added them to my stockpot. Heart was a delicious discovery for me, so I really want you to try it too—I am sure you'll love it. Why? Heart is a very versatile odd bit: you can cook it fast or braise it slowly, add it to burgers or eat it raw.

The heart is both an organ and a muscle, and the hearts of most animals are edible. As a muscle, the heart never stops working, continuously pumping blood through the animal's body. Working muscles have more flavor, and the heart is no exception, but it is also a firm-textured, toothsome piece of meat. Slowly braised, it becomes tender; quickly grilled it is flavorful and pleasantly dense; and when ground it adds a distinctive taste to a burger.

Recipes in older cookbooks love to stuff and braise heart, and while it has two cavities perfect for stuffing, it takes a brave host to present a whole heart to guests and a braver guest to tackle it. Better to braise heart slowly, then carve it into slices before serving. Or cut it open and prepare it so it can be cooked very quickly or chopped to make heart tartare. How does it taste? Well, it's dense and meaty with a slight gamy or livery taste.

> *. . . the heart is not, as you might imagine, tough as old boots due to all the work it does, but in fact firm and meaty but giving.*
> FERGUS HENDERSON

Where to start with heart? Heart Burgers, of course (page 122). The heart is ground and, while it disappears into the mixture, you'll discover its distinctive taste.

How to Choose

Well, you won't have any problem recognizing a heart, and its size is proportional to the animal. The heart pumps blood, so its color ranges from pink to dark reddish brown. Poultry, lamb, pork, game, and veal hearts are commonly sold whole, while larger beef heart is also available sliced. Animal hearts are interchangeable in most of the recipes here; just understand that the hearts from older animals have a more intense flavor.

> *The heart may be singled out as the most neglected variety meat of all, mostly because of the prejudices that have long been associated with it.*
> JANE ALLEN AND MARGARET GIN

Government regulations in most countries require that hearts are cut open for inspection, so you'll notice one or two slits in the heart when you buy it. Look for hearts that are firm and moist. A general guide to size:

Beef: 4 to 5 pounds / 1.8 to 2.25 kg
Veal: 1 to 1³/4 pounds / 450 to 800 g
Lamb and pork: 7 to 14 ounces / 200 to 400 g
Poultry: about 30 per ¹/2 pound / 225 g

How to Prepare and Cook

Generally, hearts are trimmed of the top flap and any connecting tubes. If not, cut off these and any fibrous tissue around them. Give the heart a rinse under cold running water to remove any blood that might still be in the ventricles, and pat dry. There is a layer of fat around the top of the heart, often sweeping down the sides: in most cases you can leave this on, as it helps baste the heart while it cooks. If you are preparing heart to be grilled, you should cut most of it off and set it aside to render (see page 229). If you are grinding heart for burgers, add it to the mixture.

Poultry hearts are left whole; simply trim off any tubes and leave the fat. Rinse well and pat dry.

If you're not cooking the heart whole, slice it open lengthwise to expose the chambers. Inside the heart you will see that the chambers are lined with silverskin and held together with sinews. Sever these sinews and open up the heart; it will naturally divide into thinner and thicker sections. Cut these sections apart and use a sharp knife to remove all the sinews and silverskin, leaving clean, solid pieces of meat. If you buy sliced heart, check to make sure all the sinews and silverskin have been removed before cooking.

When cooking heart you have two choices: slow or fast. Anywhere in between will result in a very tough piece of meat. You can braise heart as you would neck, shank, tail, or shoulder, so add or substitute it in any recipe you have that requires long, slow cooking. Adding some heart to your favorite stew is a good way to try it for the first time.

Slicing the whole cooked heart is quite straightforward. Place it on a carving board and cut it open along the inspection slit then cut it into slices lengthwise. Or cook heart quickly so it is still pink and juicy at the center. Sliced or diced heart can be grilled, sautéed, or cooked in a stir-fry. Leftover cooked heart makes delicious sandwiches, hash, pasta sauce, or salad (page 124).

Peruvian Heart Kebabs

MAKES 8 TO 10 SKEWERS

It was the photograph of a smiling shoeshine boy in my copy of the Latin American *Foods of the World* cookbook that convinced me to try this recipe. He looked so happy eating his wooden skewer of *anticuchos*. *Anticuchos*— small skewers of grilled meat—are a popular street food in Lima, and while they are often made with everything from seafood to beef, the authentic ones are chunks of beef heart in a spicy marinade. Once you try heart like this, you'll be ready for heart in any of its permutations. For this preparation, it is important to cook the heart only to rare or medium-rare and no more.

13 ounces / 375 g trimmed beef heart (see page 121)

1 teaspoon cumin seed

1 teaspoon coarse sea salt

$1/2$ teaspoon black peppercorns

2 serrano chiles, stems removed

1 clove garlic, germ removed

3 tablespoons red wine vinegar

1 tablespoon extra virgin olive oil

Cut the heart into $3/4$-inch / 2-cm cubes and place in a bowl.

Toast the cumin seed in a small frying pan until fragrant, about 1 minute. Place in a spice grinder with the salt and peppercorns, and grind. Add the chiles and garlic and grind again, then transfer the mixture to a small bowl and whisk in the vinegar and olive oil.

Pour the mixture over the heart pieces in the bowl and toss to coat, then cover and refrigerate for 24 hours.

Preheat the grill to high. Thread the heart pieces onto 8 to 10 wooden or metal skewers and grill over high heat for about 4 minutes total, turning once.

Alternatives: Veal heart, lamb heart, whole poultry hearts, gizzards, or liver slices, but only marinate liver 3 to 4 hours

Heart Burgers

My husband came up with this idea while we were enjoying Brisket Burgers. He thought that heart would add a gamy flavor to the burger, and he was right. This is a great way to try heart for the first time, as it is mixed with an equal amount of brisket; you can use even less on your first try. Keep the fat when trimming the heart and grind it with the meat. By grinding your own meat, you can control the quality (I also doubt you'll find any ground heart anywhere).

Follow the recipe for Brisket Burgers (page 89), replacing half the brisket with beef heart. This recipe is infinitely variable: the proportion of heart to brisket can be changed and the meats varied. After beef, my next choice is lamb—lamb heart mixed with a good piece of fatty lamb belly or shoulder plus some garlic and rosemary leaves. Veal heart and veal breast with fresh tarragon is delicious, as are pork burgers and even chicken burgers with added heart—it's up to you. Just remember two things: grind your own meat, unless you're lucky enough to have a butcher who will grind it to order; and make sure there is about 30 percent fat to keep the burgers juicy.

Salad of Duck Hearts

SERVES 4

Many of the recipes in this book take time to cook, but some odd bits can make a quick, tasty meal; heart is one of them—fast food at its best. This salad should be made with greens that can take some heat and have some pungency or bitterness so, depending on the season, dandelion, arugula, and escarole are all good choices.

24 duck hearts, about 5 1/2 ounces / 155 g, prepared (see page 121)

Coarse sea salt and freshly ground black pepper

10 to 12 cups / 2 1/2 to 3 l mixed salad greens

1/4 cup / 1 3/4 ounces / 50 g duck fat or confit fat

1 shallot, finely chopped

2 tablespoons sherry vinegar

Pat the hearts dry and season well with salt and pepper.

Rinse and dry the greens well and place in a salad bowl. In a frying pan over medium heat, melt the fat. Add the shallot and cook, stirring, until translucent. Increase the heat to medium-high and add the hearts. Cook, stirring, until the hearts are cooked but still pink in the center, about 4 minutes. Using a slotted spoon, transfer the hearts to the salad bowl.

Add the vinegar to the pan, bring to a boil, and deglaze the pan, using a wooden spoon to scrape up the browned bits from the bottom. Season the dressing with salt and lots of freshly ground pepper, and quickly pour the hot dressing over the salad and hearts. Toss well and serve immediately.

Alternatives: Poultry hearts, fresh or confited; confited gizzards (page 149); slices of liver or heart

Heart Salad

SERVES 4 AS AN APPETIZER

This recipe is an easy way to use up any leftover heart. If you have a slicing machine, use it; otherwise cut the meat as thinly as you can.

7 ounces / 200 g braised beef heart (see opposite)

2 tablespoons finely diced red bell pepper

3/4 cup / 11 g flat-leaf parsley or cilantro (coriander) leaves

3 cornichons

1 clove garlic, crushed

2 teaspoons red wine vinegar

2 teaspoons heart cooking liquid or Beef Stock (page 232)

1 teaspoon Dijon mustard

1/4 cup / 60 ml extra virgin olive oil

Coarse sea salt and freshly ground black pepper

1/2 teaspoon finely grated lemon zest

Slice the heart very thinly and arrange on a platter, sprinkle with the red pepper.

Place the parsley, cornichons, garlic, vinegar, cooking liquid, and mustard in the small bowl of a food processor. Blend until the parsley is finely chopped, then, with the motor running, slowly add the olive oil. Check the seasoning and stir in the lemon zest. Drizzle over the heart slices and serve.

Alternatives: Veal, lamb, pork heart, or braised cheek

Moroccan-Style Braised Heart

SERVES 4 TO 6

I love this combination of spices, carrots, preserved lemon, and dates, and it complements the rich flavor of beef heart. You can substitute the equivalent weight of veal or lamb heart; just use the appropriate stock and check the heart after two hours of cooking. The cooked heart is sliced and reheated in the sauce, so this is a perfect dish to make ahead and an easy way to introduce heart to the novice eater. I often cook some extra heart so that I can make Heart Salad (see opposite). Serve this with cooked fresh white beans or couscous.

1³/4 pounds / 800 g beef heart, in one piece

Coarse sea salt and freshly ground black pepper

2 tablespoons beef dripping or lard

2 onions, halved and sliced

2 stalks celery, sliced

3 cloves garlic, crushed

6 cilantro (coriander) stems, preferably with roots attached

1 teaspoon ground ginger

1 teaspoon cumin seed

Two 5-inch / 13-cm cinnamon sticks

1 fresh bay leaf

1¹/2 to 2 cups / 375 to 500 ml Beef Stock (page 232)

2 large carrots, peeled and cut into ¹/2-inch / 1-cm slices

1 preserved lemon, quartered

6 Medjool dates, pitted and cut into quarters

1 cup / 15 g cilantro (coriander) leaves, chopped

Preheat the oven to 275°F / 140°C.

Pat the heart dry and season with salt and pepper. In a heavy flameproof casserole or Dutch oven just a little larger than the heart, melt 1 tablespoon of the dripping over medium-high heat. Add the heart and brown, then transfer the heart to a plate. Add the remaining dripping to the pan with the onions and celery and cook, stirring, until the onions begin to brown.

Add the garlic, cilantro (coriander) stems, ginger, cumin, cinnamon, and bay leaf and stir until you can smell the spices. Deglaze the pan with 1 cup / 250 ml of the stock, scraping up the browned bits from the bottom with a wooden spoon. Add the heart and enough stock to come halfway up the meat, and cover the meat with a piece of wet parchment paper and the lid. Transfer to the oven and cook for 2¹/2 to 3 hours, or until very tender. Meanwhile, cook the carrot slices in boiling salted water and then drain and refresh under cold running water. Remove and discard the pulp from the lemon quarters, then dice the skin; set the carrots and lemon aside.

Remove the pan from the oven and lower the oven to 200°F / 100°C.

Transfer the heart to a cutting board.

Strain the cooking liquid through a sieve, pressing on the vegetables to extract all the juice. Discard the vegetables and spices and let the cooking liquid stand for 5 minutes. Skim off any fat, and set the fat aside for another use. Return the cooking liquid to the pan and bring to a boil over medium-high heat. Continue to boil until the liquid is reduced to about 1¹/4 cups / 310 ml.

Cut the heart into thick slices (see page 121) and add them back to the sauce along with the carrots, lemon, and dates. Place in the oven for about 20 minutes or until everything is heated through, and serve.

Alternatives: Lamb heart, neck, shanks, or shoulder; beef cheeks, shank, or shoulder; veal heart, shank, or shoulder

Heart Tartare

SERVES 2

This dish was a revelation for me. I read an article by French chemist Hervé This in which he explained that *carpaccio* or tartare could be made with any meat because by slicing it thinly you make it tender. This idea turned around in my brain, then a chef friend told me about a very flavorful heart tartare he'd enjoyed, so I decided to try it. If you are a tartare lover, you probably have your favorite mix of condiments, so go ahead and use them. Use knives to chop the meat: it gives a superior result to grinding, as you can control the texture (make sure the knives are sharp so you cut the meat rather than pureeing it). Best of all, that chopping is very therapeutic—if you are at all musical, it will beat playing air drums. Prepare the tartare just before serving.

Note that this recipe contains raw meat and egg yolks, so you must be sure of the source and freshness of your ingredients.

1 small cooked beet, finely diced

2 tablespoons finely chopped cornichons

2 tablespoons finely chopped shallot

2 tablespoons small capers, rinsed and drained well

Worcestershire sauce

Extra virgin olive oil

Fleur de sel

Freshly ground black pepper

Piment d'espelette (see below) or chile powder

1/2 pound / 225 g well-trimmed beef heart (see page 121)

2 egg yolks

Organize a platter with small bowls or piles of the beet, cornichons, shallot, and capers. Place the Worcestershire sauce, extra virgin olive oil, fleur de sel, pepper grinder, and *piment d'espelette* alongside.

Cut the heart into pieces and place them on a board. Using two large, sharp chef's knives of equal size and weight, chop the meat. Hold the knives with a loose grip and move them through the meat as you chop, stopping from time to time to pile the meat back on top of itself. Turn the chopped meat over as you work to guarantee an even texture. Imagine you are playing the drums; even if you have no natural rhythm, it will work. Continue chopping until the texture is fine.

Divide the finely chopped meat between 2 plates, then make a small depression in the top of the meat and slip in the egg yolk. Serve with forks; each diner adds his or her own combination of condiments to the meat.

Alternatives: Veal, lamb, or venison heart

PIMENT D'ESPELETTE

This pepper arrived in the Basque region of France from Mexico, and it thrived in its foreign home. If you are in the Basque region in the season, you'll see strings of these peppers everywhere. This bright red narrow pepper ranges in length from 2 1/2 to 5 1/2 inches / 6 to 14 cm and is available fresh, dried, or ground into a coarse powder. *Piment d'espelette* is fruity and flavorful with a little touch of heat, falling just below the midpoint on the Scoville scale. It received an AOC designation in 1999.

TATARS TARTARE

You can probably guess the origin of the word tartare. It comes from the Mongolian tribesman, the Tatars, who, under the leadership of Genghis Khan controlled much of Asia and Eastern Europe during the thirteenth century. They had a formidable reputation as fierce warriors and lovers of raw meat, their favorite being horsemeat. Supposedly, they placed pieces of raw meat under their saddles before setting out for a hard day of fighting and pillaging. In the evening they would stop, take out the meat (now tenderized and salty from the horse's sweat) and enjoy a tasty snack, often washed down with a glass of blood.

> . . . *a peckish gourmandism has often enabled me to relish a plate of raw beef, finely chopped, served forth with toasted sourdough bread and some watercress.*
> M. F. K. FISHER

This predilection for raw meat continued among soldiers who followed the same method. Brillat-Savarin recounts his dinner conversation with a Croatian cavalry captain. The soldier said that he and his men could eat like kings in the battlefield with little fuss. They simply killed the first animal they saw, removed thick slices of its flesh and salted them well. Then they tucked the meat in bags under their saddles and rode and rode. Brillat-Savarin agreed with his guest that raw flesh was tasty if well seasoned and also nutritious.

The French use the word tartare in the kitchen to describe two different piquant preparations: a mayonnaise sauce flavored with onions, gherkins, capers, and hard-boiled egg yolks; and a dish of raw chopped meat seasoned with many of the same ingredients. In the nineteenth century, Elizabeth Acton introduced tartare sauce to the English, but it was not until the beginning of the twentieth century that steak tartare became a popular dish on the English side of the Channel.

Melancholy Spleen

You've probably only considered venting your spleen, not eating one. Also known as *melt* or *milt*, the spleen's role in the body is to maintain the quality of the animal's blood. Spleen is part of the collective known as pluck (see page 147), and usually ends up mixed with other pieces of odd bits in stuffings, pâtés, and soups, but sometimes it wanders into the spotlight.

Beef spleen is large, and it is often available at kosher butchers. My experience is with pork spleen, which is easy to find and smaller. If you love liver, you'll like spleen.

How to Choose

Pork spleen is a long flat piece of meat about 16 inches / 40 cm long, rounded at one end and tapering off to a point at the other. The rounded end is thicker and the spleen becomes progressively narrower and thinner toward the tail end—think of a giant tadpole. Its color is very dark red, and it has a strip of fat running from one end to the other right down the middle. The spleen closely resembles liver, so select it as you would liver (see page 131).

How to Prepare and Cook

Usually, the outer membrane is already taken off, but if it is still on, remove it as you would for liver (see page 131). Leave the central ribbon of fat in place; the spleen requires no other preparation.

> *se mettre la rate au court-bouillon—literally, "to put the spleen in the court bouillon": to make a mountain out of a molehill*

You can add spleen to sausage and pâté mixtures or braise it in stock, but my suggestion is to cook it like Rillons (page 152). This gives the spleen a mildly spicy flavor and really improves its taste. Replace some of the pork belly in the recipe with spleen.

Cut the spleen into four pieces crosswise and marinate the pieces with the pork belly overnight. Don't brown the spleen with the pork, but instead roll up the pieces with the fat on the inside and secure the rolls with a toothpick. Add them to the pan with the browned belly when you lower the oven temperature and cook them for an hour, or until they are tender. Let the spleen rolls cool, then remove the toothpicks. Cut the rolls into thin slices like a jelly roll and serve with drinks or in a salad.

> *Spleen, also called melt by butchers is commonly seen in American supermarkets labeled 'pet food'*
> CALVIN SCHWABE

One of the most famous culinary dishes made with spleen is found in Sicily. Spleen is the star of Palermo's street food, served in a sandwich called a *vastedda*. The spleen slices are cooked in lard and piled onto a bun, then topped with ricotta salata, a squeeze of lemon juice and a sprinkle of salt. My Italian friend Francesco tells me that while the most famous place to eat this sandwich is Antica Focacceria di San Francesco in the Kalsa neighborhood, there are spleen sandwich carts around town that make, in his opinion, even better sandwiches. Sicilian immigrants in New York have been able to enjoy *vastedda* for over a century at spots like Ferdinando's Focacceria in Brooklyn, where they are topped with fresh ricotta and grated *caciocavallo* cheese.

Luscious Liver

Liver, liver, Makes me shiver
SYLVIA PLATH

Perhaps your reaction to liver is the same as Sylvia Plath's. Well, that's a shame, because liver is not only delicious, it is very good for you. Liver elicits strong feelings. If you think it has no flavor and the texture of shoe leather, then you've eaten it badly overcooked—or perhaps you haven't eaten it, but just know instinctively that you don't like it. Have you enjoyed a good coarse country-style terrine? Then you like liver. What about a velvety duck pâté, or smooth, rich, creamy foie gras? Liver, liver—are you still shivering?

Every cuisine has its liver specialty: the Italian *fegato alla veneziana*; Jewish chopped chicken liver; Eastern European liver dumplings and liver in cream sauce. The Chinese stir-fry liver; the Germans have braunschweiger, a liver sausage; and the English enjoy liver and bacon. In Finland, they make *maksalaatikko*, a liver and rice pudding flavored with syrup and raisins, and serve it for dessert. Fans of the television show *Iron Chef* may recall chef Michael Symon's chocolate liver truffles. Liver is a very versatile odd bit.

There is a lot of misunderstanding about the liver's role in an animal's body. The liver is one of the largest and most important organs: it breaks down metabolic compounds in the animal's system for reuse or removal via its urine. Most of these compounds, with the exception of ammonia, are harmless. The liver processes fats and stores nutrients and vitamins, which is why it is such an important and valuable food source. It does not, as many people think, accumulate harmful toxins. Liver from well-raised animals is an excellent food, nutritionally dense, with more protein than a steak, and a good source of vitamins A, B, and C, and iron. Liver not only is a very nutritious odd bit, it is also rich and satisfying.

Seared crisp on the outside and meltingly tender on the inside, enriched with butter and spread on toast or quickly grilled with a warm and creamy center—well-prepared liver is sublime.

So if you think you don't like it, try it again.

How to Choose

The livers of most animals and birds are edible, and their texture and taste vary from creamy and smooth to granular and strong, depending on the animal and its age. The livers from poultry and veal are the mildest in flavor and have the finest texture. As with any odd bit, its provenance is important, and it must be used within two days of purchase or be frozen.

Throughout my childhood and early youth I shared the predominant modern Anglo Saxon squeamishness about eating the 'organs and edges' of our meat animals. It's hard to say where this squeamishness comes from. Childish reactions (in every sense) to these foods seem almost inbuilt in our culture, so that school age kids are saying 'liver, yuk!' and 'Eurrgghh! Not tongue' before they have the least idea of what either meat tastes like.
HUGH FEARNLEY-WHITTINGSTALL

Livers consist of two lobes, one slightly larger than the other. They range from pale to dark brown depending on the animal and its age. All liver, no matter what the animal, should be resilient to the touch and shiny with no smell, with its outer membrane intact. This membrane keeps the liver fresh, and it is preferable to buy the liver whole or in a piece, as sliced liver deteriorates more quickly. You can slice it yourself or have your butcher slice it to order. Choose smaller livers for a milder flavor and better texture.

Calf's liver ranges in size from 2 to 5 pounds / 900 g to 2.25 kg, and has the finest texture and flavor. Milk-fed veal produces a plump, pale, pinkish brown liver, while the liver from pastured veal will be smaller and darker. Beef liver is large—10 to 16 pounds / 4.5 to 7.25 kg—and dark with a stronger flavor and coarser texture than veal.

Lamb's liver is about 3/4 to 11/2 pounds / 350 to 700 g and while it's a littler drier than veal, it is still mild in flavor. Pork liver is more variable in size, depending on the pig, and can range from 11/2 to 4 pounds / 700 g to 1.8 kg. It is stronger in taste with a more granular texture. Don't overlook liver from rabbit or game animals like deer if available.

Poultry livers are probably the mildest of all in flavor and have a creamy texture; they are sold whole by the pound or kilo. They should be trimmed of tubes and be pale reddish brown in color and clean-smelling. Foie gras, the king of livers, is the enlarged liver of a goose or duck. It should be a uniform pale creamy color and free of any bruises or blood spots. A duck foie gras, more common than goose, weighs in around 11/2 pounds / 700 g.

As livers vary in size, it is hard to say how many slices or pieces to serve per person. Liver is a rich, dense meat, so about 41/2 ounces / 125 g per person is a good guide.

How to Prepare and Cook

Liver should already have all the large connective tissue removed, and the large blood vessels and ducts should be trimmed. Before slicing, remove the membrane covering the liver by slipping the point of a knife between it and the liver to loosen it. Pull it up, placing your finger on the liver and pressing down on it to prevent it from tearing as you peel off the membrane. If you buy the liver sliced, check to see that the membrane has been removed; more often than not it is left on. Why bother removing it? The membrane causes the liver slices to curl up in the pan.

Slice the liver about 1/2 to 3/4 inch / 1 to 2 cm thick, slightly on the diagonal to create larger slices. If the slices are too thin, they will easily overcook. Often the liver slices have small holes in them; this is normal. If any contain blood, cut them out.

With poultry livers, including foie gras, the membrane is so thin that it can be left on, but make sure there is no gall bladder attached to the liver. This small, dark green sac is usually removed before sale because if the inedible gall bladder splits, its dark green bile will turn the liver bitter. This is why recipes often instruct you to cut away any traces of green from the liver—it's the bile. Trim away the connecting threads and separate the poultry livers into two lobes. With poultry livers, the blood vessels are so small you don't have to worry about them. The exception is foie gras. To remove the blood vessels from foie gras, leave it at room temperature for about thirty minutes, then separate the liver into two lobes, carefully cutting the veins where the lobes join. Pull the larger veins out of the liver with tweezers before slicing.

The most common way to cook liver is to sauté or grill it. Strongly flavored livers like pork and beef are often added with other ground meats to pâté and sausage mixtures or braised. Livers from animals and birds are interchangeable in most recipes; it's just a question of taste. Liver can be cooked quickly, making it a perfect food for today's time-conscious cook.

Grilled Liver with Red Currant Sauce

SERVES 2

Michel Troisgros inspired this sauce. The bright tart flavor of red currants is a perfect foil for liver. As the sauce doesn't rely on pan juices, it is perfect to cook outside on the grill.

About 8³/₄ ounces / 250 g calf's liver, cut into ¹/₂ inch / 1 cm-thick slices

Olive oil

Coarse sea salt and freshly ground black pepper

¹/₄ cup / 2 ounces / 60 g unsalted butter

3 tablespoons toasted slivered almonds

¹/₄ cup / 1³/₄ ounces / 50 g stemmed red currants

20 mint leaves, finely sliced

Preheat the grill to medium-high.

Brush both sides of the liver slices with olive oil and then season with salt and pepper. Grill the liver until you see beads of blood on the top surface of the slices, 45 seconds to 1 minute, turn, and cook on the other side for about 30 seconds or until you again see the blood beads form. Transfer the slices to a plate and let them rest in a warm place while you make the sauce, which takes no time at all.

Heat the butter in a frying pan over medium heat. When the butter begins to color, add the almonds and currants and stir to combine. Cook for a minute or two, just until the berries soften. Remove the pan from the heat, stir in the mint leaves, pour the sauce over the liver slices, and serve.

Alternatives: Pork or lamb liver or beef, veal, or lamb heart

Calf's Liver with Onions, Bacon, and Sage

SERVES 2

The Italians are justly famous for their liver dishes, and they love to cook them with onions or sage. So do I. This is my favorite way to eat liver. It is a quick meal, but does need your full attention so it doesn't overcook. Serve it with a watercress salad.

In the summer, try grilling liver. Replace the dusting of flour with a brush of olive oil and grill quickly over high heat. Add the vinegar to the onion mixture and serve alongside the liver.

2 thick slices bacon, double smoked if possible, about 3 ounces / 90 g

¹/₄ cup / 1³/₄ ounces / 50 g duck fat

3 onions, halved and thinly sliced

Coarse sea salt and freshly ground black pepper

16 sage leaves, finely shredded

About 8³/₄ ounces / 250 g calf's liver, cut into ¹/₂-inch- / 1-cm-thick slices

Flour

1 tablespoon sherry vinegar

Preheat the oven to 200°F / 100°C. Place a plate in the oven.

Cut the bacon into ¹/₄-inch / 6-mm strips. Heat half the fat in a frying pan over medium heat and add the onions and bacon. Season with salt and pepper and cook, stirring often, until the onions are softened and colored, then stir in the sage and keep warm in the oven.

continued

Dust the liver slices very lightly with flour and season with salt and pepper. In another frying pan just big enough to hold the liver slices, heat the remaining fat over medium-high heat. When the fat is hot, add the liver and cook until you see beads of blood on the top surface of the liver, 45 seconds to 1 minute, turn and cook on the other side for about 30 seconds, or until you again see the blood beads form. Transfer the liver to the plate in the oven and turn the oven off.

Add the vinegar to the pan and stir to deglaze, scraping up the browned bits from the bottom, then add the pan juices to the onion mixture. Place the liver on warm serving plates, top with the onion mixture, and serve.

Chicken Liver Crostini

MAKES ABOUT 1 CUP / 200 G, ENOUGH FOR 20 CROSTINI

Chicken liver, with its mild flavor, is a good way to reintroduce people to this odd bit. Crostini are a popular snack with drinks in Italy, and also make a good starter served with a salad. The liver mixture can be made ahead but bring it to room temperature before proceeding. You can also pack this mixture into a dish and serve as a spread with crackers.

> 3 tablespoons duck fat or unsalted butter
>
> 1 shallot, finely chopped
>
> 2 sprigs rosemary
>
> 7 ounces / 200 g chicken livers, prepared (see page 131)
>
> Coarse sea salt and freshly ground black pepper
>
> 1 tablespoon small capers, rinsed and dried
>
> 2 tablespoons dry vermouth
>
> 1 teaspoon red wine vinegar
>
> 20 slices baguette
>
> Olive oil
>
> 1 clove garlic

In a frying pan over medium-low heat, melt the fat. Add the shallot and rosemary and cook gently for about 5 minutes, or until the shallot is softened but not colored.

Meanwhile, pat the livers dry and season them with salt and pepper. Add them to the pan and cook, stirring, until the livers are just pink in the center, about 3 minutes per side. Cut a liver in half to check. Remove the pan from the heat and, using a slotted spoon, transfer the livers and shallot mixture to a food processor, discarding the rosemary sprigs. Add the capers.

Pour the vermouth in the pan, and return it to the heat. Bring the vermouth to a boil and, using a wooden spoon, stir to deglaze the pan and scrape up the browned bits from the bottom. Boil the vermouth until it is reduced by half. Add $1/2$ teaspoon of salt and the vinegar, stir, and pour over the livers. Pulse the food processor to chop into a coarse paste, check the seasoning, and transfer the mixture to a bowl.

Preheat the broiler to high.

Brush the baguette slices with a little olive oil and toast them. Cut the garlic in half and rub the toasted bread on one side with the garlic, then top with a spoonful of liver mixture and serve.

Alternative: Any poultry livers

Liver with Dubonnet and Orange

SERVES 4

Today English cooking is getting more respect than it has for a long time, but the renaissance didn't start with Nigella, Jamie, and Gordon. Margaret Costa was one of England's great cookery writers. In 1965, she took over from the colorful Robert Carrier at the *Sunday Times*. Later, she published her book *Four Seasons Cookery* and ran a restaurant with her husband, Bill Lacey, in London during the 1970s. This recipe is a version of one the most popular dishes at her restaurant; it makes it worth adding Dubonnet to your liquor cabinet.

1 orange

2 tablespoons flour

Coarse sea salt and freshly ground black pepper

About 17 1/2 ounces / 500 g calf's liver, cut into 1/2 inch- / 1 cm-thick slices

3 tablespoons duck fat or lard

2 shallots, finely sliced

1/2 cup / 125 ml red Dubonnet

2 tablespoons chopped flat-leaf parsley

Preheat the oven to 200°F / 100°C. Place a serving dish in the oven.

Finely grate the zest from the orange, then squeeze 2 tablespoons of juice; set the zest and the juice aside separately.

Put the flour in a shallow dish and season with salt and pepper, then dip in the liver to coat lightly, shaking off the excess.

Heat 2 tablespoons of the fat in a large, heavy frying pan over medium-high heat. When the fat is hot, add the liver in a single layer, in batches if necessary, and cook until you see beads of blood on the top surface of the liver, 45 seconds to 1 minute. Turn and cook on the other side for about 30 seconds, or until you again see the blood beads form. Transfer the liver to the warm serving dish in the oven and turn the oven off.

Wipe out the pan, place over medium heat, and add the remaining fat. Add the shallots and cook until just beginning to soften. Pour in the orange juice and Dubonnet and deglaze the pan, using a wooden spoon to scrape up the bits from the bottom. Boil until reduced to about 1/4 cup / 60 ml, then add the zest and parsley and pour the sauce over the liver. Serve immediately.

Alternatives: Pork, lamb, or chicken liver

DUBONNET AND THE ZAZA

In 1846, wine merchant Joseph Dubonnet created a wine-based aperitif that he modestly named after himself. It was his way of making the bitter quinine used to fight malaria more palatable for the soldiers serving in the French Foreign Legion. Today Dubonnet is still made using his original recipe, which includes citrus, herbs, spices, coffee beans, and quinine. Try a Zaza cocktail, named after the actress Zsa Zsa Gabor. Simply pour equal amounts of gin and Dubonnet into a cocktail shaker, add ice, shake well and strain into a cocktail glass. Add a lemon twist and it's ready to drink. Enjoy one while you cook liver and you'll be in good company: the Zaza is allegedly a favorite tipple of Queen Elizabeth II, though I doubt she cooks liver while drinking it.

Spicy Indian-Style Liver

SERVES 4

I've always thought it strange that you rarely see recipes for odd bits in South Asian cookbooks. Is it the authors or the editors who banished them? I know that these tasty pieces of quality protein are eaten there. Spicy, complex flavors match well with stronger flavored odd bits, and lamb's liver is perfect in a spicy sauce. Traditionalists will want to pound the spice mixture in a mortar: well, go ahead. Some days I hoist my stone mortar onto the table, but just as often I throw everything in the food processor. If your processor has a small bowl, use it; you won't have to scrape down the sides of the bowl so often. The sauce can be made ahead, but cook the liver just before serving and make sure you keep it pink. If your bunch of cilantro (coriander) still has the roots, remove the largest ones, peel them, and add them to the spice mixture.

1 onion, chopped

3 cloves garlic, germ removed

One 1^1/2-inch / 4-cm piece fresh ginger, peeled and chopped

1 teaspoon cumin seeds, toasted

Coarse sea salt

^{1}/2 teaspoon turmeric

^{1}/2 teaspoon black peppercorns, crushed

4 cardamom pods

1 serrano chile

1 fresh bay leaf, torn

3 tablespoons water

2 tablespoons ghee or clarified butter (see page 94)

1^3/4 cups / 425 ml Lamb Stock (page 234)

17^1/2 ounces / 500 g lamb liver, prepared (see page 131)

Freshly ground black pepper

1 tablespoon freshly squeezed lemon juice

3 tablespoons chopped cilantro (coriander)

Place the onion, garlic, and ginger in a food processor. Add the cumin, ^{1}/2 teaspoon of the salt, and the turmeric and peppercorns. Crush the cardamom pods, remove the seeds, and add them to the food processor. Trim and halve the chile and discard the seeds. Chop the chile and add it with the bay leaf to the food processor. Pulse, then add the water and pulse to make a soupy paste. Set aside.

Add 1 tablespoon of the ghee to a large frying pan over medium heat. Add the spice paste and cook, stirring from time to time, until the mixture begins to stick on the bottom of the pan.

Add 1 cup / 250 ml of the stock and bring to a boil. Deglaze the pan, using a wooden spoon to scrape up the bits from the bottom of the pan. Reduce the heat and simmer until very thick, about 10 minutes.

Meanwhile, cut the liver into ^{1}/2 by 1-inch / 1 by 2.5-cm pieces. Pat dry and season with salt and pepper.

Push the thickened spice paste to the sides of the pan, and then add the remaining ghee to the pan. When it is hot, add the liver and cook, stirring, until colored on all sides. Add ^{1}/2 cup / 125 ml of the remaining stock and cook, stirring, until the liver is just done but still pink in the center, about 4 minutes.

Check the consistency of the sauce—I like it just coating the liver pieces—and add more stock if necessary. Stir in the lemon juice, check the seasoning, sprinkle with the cilantro (coriander), and serve.

Alternatives: Lamb heart, kidneys, chicken livers, or young beef calf's liver

LIVER: MYTH, HISTORY, AND A SAUSAGE

Anyone familiar with Greek mythology will recall the fate of Prometheus. This poor Titan, who defied Zeus by revealing the secret of fire to mankind, received a cruel punishment for his crime: he was chained to a rock, and an eagle devoured his liver. Unfortunately for Prometheus, the liver is the only organ that regenerates, and each night his liver grew back and every morning the eagle returned. His agony continued until Hercules arrived, slew the eagle and set him free.

Liver played a role in a real hero's life. There are many Antarctic heroes, but for Australians, Douglas Mawson is one of the greatest. He didn't join Scott's doomed race to the South Pole, but decided instead to lead an expedition to explore the region west of Cape Adare on the Ross Sea. His team broke into several parties and Mawson headed off with Xavier Mertz and Belgrave Ninnis on a voyage that turned into a horrific test of endurance. Early in the trek Ninnis fell into a crevasse and died. Not only was his death a blow to the morale of the two remaining men, Ninnis had been carrying most of their supplies, including the food, which disappeared with him.

Mawson and Mertz had no choice but to return to base, and to survive the journey they killed and ate their dogs en route. They were almost two-thirds of the way back when Mertz became very ill and was too weak to move. They made camp and Mawson stayed with him until he died. Mawson wrote in his diary that Mertz had died of "weather exposure and want of food." Despite being on the brink of starvation himself—and tumbling into a crevasse on the way—Mawson finally made it back to base camp. It was a remarkable journey and a true test of physical and mental endurance.

In 1969, a medical study looking into Mawson's ill-fated expedition concluded that Mertz had died from vitamin A poisoning. Mawson fed his friend the dog's liver, knowing that it was rich in vitamins and hoping it would help him recover. All liver contains vitamin A, and very high concentrations of vitamin A can be toxic to humans. However, a later study in 2005 dismissed this theory and said that Mertz probably died from starvation and low tolerance for a high meat diet—Mertz had been a vegetarian.

When you think of liver sausage, you probably think of liverwurst. Well, in France they make dry-cured sausages using pig's liver. As they age and dry, these sausages develop a lightly candied taste. Some of the best come from the Pyrenees, and my favorite is the sausage from the town of Foix. I can't swear it is tastier than other similar liver sausages, but its name is much more fun to say: *la saucisse de foie de Foix*. And as you might guess, the residents of the town of Foix have created the Confrérie des Chevaliers de la Saucisse de Foix—a brotherhood of Foix sausage aficionados—which gives them an excuse to celebrate their sausage with a festival.

Tremendous Tripe

Tripe evokes a strong reaction, even from those who have never even tried it. True, tripe is challenging on several levels. There is its texture: cooked tripe can be pleasantly chewy and slippery or meltingly tender depending how long it is cooked. Then there is the smell: often gutty while it's cooking, but like many foods, its odor is stronger than its taste. Finally, there is its name. While *tripe* refers to a ruminant's stomach prepared for eating, it also means worthless, rubbish, or nonsense. Tripe has some very serious image problems.

> Tripe, when made with care at home, is a great delicacy and it is worth the effort to prepare it at home, if only a few times a year.
> OLD POLISH TRADITIONS IN THE KITCHEN

First, I should explain exactly what tripe is. It is the stomach of ruminants: buffalo, sheep, deer, goats, antelope, and cow, with beef tripe being the most common, although lamb is also often available. From earliest times, the stomach's shape meant it was a popular cooking vessel; it could be filled with a mixture of meat and odd bits and suspended over a fire. Later, stuffed stomachs were boiled in a pot, so both the stomach and the filling were enjoyed.

There are four chambers in a cow's stomach, which means there are four kinds of tripe. The first stomach, the rumen, is the biggest. It has a rough texture and more fat than other tripe, and it varies in thickness. It's called blanket tripe, but I think a better name would be shag tripe, because it looks more like a trimmed shag rug than a blanket. The recticulum is the second stomach, and it is shaped like a bag. The French call it *bonnet* and it does look like a bathing cap.

This stomach yields the meatiest and reputedly the most tender tripe; it is also the most familiar, with the distinctive honeycomb pattern that gives it its name. The omasum, the third stomach, is appropriately called book tripe, with its lining of overlapping folds that resemble the pages of a book. The final and true stomach of the cow is the abomasum, with rough ridges. It's called reed tripe or, in the north of England and less poetically, slut or black tripe. It is an ingredient in son-of-a-bitch stew (see page 167), but it's not commonly available.

> *non c'è trippa per gatti*—literally, "there is no tripe for cats": your request is impossible

In North America, the most widely available tripe is honeycomb, whereas in Europe, where tripe is more popular, you'll be offered a choice of blanket, honeycomb, and book tripe. Some recipes are specific on what tripe to use, and tripe aficionados appreciate the different textures of each stomach. I've tried tripe from the first three stomachs, and I prefer honeycomb for most recipes.

> *la trippa di zianata*—literally, "Your aunt's tripe!": A Sicilian insult from the world of the American mafia

While tripe refers to the stomach of ruminants, or cud-chewing animals, it is sometimes extended to include a pig's stomach, which is also known as maw. The recipes here are made with beef tripe, but you can substitute lamb tripe or even pig's stomach.

I doubt that I'll restore tripe to every table, but I hope you'll give it another chance. If I can learn to love it I know you can too, and I think you'll be surprised by just how tasty it can be.

How to Choose

While honeycomb tripe is sold fresh, it has already been scalded, bleached, and partially cooked. The word "fresh" distinguishes it from completely cooked or pickled tripe. The amount of cooking and bleaching varies greatly, and there is really no way to tell by looking at the tripe. In North America, tripe is bleached more and cooked longer than in Europe, resulting in a much more muted flavor.

The color of tripe ranges from creamy to brilliant white from bleaching. In Europe, it is beige in color and stronger in flavor. Wherever you buy it, the tripe should be moist and smell fresh. If you can, give the tripe a poke with your finger: it should feel firm and bouncy to the touch. Don't buy tripe that is very soft or plumped with water. Keep tripe refrigerated and cook it within twenty-four hours, or freeze it.

There is also "green tripe," which is tripe that has been cleaned but not cooked. It is not really green but a dirty brown color with a greenish tinge, its color varying depending on what the animal ate. It is usually sold as animal food.

How to Prepare and Cook

Tripe should be rinsed and then briefly blanched again before proceeding with the recipe. This second blanching removes any residual bleach.

Trim away any extraneous pieces of fat from the tripe and make some shallow slashes on the back, or smoother side, of the tripe to prevent it from curling. If you have any very thick pieces (often there are pieces that look like they have been folded over and glued together), butterfly them (see page 80) so that all the pieces are about the same thickness. Cut the tripe into squares about 3 inches / 7.5 cm. This doesn't have to be exact (often tripe comes cut into odd pieces); just make sure they are roughly equal-sized pieces.

> *It is easy to cook a filet mignon, or to sauté a piece of trout, serve it with browned butter à la meunière, and call yourself a chef. But that's not really cooking. That's heating. Preparing tripe, however, is a transcendental act: to take what is normally thrown away and, with skill and knowledge, turn it into something exquisite.*
> THOMAS KELLER

To blanch, place the pieces of tripe in a saucepan and for each 1 pound / 450 g, add 4 cups / 1 l of water and 1 teaspoon of coarse sea salt. Squeeze the juice from half a lemon into the pan and then add the lemon half. Place the pan, uncovered, over medium heat and bring to a boil. Remove from the heat and drain the tripe and rinse it under cold running water. Squeeze out any excess water, then pat dry and set aside.

Tripe has no natural gelatin, so often it is cooked with a calf's or pig's foot or a piece of pork skin, all of which add gelatin and improve the texture of the final sauce.

As tripe is precooked, estimating cooking times for any recipe is tricky. Even tripe from the same supplier can vary between batches, so it is essential to check it several times while it is cooking. The cooking times in these recipes are only a rough guide.

Beginner's Tripe

This is the tripe dish inspired by two British food writers of different generations, Jane Grigson and Hugh Fearnley-Whittingstall, and it will win you over. If you are still a little hesitant, serve the tripe with cooked pasta. Choose a pasta shape that mimics the tripe pieces; that way the tripe will be less evident.

3/4 cup / 5 ounces / 140 g dried chickpeas, soaked overnight, or 2 cups / 11 1/2 ounces / 325 g canned chickpeas, rinsed well and dried

1 pound / 450 g tripe, blanched (see page 139)

2 tablespoons beef dripping or lard

1 onion, chopped

1 carrot, peeled and finely chopped

2 stalks celery, finely chopped

2 cloves garlic, finely chopped

1 large sprig thyme

1 fresh bay leaf

Strip of lemon zest

1/2 teaspoon chile flakes

One 28-ounce / 796-g can San Marzano tomatoes

1/2 cup / 125 ml Beef Stock (page 232)

Coarse sea salt and freshly ground black pepper

2 tablespoons olive oil

2 1/2 ounces / 75 g hot or sweet chorizo, diced

1 red bell pepper, seeded and diced

1/4 cup chopped flat-leaf parsley

Drain the soaked chickpeas and place in a saucepan; if you are using canned chickpeas, skip to the next paragraph. Cover with 1 inch / 2.5 cm of cold water, place over medium heat, and bring to a boil. Skim, lower the heat, and simmer, partially covered, for 45 minutes to 1 hour, or until cooked. Drain well.

Spread the chickpeas on a paper towel–lined baking sheet and place, uncovered, in the refrigerator for a couple of hours before frying, so they crisp up better in the pan.

Cut the tripe into 1/2 by 3-inch / 1 by 7.5-cm strips; set aside.

In a heavy flameproof casserole or Dutch oven, melt the dripping over medium heat. Add the onion, carrot, and celery, and cook, stirring occasionally, until the vegetables soften and begin to color, about 10 minutes.

Add the garlic, thyme, bay leaf, lemon zest, and chile flakes, and cook, stirring, until fragrant. Pour in the tomatoes with all their juices and bring to a boil. Reduce the heat so the sauce bubbles gently and cook, stirring from time to time, until the sauce becomes very thick. As it thickens, it will splutter, so use a splatter screen or leave a wooden spoon in the sauce; it helps to limit the spluttering.

Preheat the oven to 300°F / 150°C.

Pour in the stock, add 1 teaspoon of salt, and season with pepper. Stir in the tripe to coat with the sauce and bring back to a boil. Cover and transfer to the oven and cook for 2 hours or until the tripe is very tender. Check the tripe after 1 hour, as it may cook faster. Remove and discard the thyme, bay leaf, and lemon zest.

Place a large frying pan over medium heat, add the olive oil and when hot add the cooked, dried chickpeas and cook until they begin to brown, about 10 minutes. Meanwhile, slice the chorizo into 1/4-inch / 6-mm slices. Add the chorizo and red pepper to the pan and continue to cook until the chickpeas are crunchy and the red pepper has softened slightly.

Stir the chickpea mixture into the cooked tripe, check the seasoning, sprinkle with parsley, and serve.

Alternative: Chitterlings

Calvados Tripe

SERVES 6

This is a wonderful way to prepare tripe, because it cooks while you sleep and you wake up to a wonderful smell of tripe and apples. Of course, if you don't like the smell of tripe, this may not be the dish for you. This is a version of the French classic dish inspired by Jane Grigson. It is important to cut the tripe initially into pieces no smaller than 3 inches / 7.5 cm to prevent it from overcooking—especially in North America where the tripe is precooked longer than in Europe. The tripe in this dish will be very soft and melting. Make sure to serve it very hot in warmed soup plates to keep the gelatinous sauce liquid, accompanied by boiled potatoes or crusty bread.

> 1 large piece pork skin (see page 228)
>
> 3 onions
>
> 6 cloves
>
> 2 leeks, halved lengthwise, rinsed well and cut into 1-inch / 2.5-cm slices
>
> 2 large carrots, peeled, quartered lengthwise, and cut into 2-inch / 5-cm pieces
>
> 2 large apples, peeled, cored and sliced
>
> 2 stalks celery, cut into 1-inch / 2.5-cm slices
>
> Coarse sea salt and freshly ground black pepper
>
> 2 1/4 pounds / 1 kg blanched tripe, (see page 139)
>
> 2 cloves garlic, germ removed
>
> 2 stems flat-leaf parsley
>
> 2 fresh bay leaves
>
> 2 large sprigs thyme
>
> 1 calf's foot, prepared (see page 100)
>
> 6 cups / 1.5 l dry sparkling alcoholic cider
>
> 1/4 cup / 60 ml Calvados or brandy
>
> 1/4 cup chopped flat-leaf parsley

Preheat the oven to 250°F / 120°C.

Line a large heavy casserole or Dutch oven with a tight fitting lid with the pork skin.

Cut each onion into 6 wedges, and insert a clove into 6 of the wedges. Place them in a large bowl and toss together with the leeks, carrots, apples, and celery and season well with salt and pepper. Place one third of the vegetable mixture in the pan and then add half the tripe pieces, half the garlic, 1 parsley stem, 1 bay leaf, and 1 thyme sprig.

Add another third of the vegetable mixture, then the remaining tripe, garlic, parsley, bay leaf, and thyme and season well with salt and pepper. Finish with a final layer of vegetables and place the calf's foot on top. Pour over the cider, then cover with a piece of wet parchment paper and the lid. Place in the oven and cook for 12 hours or overnight.

Remove the pan from the oven and discard the paper and the calf's foot. Using a slotted spoon, remove the tripe pieces and carrots, and set aside. Strain the cooking liquid (you should have about 4 to 5 cups / 1 to 1.25 l), and let stand for 5 minutes. Discard the remaining vegetables and herbs. Skim the cooking liquid, then pour it into a saucepan, bring to a boil over medium-high heat, and boil until reduced by half.

Meanwhile, cut the tripe pieces in half and place them in a clean pan. Add the reduced cooking liquid along with the Calvados, check the seasoning, and reheat gently. When hot, serve sprinkled with parsley.

> *The trouble with tripe is that in my present dwelling place, a small town in Northern California, I could count on one hand the people who would eat it with me.*
> M. F. K. FISHER

TRIPE AROUND THE WORLD

As we know, the French take their food seriously, and they appreciate odd bits. Three cities in France are famous for their tripe dishes. Lyon has its *tablier de sapeur* or "fireman's apron," a dish of thick blanket tripe cooked, then coated in bread crumbs and fried. In Caen, it is *tripes à la mode de Caen* (page 141), a dish of tripe cooked with the apples, cider, and Calvados from Normandy. Lamb tripe is stuffed with a mixture of pork and garlic and cooked in white wine with lamb's feet to create *pieds et pacquets* in Marseille. The French don't have the monopoly on tripe eating, though: the Italians are serious tripe lovers, too, and throughout Italy, Saturday is the customary day to enjoy it. *Buseca* is a tripe soup from Lombardy; in Turin they add wild mushrooms to their tripe; and in Naples, tripe is simply boiled and served with salt and lemon.

In Portugal, it is the residents of Porto who are renowned as tripe eaters. During the eighteenth century, Porto was a strategic port for the British navy, supplying them with large amounts of salt beef. This left behind lots of cheap innards that the locals cooked up to make *tripas à moda do Porto,* tripe flavored with cumin and served with white beans. The Mexicans are famous for their spicy menudo, a soup made with tripe that is reputedly a cure for a hangover. The Turks, too, believe that tripe soup, *iskembe çorbasi,* is an antidote for a night out drinking. Restaurants specializing in this dish stay open all night so that revelers can sober up before returning home. Northern England is well known for tripe and onions in white sauce, the dish that traumatized my childhood, and, while you might not believe it, the offal-fearing Americans can also claim a tripe dish, pepper pot soup.

Pepper pot soup entered American culinary folklore as the soup that won the war by saving Washington's troops from starvation. In the winter of 1777 to 1778, George Washington set up his army quarters in Valley Forge, northwest of Philadelphia. It was an excellent defensive location and the soldiers were able to build log cabins, but they lacked food and clothing. One story from this time recounts that the soldiers survived thanks to a local butcher. He gave the army large quantities of tripe that Washington's chef made into pepper pot soup. Well, Washington's personal chef was African, and his army included black slaves, so perhaps a spicy soup did help the army survive the long winter. But if there was tripe—a highly perishable odd bit—there were probably other parts of the cow available for the soldiers to eat as well. We all know the Continental Army went on to victory, but it wasn't because they ate tripe. The victory over the English was the result of excellent training during their stay at Valley Forge from the Prussian military expert Baron von Steuben.

While pepper pot soup is linked to Philadelphia, and George Washington's army, the recipe is not American in origin. Recipes for pepper pot soup appear in several British cookbooks dating from the mid-eighteenth century, and the soup may have arrived in Philadelphia with British immigrants. Or it perhaps it came with the African slaves, who arrived in America after a sojourn in the Caribbean islands. There they would have eaten the West Indian pepper pot stew. In Jamaica, pepper pot stew is made with a variety of ingredients, including tripe, pig's feet, fish, and vegetables, and is flavored with crushed peppercorns or hot red peppers. Merchant ships transported not only slaves, but produce and spices from the Caribbean, making these ingredients readily available in Philadelphia.

Whatever the origins of pepper pot soup, the Pennsylvania Dutch continued to cook it using tripe and veal knuckles, and throughout the nineteenth century it was sold on the street corners from milk cans. As with many dishes made with odd bits, the soup fell out of favor, and today when it is made, it rarely includes tripe.

Soldiers in Washington's army also reputedly ate rock tripe during their winter stay at Valley Forge, but rock tripe isn't one of the linings of a cow's stomach. It is a hardy lichen that survives in cold, Arctic climates and drought conditions. In North America, the Cree used this lichen to thicken fish soups, while other Native Americans thought of it only as food of last resort. Rock tripe gives the eater a sense of fullness, and early European explorers ate it to ward off starvation. According to one explorer, it was palatable, but even gummier than sago, a starch extracted from tropical plants and used, like tapioca, to thicken soups and puddings. Rock tripe helped members of Sir John Franklin's first voyage to find the Northwest Passage survive, but then they also ate the leather soles of their shoes.

In Japan, a variety of rock tripe called *iwatake* is a sought-after delicacy, while in China rock tripe is used medicinally. Rock tripe remains a popular food among survivalists, and tests undertaken on mice reveal that though it has limited nutritional value, it helps boost the immune system. I think I'll stick with cow's tripe.

Dickensian Tripe

A mighty fire was blazing on the hearth and roaring up the wide chimney with a cheerful sound, which a large iron cauldron, bubbling and simmering in the heat, lent its pleasant aid to swell. There was a deep, red, ruddy blush upon the room; and when the landlord stirred the fire, sending the flames skipping and leaping up—when he took off the lid of the iron pot and there rushed out a savoury smell, while the bubbling sound grew deeper and more rich, and an unctuous steam came floating out, hanging in a delicious mist above their heads—when he did this, Mr. Codlin's heart was touched . . .

"It's a stew of tripe," said the landlord, smacking his lips, "and cow-heel," smacking them again, "and bacon," smacking them once more, "and steak," smacking them for the fourth time, "and peas, cauliflowers, new potatoes, and sparrow-grass [asparagus], all working up together in one delicious gravy."

—The Old Curiosity Shop

Minted Tripe and Pea Salad

SERVES 4 AS AN APPETIZER

Maggie Beer is an Australian chef and food writer and, like me, she is a late convert to tripe: her epiphany occurred in Italy. This is a version of one her recipes for lamb tripe, which is more readily available in Australia, so if you can't find it beef tripe works too. I like the slightly crunchy texture of this salad. You'll need about 1 pound / 450 g of peas in the pod, but good quality frozen peas are also acceptable. You could substitute favas or asparagus tips in the spring or fresh cooked cranberry beans in the autumn. Serve it at room temperature, not cold.

1 pound / 450 g lamb or beef tripe, blanched (see page 139)

2 tablespoons unsalted butter

2 tablespoons olive oil

2 leeks, trimmed, rinsed well and sliced into $1/2$-inch / 1-cm slices

1 cup / 250 ml Poultry Stock (page 233)

$1/4$ cup / 60 ml verjuice or apple cider vinegar

1 large sprig thyme

1 fresh bay leaf

1 teaspoon coarse sea salt

Freshly ground black pepper

$1^3/4$ ounces / 50 g pancetta

Olive oil

1 cup / $4^1/2$ ounces / 130 g shelled fresh peas

2 tablespoons shredded fresh mint leaves

Cut the tripe into $1/2$ by 3-inch / 1 by 7.5-cm strips and pat dry very well.

In a frying pan over medium-high heat, add the butter and olive oil, and when the butter begins to foam, add the tripe. Stir from time to time and cook until lightly colored; the tripe will spit and splutter. If some pieces stick, don't worry; they will be dislodged when the pan is deglazed. Using a slotted spoon, transfer the browned tripe to a medium saucepan and add the leeks.

Add the stock and verjuice to the pan and bring to a boil, then deglaze the pan, using a wooden spoon to scrape up bits from the bottom. Pour the liquid over the tripe and leeks in the saucepan and add the thyme, bay leaf, and salt and season well with the pepper.

Cover and simmer gently until the tripe is cooked but still has a little texture, like a cooked green bean. The time is hard to estimate: the tripe may be cooked in an hour or it can take up to 2 hours, so check the tripe often after the first hour.

Meanwhile, cut the pancetta into $1/8$ by $1/4$-inch / 3 by 6-mm strips, and place in a frying pan. Cook over low heat until crispy, adding a little olive oil if necessary. Transfer the cooked pancetta to a small dish and set aside.

With a slotted spoon, transfer the tripe and leeks to a bowl, removing and discarding the thyme and bay leaf. Bring the cooking liquid to a boil over medium heat and boil, until thick and syrupy and reduced to about $1/4$ cup / 60 ml. Pour the liquid over the tripe and let it cool to room temperature.

Bring a saucepan of water to a boil, add some salt and the peas, and simmer until just the peas are cooked. Drain the peas and rinse them under cold water, then add to the cooled tripe with the mint leaves and stir to mix. Check the seasoning and serve sprinkled with the pancetta.

TRIPE DRESSERS

A tripe dresser is not someone who goes out wearing a tripe dress, but a man—and historically they were always men—who makes bovine odd bits edible.

At the abattoir, after an animal is slaughtered, its stomach is removed and given an initial cleaning. It is then sent out for further processing, along with other odd bits like udders and feet. In the past, tripe dressing was very labor intensive, as each stage was done by hand. First the stomachs were scalded in large tanks of boiling water, then they were transferred to tables where they were scrubbed with brushes to remove the membranes. After that, they were cooked and bleached before being dressed or trimmed for sale. Today machines do most of this work. The stomachs are washed in hot water in a machine that resembles a very large domestic washing machine. Then they are placed in a Parmentière—a machine with an abrasive interior that removes the membranes and fat. If you are familiar with the classic French garnish, you might have guessed by its brand name that this machine was originally designed for cleaning potatoes. Finally the stomachs are cooked, bleached, and trimmed.

Tripe dressers also prepare udders and feet. The udders are skinned, cleaned of any residual milk that would cause the meat to spoil, and cooked for a very long time (see page 168). During the cooking, they give off a lot of fat, which in the past was reclaimed and used for frying fish and chips, but not today thanks to an erroneous fear of animal fat. The cow's feet are thoroughly cleaned and then boiled. The fat from feet is still sold as neat's foot oil for treating leather, *neat* being an old English word for cattle. Tripe dressers often make blood puddings as well.

Many of these businesses are family run, and not surprisingly the younger generation is not always keen to continue the family tradition, especially when sales are declining and expensive machinery has increased operating costs. Figures from Northern England, where tripe has always been a popular and a common prepared food, picked up for supper on the way home from work, reveal the dramatic decline in this profession. At the beginning of the twentieth century, there were 260 specialist tripe shops in Manchester alone; by the century's end not one was still operating.

> In all these cases the tripe must have long stewing, unless it has been done very nearly enough by the regular tripe-dresser of whom it was bought.
> **CASSELL'S HOUSEHOLD GUIDE**

All is not lost. There are still a handful of tripe dressers remaining in England today, though most of their product is shipped to central Europe, where the market is bigger. In France, tripe is still popular, and cleaned tripe for cooking and calf's feet are standard items at markets and butcher shops. Ready to eat tripe is also available and can even be purchased in supermarkets.

> . . . a most excellent dish of tripes.
> **SAMUEL PEPYS**

Giblets, Pluck, Haslet, and Pettitoes

Giblets is a collective term for poultry's edible organs. In the past, it included the heart, liver, kidneys, gizzard and also the head, neck, feet, and wing tips. Giblets were prized morsels, and there are numerous recipes for stews made using the giblets of larger birds. The word comes from the Old French word *gibelet*, meaning game stew, a derivative of the French word for game, *gibier*. Today, however, giblets are typically just the internal organs of the bird and its neck.

> . . . take particular care of the giblets, they bear a very good price in the market . . .
> HENRY FIELDING

Packaged together and tucked inside a fresh bird, giblets are lucky to be tossed into the stockpot. More often than not they end up in the garbage, as we are unsure what to do with them. If you find giblets in your bird, separate out the liver and add the rest to your stockpot, or make a quick broth to use for gravy or sauce for your bird. The liver can turn a stock bitter: it's best sautéed quickly and enjoyed on a slice of toast, a cook's treat. If you eat lots of poultry, you might want to squirrel away the hearts, livers, and gizzards separately in the freezer to use in another recipe. With larger birds, the neck can be very meaty, so I often roast it with the bird. It boosts the sauce and is full of tasty nuggets of meat for those who like to gnaw on a bone.

Unfortunately, giblets are disappearing. Now when I buy a bird, it doesn't even come with its neck, let alone its internal organs. Where do all the giblets go? A lot of chicken is sold in pieces, so giblets are available separately, making it easier to try recipes that use them. Good poultry suppliers will sell gizzards, and hearts and liver by the pound, and sometimes you can find necks too.

Pluck is a collective noun referring to an animal's edible visceral organs: the heart, liver, and lungs and sometimes also the windpipe and spleen (see page 129). These vital organs are also associated with personal courage—for example, you can be "plucky," meaning courageous and determined, or you can "pluck up courage." You might be a person of kidney, which means you are brave. On the other hand, you could well be lily-livered (that is, with a white liver), or liver-hearted; in both cases, you'd be a coward.

Haslet or *harslet* was a dish of fried pig's organs, but now it describes a meatloaf made from ground pig's organs and wrapped in caul fat.

> Hij heeft een hazenhartje—literally, "he has a rabbit's heart": he's scared of everything

Pettitoes are not trotters, as you might think, but a special dish made with the feet, heart, liver, and lights (lungs) of a pig. They are cooked, then minced, then blended with the cooking liquid and thickened and enriched with egg yolks. The mixture is then served with toast—like haggis without the stomach.

Give Gizzard a Go

... there should be no taste prejudice against eating gizzards. Like mammalian tongue, they are just plain ordinary meat.
CALVIN SCHWABE

The gizzard is the bird's stomach, usually included with the giblets (see page 147). It is not a pouch where food is digested, but a mechanism for grinding up and breaking down the bird's food before it passes through its alimentary canal. The bird swallows small bits of stone and grit that it stores in a sac inside its gizzard to help with this grinding process, and as you can imagine, the gizzard is a very tough muscle. Why should you think of eating it? Well, because it is a working muscle, it is very tasty and while small it is a solid piece of meat. When cooked, it is toothsome and delicious.

How to Choose

Gizzards should be plump, shiny and reddish brown, and meaty. They are usually split with the gravel sac and the connective tissue already removed.

How to Prepare and Cook

Remove any fat and set aside. If the gizzards are still intact, slit them open from one side, cutting through the flesh and tough connective tissue inside. Pull apart the flesh at the slit to expose the gravel sac, pull it out, and discard it. Peel away any membrane and cut the hard connective tissue away from the flesh.

... till, crammed and gorged, nigh burst with sucked and glutted offal. ...
JOHN MILTON

The gizzard, like heart, must be cooked fast or slow: in between it is just tough. It can be quickly grilled or added to the stockpot, but my favorite way is to cook them is to confit them slowly in duck fat.

Confit of Gizzards

Cooking gizzards slowly in duck fat is an excellent way to handle these tough muscles. It renders them succulent and tender. Once cooked, they can be kept covered in fat for six months or longer in the refrigerator. With some gizzards resting under a blanket of fat in my refrigerator, I know I can make myself a fast, tasty meal by simply heating them up and serving them with a green salad. Use confited gizzards instead of heart in the Salad of Duck Hearts (page 124).

> 10^1/$_2$ ounces / 300 g gizzards, prepared (see opposite)
>
> 1^1/$_2$ tablespoons / ^{3}/$_4$ ounce / 20 g Confit Salt (see below)
>
> 1 clove garlic
>
> Melted duck fat or lard

Sprinkle the gizzard halves with the salt, turning to coat. Cover and refrigerate for 1 day.

Preheat the oven to 200°F / 100°C.

Rinse the gizzards to remove the excess seasoning mixture and pat dry. Place them in a small, heavy flameproof casserole or Dutch oven and add the garlic clove and just enough fat to cover the gizzards. Place the pan over medium heat, and when you see the first bubble in the fat, remove the pan from the heat and transfer to the oven. Cook, uncovered, until the gizzards are very tender, about 3 hours.

Using a slotted spoon, transfer the gizzards to a sieve placed over a bowl and let cool. Strain the fat into a large measuring cup and let stand for about 10 minutes so the cooking juices sink to the bottom.

Place the gizzards in a clean container and then pour enough of the fat over to cover them completely. Discard any cooking juices at the bottom of the measuring cup, and reserve any extra fat for another use.

Alternatives: Poultry hearts, spleen

Confit Salt

MAKES ABOUT 1^1/$_2$ OUNCES / 40 G

This is a simple mixture that you can change following your taste. Sage and fennel seeds are excellent additions.

> 3 large sprigs thyme
>
> 2 fresh bay leaves, torn
>
> 1^1/$_2$ ounces / 40 g coarse sea salt
>
> 2 teaspoons black peppercorns
>
> ^{1}/$_4$ teaspoon freshly ground nutmeg

Remove the leaves from the thyme stems and discard the stems. Combine the thyme and bay leaves, salt, peppercorns, and nutmeg in a spice grinder and grind until powdery. Store in an airtight container; it will keep for several months.

Restaurant Darling—Belly

Breast or belly? Well, it seems to depend on the animal. We're all familiar with poultry breasts, one of the popular cuts that have no place in this book; other breasts and bellies do belong here. Think of pork belly. Only a few years ago, it wasn't fashionable at all; it was curiously over-shadowed by its bones—spare ribs. Times have changed, and chefs have rediscovered pork belly, due in part to the revival of heritage pork breeds. These animals put on fat and produce a well-marbled belly that is simply one of the best cuts to roast, braise, and eat. Now it is the darling of the restaurant menu, and it is slowly working its way into home kitchens. This is how less-loved pieces of the animal win the respect they deserve. Chefs cook and serve them, food writers popular-ize them, then recipes using them appear in the food media. And finally we ask our butcher for them. Belly is an excellent cut to cook because, even if you think you can't cook, you can cook pork belly. Its layers of fat keep it moist and juicy, so you really can't overcook it. Pork belly's rise to stardom gives me hope that every odd bit in this book can one day become mainstream.

> *. . . short ribs, veal breast—they become completely different entities after they are cooked. They transcend themselves, developing complex, satisfying aroma.*
> THOMAS KELLER

Lamb belly, more commonly called breast, however, is still a very underrated cut. The easiest way to approach it is to buy a rack of lamb spare ribs; these are often called riblets to distinguish them from a rack of lamb.

Beef belly, also called the flank, is divided into two sections. The hindquarter is where the skirt or flank steak is cut; the rest is usually ground. The forequarter flank, also called the plate, is what interests us in this book. In this section are the ends of the rib bones, and so we find short ribs, another chef favorite. Like pork belly, chefs have made this cut so popular that it has just about lost its odd bits status—another success story.

How to Choose

Apply the same criteria as you would when buying any meat. The front end of the belly closest to the animal's head is thicker and meatier and has bones, and is the preferred piece. The tail end of the belly is thin and boneless.

You can buy belly with and without the bones. I am a great fan of bones, and like to take them even if the recipe doesn't require them, and put them aside for stock. With the forequarter flank of beef, the choice cut is the beef short ribs. Pork belly, however, is more difficult to find on the bone because of the popularity of pork spare ribs. With pork belly, try to buy it with the skin: it is easy to cut off if the recipe requires it, and the skin is very useful (see page 228).

Lamb breast is fatty and is often sold boned and rolled. My preference is for the trimmed lamb spare ribs, as they are more versatile and there is a better ratio of meat to fat. This cut resembles a smaller version of pork spare ribs, with six to eight rib bones. It should be well trimmed with the breastbone removed.

How to Prepare and Cook

Beef short ribs need only to be cut into pieces on the bone. Depending on the recipe, remove the skin from the pork belly and set aside for another use.

Lamb spare ribs should have the outer layer of fell, the thin papery membrane just below the hide, removed, leaving only the fat. However, if it is still there, place the ribs bone side down and insert a small knife between it and the fat. Using a cloth to help your grip, grab the edge of the fell and pull it back, then take a knife and cut it away from the fat. Turn the ribs over and pierce the thin opaque membrane covering the bones with the knife. Using your cloth again, take hold of the membrane and pull it off, gently. If you are too gung ho, it will tear and make the job more difficult. As you pull, you will notice a flap of meat on the bone side of the ribs: leave it on if you are braising the ribs whole; if you're not, cut it off and braise it with the pieces of ribs. To cut the ribs into individual pieces, begin at the wide end and slice through between the bones. As you reach the short end, there is a small curved piece of cartilage: cut around this and remove it and set aside for the stockpot. Lamb riblets can be cooked like pork ribs, braised and finished in a hot pan or on a grill to add a crisp texture.

Rillons, Endive, and Apples

SERVES 4 AS AN APPETIZER

This is a good way to serve rillons (see page 152). The bitter endive and the sweet apple pair perfectly with the fatty, spicy, crispy pork. Sometimes I add some radicchio, or escarole. I serve this as an appetizer, so one rillon per person is enough, but if you wanted to make this a lunch dish you could add an extra two rillons and cut them in half. I like hazelnuts because I find that prepackaged walnuts are often rancid. If you use walnuts, replace the hazelnut oil with walnut.

2 tablespoons rillon fat or lard

4 rillons (page 152)

3 to 4 heads of Belgian endive, cut crosswise into 1¹/₂-inch / 4-cm pieces

1 apple, peeled, cored, quartered, and sliced crosswise

1 tablespoon brown sugar

1 tablespoon brandy

2 tablespoons coarsely chopped toasted hazelnuts

1 tablespoon hazelnut oil or olive oil

Melt the fat in a frying pan over medium heat, add the rillons, and cook, turning often, until they heated through and crisp on all sides.

Add the endive and apples slices and cook, stirring until slightly softened. Stir together the sugar and brandy and pour into the pan, stirring to deglaze the pan. Stir in the hazelnuts and hazelnut oil and serve immediately.

Rillons

MAKES 12 PIECES

If you like rillettes but don't like the work, rillons are for you: chunks of pork belly caramelized on the outside then cooked in seasoned fat until they are moist and tender in the center. They keep for several months if covered with fat and refrigerated, although mine rarely last the week. I love them so much that I only make them in small batches; that way I don't eat too many. However, if you have more willpower than I, this recipe is easily doubled. Serve them as a snack with a glass of white wine, add them to a charcuterie platter, or pop them into a salad (page 151). They can be eaten cold, but I prefer them warm so the fat is soft and melting.

2¼ pounds / 1 kg boneless pork belly, skin removed (see page 150)

1 tablespoon Spiced Seasoning Salt (page 28)

About ⅓ cup / 2¼ ounces / 65 g lard

4 cloves garlic, crushed

4 large sprigs thyme

1 fresh bay leaf

1 teaspoon hot pimentón (smoked paprika)

½ cup / 125 ml white wine

½ cup / 125 ml water

Freshly ground black pepper

Brandy (optional)

Cut the pork belly into equal large cubes about 2½ inches / 6 cm by the thickness of the belly. (I usually get about 12 pieces.) Place them in a large bowl and sprinkle with the seasoned salt. Toss together, cover, and refrigerate overnight.

Remove the pork from the refrigerator, discard any liquid, and pat dry the pieces.

Preheat the oven to 400°F / 200°C.

In a large, heavy frying pan melt 2 tablespoons of the lard and brown the pieces of belly on all sides; they should be dark and caramelized.

Using a splatter screen during the cooking is a good idea, and it makes cleaning up easier.

Transfer the pieces to a flameproof casserole or Dutch oven just big enough to hold them in a single layer. Add the garlic, thyme, bay leaf, and pimentón. Carefully strain the fat from the frying pan, leaving behind any debris, then pour it over the meat along with the wine and water and season with pepper. Place the pan over medium heat and bring to a simmer, then transfer to the oven, and cook, uncovered, for 30 minutes, stirring every 10 minutes.

Lower the oven temperature to 300°F / 150°C. Check the amount of cooking liquid in the pan: it should be about halfway up the pieces of belly; if it's not, add some of the remaining lard and if necessary a little more water. Cover and return to the oven and cook, stirring a couple of times, for another 2 hours, or until the pieces are very tender. Let them cool slightly in the pan.

You can eat the rillons right away warm, or at room temperature, or refrigerate for up to a week. To keep the rillons longer, transfer them to a clean container and strain the cooking fat from the pan over them. Melt the extra lard and pour enough of it over the rillons to cover them completely. Cool, cover, and refrigerate in the fat.

To eat, remove the rillons from the refrigerator and let them come to room temperature. You should now be able to pull them out of their fat. Place them with some of their fat in a frying pan over medium heat and cook, turning until heated through and crisp on the outside. Add a slug of brandy and flambé, and then serve.

Alternatives: Replace some of the pork belly with rolled spleen

Horseradish Braised Short Ribs

This recipe taught me a lot about horseradish. I have memories of grating horseradish and barely being able to stay in the room, so powerful were its volatile oils. When I grated horseradish for this recipe it wasn't very strong, and after cooking I hardly knew it was there. Well, the reason you eat horseradish fresh or preserved with vinegar is because heat destroys its power. The strength of horseradish also varies with the season, so you may want to add more or less than I call for here. Serve this with mashed potatoes or cooked noodles.

12 beef short ribs, about 5 pounds / 2.25 kg, prepared (see page 150)

Coarse sea salt and freshly ground black pepper

2 tablespoons beef dripping or lard

2 onions, halved and sliced

2 stalks celery, sliced

3 cups / 750 ml Beef Stock (page 232)

2 cups / 500 ml canned tomatoes

6 cloves garlic, crushed

3 large thyme sprigs

2 fresh bay leaves

1 tablespoon mustard powder

1 teaspoon fine sea salt

18 cipollini onions

2 tablespoons unsalted butter

1 tablespoon sugar

3 tablespoons water

2 packed cups / 6^1/$_4$ ounces / 175 g coarsely grated fresh horseradish

Remove the ribs from the refrigerator 30 minutes before cooking. Preheat the oven to 250°F / 120°C.

Pat the ribs dry, and season the meat with salt and pepper. In a large, heavy flameproof casserole or Dutch oven, heat half the dripping over medium high-heat and brown the ribs in

batches, adding more fat as necessary. Transfer the browned ribs to a plate.

Add the onions and celery to the pan and cook, stirring, until the onions begin to brown. Pour in the beef stock and bring to a boil then deglaze the pan, using a wooden spoon to scrape up the browned bits from the bottom. Add the tomatoes, garlic, thyme, bay leaves, mustard, and fine sea salt and return to a boil. Return the ribs to the pan with any juices and cover the ribs with a piece of wet parchment paper and the lid and transfer to the oven. Cook for 4 hours, or until the beef is very tender.

Remove the pan from the oven and, using a slotted spoon, transfer the ribs to a serving dish. Strain the cooking liquid, pressing hard against the vegetables in the sieve to extract all the juice. Let the liquid stand for 5 minutes; discard the contents of the sieve.

Skim the excess fat off the liquid and set aside the fat for another use. Return the liquid to the pan (you should have about 5 cups / 1.25 l) and bring to a boil. Continue to boil until the liquid is reduced by half. Check the seasoning. (You can cover and refrigerate the ribs and sauce separately overnight and continue the recipe the next day if you wish.)

Lower the oven to 200°F / 100°C.

Place the ribs in the oven to keep warm. Place the cipollini onions in a saucepan and cover with water. Bring to a boil over medium heat, then lower the heat and simmer for 2 minutes. Drain and peel the onions, leaving a little of the root intact so that the onions stay whole.

In a frying pan with a lid, melt the butter over medium heat and then add the sugar, peeled onions, and 2 tablespoons of the water. Toss to coat, season with salt and pepper, then cover and cook until the onions are tender, about 10 minutes. Uncover and cook until the onions begin to caramelize, then add the remaining water to deglaze the pan, add to the ribs.

Meanwhile, place the sauce in a saucepan over low heat. Stir in the horseradish, then spoon the sauce over the ribs and serve.

Alternatives: Beef cheeks, chuck, shank, or oxtail

Tamarind Glazed Lamb Ribs

SERVES 2 TO 4

Lamb ribs have never caught on like pork ribs, which is a shame, because they are tasty and cheap. The problem was that butchers didn't care about them, and sold them covered in fat and skin. That has changed, and now I can buy well-trimmed lamb ribs that have the skin and excess fat removed. The tamarind glaze here is a good contrast to the rich, fatty lamb. Tamarind is the fruit of an Asian tree and has a sour flavor that intensifies as it dries. The pulp can be found compressed into small packages, seeds and all, in Asian, Caribbean, and Latin markets. It must be soaked before using, then squeezed to remove the excess water and seeds.

> 4 racks lamb spare ribs, about 2 1/4 pounds / 1 kg, prepared (see page 151)
> Coarse sea salt and freshly ground black pepper
> 1/2 teaspoon five-spice powder
> 1/4 cup / 1 3/4 ounces / 50 g tamarind pulp
> 1/2 cup / 125 ml boiling water
> 1/2 cup / 3 ounces / 90 g brown sugar
> 2 tablespoons Asian fish sauce
> 1 tablespoon lime juice
> 1 teaspoon very finely grated fresh ginger
> 1 whole serrano chile

Preheat the oven to 325°F / 160°C.

Season the ribs on both sides with salt, pepper, and five-spice powder. Place them on a rack in a shallow roasting pan and add enough water to cover the bottom of the pan.

Cover the pan with aluminum foil and bake for 1 to 1 1/2 hours, or until the meat can be easily pierced with a knife and shrinks back from the bones. The ribs can be cooked in advance. If they are cold, they must be reheated on the grill for about 5 minutes before you brush them with the glaze.

Meanwhile, make the glaze. Place the tamarind pulp in a saucepan, pour over the boiling water, stir to mix, and let stand for 30 minutes.

Add the sugar, fish sauce, lime juice, ginger, and chile to the saucepan and place over medium heat. Bring to a boil, stirring to dissolve the sugar. Lower the heat and simmer for 10 minutes.

Using a rubber spatula to press on the solids, pass the glaze through a coarse sieve into a bowl; discard the solids in the sieve. You will have about 1/2 cup / 125 ml of glaze.

Preheat the grill or broiler to medium. Brush the ribs with the glaze and cook for another 10 minutes, or until crisp. Serve the ribs with any remaining glaze.

POETIC ODD BITS

Haggis is often the butt of jokes, along with the Scottish people for eating such a bizarre dish. However, those who repeat these jokes have probably never eaten the real thing, which is very tasty. A dish born of thrift, haggis is a way to use the liver, lungs, and heart, very perishable odd bits, in what is really a giant sausage. Recently, English historian Catherine Brown created a stir when she audaciously suggested that haggis is not Scottish at all, but an English creation. To back up her claim, she pointed out that in *The English Housewife* (1615) by Gervase Markham, there are several references to haggis. Markham, an Englishman, reveals that haggis was eaten in England before being popularized by the Scots. Scottish haggis maker Robert Patrick was not impressed with Brown's suggestion or with Markham's claim, responding that everyone wants a piece of Scotland's heritage. He cited the Dutch and Chinese, who both assert that they invented golf. However, Brown is not the first to point out the English claim: the English cookery writer Jane Grigson stated much earlier that haggis "is no more Scottish in origin than goulash." Like Brown, Grigson referred to numerous recipes of the English court dating from the Middle Ages through to the seventeenth century. What the Scots did for haggis, Grigson noted, was to serve it with neeps (turnips) and whisky, an inspired combination. Haggis remained popular throughout England until the turn of the eighteenth century, and in certain pockets well into the nineteenth century.

What sets haggis apart from other sausages is that the mixture of odd bits, minced suet, onion, and oatmeal is enclosed in a sheep's stomach and not stuffed into intestines or wrapped in caul fat. I think knowing the mixture is cooked in the animal's stomach puts people off, not the mixture itself. Anyone who has eaten processed meats has probably eaten the same ingredients in a much less tasty package.

In her book *The Scots Kitchen,* F. Marian McNeill gives three recipes for haggis, one of them a prizewinner from Edinburgh. She even suggests that the stomach really isn't necessary; haggis, she advises, can be cooked in a jar or a pan, as it is the sausage mixture that gives it the flavor, not the stomach.

Whichever way you make it, and even if it is English in origin, today haggis is inextricably linked to Scotland, thanks to the Scottish bard Robert Burns. The eighteenth-century poet made haggis famous in verse, and every year on January 25 his birthday is celebrated with a dish of haggis. For this grand fete, the haggis, preceded by a piper, is borne into the room with much ceremony, then Burns's famous poem, "Address to a Haggis," is recited before the haggis is cut. Now, I can't believe that the occasion would be nearly as special if the haggis were cooked in a jar.

> *Fair fa' your honest, sonsie face,*
> *Great chieftain o' the puddin-race!*
> *Aboon them a' ye tak your place,*
> *Painch, tripe, or thairm:*
> *Weel are ye wordy o' a grace*
> *As lang's my arm*

> *All hail your honest rounded face,*
> *Great chieftain of the pudding race;*
> *Above them all you take your place,*
> *Stomach, tripe, or guts:*
> *You're worthy of a grace*
> *As long as my arm*

At the time I write this, haggis from the United Kingdom is still banned in the United States. During the mad cow crisis of the 1990s, the USDA decided that Scottish haggis could be lethal. They feared that the sheep's organs might carry a disease related to BSE known as scrapie. In 2009, the World Health Organization ruled that sheep organs were again safe to eat, and this has forced the USDA to reconsider its position. Americans of Scottish descent and Scots living in the United States are all hoping for a change in the ruling, claiming that haggis made in America is just not the same as the real thing. In the United Kingdom, haggis sales are booming—up almost 20 percent in a year.

The famous French specialty of rillons also inspired a poem:

Rhyming Rillons
Rillons, Rillettes, *they taste the same,*
And would by any other name,
And are if I may risk a joke,
Alike as two pigs in a poke.

The dishes are the same and yet,
While Tours provides the best Rillettes,
The best Rillons *are made in Blois.*
There must be some solution.
                    Ah!—
Does Blois supply, so you suppose,
The best Rillettes de Tours, *while those*
Now offered by the chefs of Tours
Are, by their ancient standards, poor?

Clever but there remains a doubt.
It's a thing to brood about,
Like non-non-A, infinity,
Or the doctrine of the Trinity.
                    —*Richard Wilbur*

Spiced Lamb Ribs with Beans and Spinach

SERVES 4 TO 6

Matching fatty lamb breast ribs with beans is a good way to exploit their fat, which enriches and flavors the dried beans. Often I remove the bones from the ribs—they simply slip out when they are cooked—and stir the lamb meat through the beans. This dish improves with reheating, as the flavors mellow and blend, but if you decide to cook it ahead, don't add the spinach and lemon until just before serving. Remember that the beans must be soaked overnight before you begin the recipe. Serve this with a cucumber salad.

2 cups / 12 ounces / 350 g dried pea beans, rinsed and soaked overnight in cold water

2¼ pounds / 1 kg lamb ribs, prepared (see page 151) and cut into ribs

Coarse sea salt and freshly ground black pepper

2 tablespoons rendered lamb fat or lard

2 tablespoon garam masala

2 teaspoons ground coriander

2 teaspoons ground allspice

2 teaspoons turmeric

1 teaspoon chile powder

2 cups / 500 ml Lamb Stock (page 234)

2 cloves

1 onion, halved

3 cloves garlic, crushed

2 fresh green chiles

2 fresh bay leaves

8¾ ounces / 250 g rinsed, stemmed spinach leaves

1 cup / 15 g fresh cilantro (coriander) leaves, coarsely chopped

1 lemon

Drain the beans, place them a saucepan, and cover them with cold water. Place over medium-low heat and bring slowly to a boil, then skim off the foam, lower the heat, and simmer for 10 minutes. Strain the beans, keeping 2 cups / 500 ml of the cooking water, and set the beans and reserved water aside.

Preheat the oven to 300° F / 150° C.

Pat the lamb dry, and season with salt and pepper. In a Dutch oven or flameproof casserole, heat 1 tablespoon of the fat over medium heat and brown the ribs in batches. As the ribs brown, transfer them to a plate. Only add more fat if you need to; enough fat should render from the ribs as they brown.

When all the ribs are browned, remove the pan from the heat and add the garam masala, coriander, allspice, turmeric, and chile powder. Stir the spices into the fat and continue stirring for 1 minute. Return the pan to the heat and pour in the stock; bring to a boil, deglazing the pan by scraping up the browned bits from the bottom.

Insert a clove in each onion half and add the onion to the pan with the garlic, chiles, bay leaves, and 2 teaspoons of salt. Add the drained beans and browned ribs; the liquid should almost cover the beans—add a little of the bean cooking water if necessary.

Cover, transfer to the oven, and cook for 1 hour. Check that the beans are still moist, adding some of the reserved bean cooking water if necessary. Cover and continue to cook another hour, or until the lamb and beans are tender. Remove the onion, chiles, and bay leaves and discard.

Finely shred the spinach leaves and stir it into the beans with the cilantro (coriander) leaves. Grate the zest of the lemon finely and squeeze its juice, then stir the zest and juice into the beans. Check the seasoning and serve.

Twice-Cooked Beer Belly

SERVES 4 TO 6

There are so many ways to cook pork belly. With this method, first you slow cook it so some of the fat renders and bastes the meat, then you cook it again on the grill, where the remaining fat is cooked until hot and crisp—a perfect combination. This is a good recipe for summer, when everyone else is buying up spare ribs and thinking that braising is only for winter. Let them eat the spare ribs with little or no meat—I'll take the belly every time.

This recipe takes advance planning, as the belly is seasoned with a rub and cured for two days before braising. Once you've braised the meat, you can keep it for several days in the refrigerator before the final grilling.

2 tablespoons Spiced Seasoning Salt (page 28)

$1/4$ cup / $1^1/2$ ounces / 45 g brown sugar

1 teaspoon cinnamon

Freshly ground black pepper

$2^1/4$ pounds / 1 kg boneless pork belly, with skin

2 tablespoons lard

2 onions, halved and sliced

2 carrots, peeled and sliced

2 stalks celery, sliced

4 cloves garlic, crushed

2 fresh bay leaves

2 cups / 500 ml pilsner beer

Remove the skin from the belly and set aside. Cut the top layer of fat into a crisscross pattern, cutting just the fat and not into the meat.

Mix the seasoning salt with half of the sugar and the cinnamon and stir in a generous amount of freshly ground pepper. Rub the mixture all over the pork and then place the meat in a glass dish with the skin. Cover and refrigerate for two days, turning once or twice.

Remove the pork from the refrigerator 30 minutes before cooking, rinse off the seasoning mixture, and pat the pork belly dry. Set the skin aside.

Preheat the oven to 300°F / 150°C.

In a heavy flameproof casserole or Dutch oven over medium-high heat, add 1 tablespoon of the lard and brown the pork, starting with the fat side. Transfer the browned belly to a plate. Lower the heat to medium, add the remaining lard, onions, carrots, and celery to the pan. Cook, stirring until the onions begin to color, then add the garlic and bay leaves.

Pour in the beer and bring to a boil to deglaze the pan, using a wooden spoon to scrape up the browned bits from the bottom. Return the pork with any juices to the pan, cover with the pork skin and the lid. Transfer to the oven and cook for 2 to $2^1/2$ hours, or until tender.

Place the cooked pork on a baking sheet, cover with a second baking sheet and weight down—with the lid from the Dutch oven, for example. Strain the cooking liquid and let the belly and liquid cool separately. Then refrigerate both the liquid and the belly with the weight overnight.

The next day, remove the pork and the cooking liquid from the refrigerator. Cut the pressed belly into 6 equal slices about $3/4$ inch / 2 cm thick. Remove the fat from the cooking liquid and set the fat aside for another use. Place the liquid in a saucepan and add the remaining sugar. Place the pan over medium heat and bring to a boil, stirring to dissolve the sugar. Boil until reduced to about $1/2$ cup / 125 ml and syrupy; set aside.

Preheat the grill to high, then lower the heat to medium. Cook the pork belly slices for about 3 minutes on each cut side and 3 minutes on the fat side, 9 minutes in total, brushing the cooked sides with a little of the glaze. Serve the pork belly slices with any remaining glaze.

Lights and Lungs: The Story of a Soup

Lights is a synonym for "lungs," and once denoted both human and animal lungs; however now it is used exclusively for animal lungs. *Lights* is Anglo-Saxon in origin, and it means (as you might guess) "not heavy"—a perfect name for lungs, which are bulky but full of air and surprisingly light despite their size.

Lungs have been forbidden for human consumption in the United States since 1971, but in many other countries they are readily available. My pursuit of lungs began by chance, and this is the story of a recipe. While researching this book, I read many accounts of cooking lungs, some with very strange instructions. A reputable cooking authority told me I would have to beat the air out them with a rolling pin before I could even consider cooking them. With my weak knowledge of anatomy, I imagined myself bursting lungs like two partially inflated balloons in my kitchen. Then a friend told me that he'd read you must cook them with the trachea still attached. Why? So it could hang over the side of the pan and allow the air in the lungs to escape. This conjured up an image of independently breathing lungs floating in my saucepan; you can imagine my trepidation as I considered cooking them.

As with many things you fear, your imagination is worse than the reality (except with writing cookbooks). My first problem was to choose a lung recipe to try—you'd be surprised how many there are. I could draw on my heritage and make haggis (see page 156), and as the lungs would be chopped up, perhaps I wouldn't have to bother trying to expel the air. But once they were mixed with all the other ingredients and spiced, how would I know which pieces were lung?

Then fate took a hand and I stumbled upon a recipe for lung soup that was the specialty of a restaurant in Berchtesgaden, Germany, close to the Austrian border. As I was considering how to further research it without flying to Germany, a friend in Paris emailed me to say his friends from Berlin, whom I'd met some years earlier, were coming to visit. On a whim I emailed him back. Could he ask Christine and Hanno if they had ever been to the Bräustüberl in Berchtesgaden to try the famous lung soup? Well, not surprisingly they hadn't (neither of them is very keen on odd bits), but Christine offered to help in the hunt. She searched the Internet in German but couldn't find out any more information, so she asked a friend who is passionate about cooking and German cuisine. Not only did Christine's friend know about the soup, she is a close friend of the chef's mother. Kitchen kismet had stepped up to my soup bowl, and I now had the email address of chef Rico Buchholz at the Bräustüberl restaurant.

I sent off an introductory message and Rico replied that he would love to chat about lung soup. He sent me his telephone number and asked me to call anytime before 10 a.m. With the time difference between Germany and North America, that meant four in the morning for me—not my finest hour. I decided to wait until I was in Paris and in the same time zone. I finally connected with him, but Rico's English is not good on the phone and my German is nonexistent, so we decided that I should send him a list of questions by email.

In his reply (eased by the translations of his English-speaking girlfriend, Mandy), Rico described the restaurant as a family-style place that can seat up to six hundred people—no wonder he had very little time to answer my questions on the telephone. The owner, Mr. Bankhammer, an Austrian by birth, is also a butcher, and the restaurant's philosophy has always been nose-to-tail eating. There are several dishes on the menu that include odd bits like brains, sweetbreads, tripe, and liver, and of course there is the famous lung soup. All of these dishes have an enthusiastic following, according to Rico.

Rico uses veal lungs, which in his words are the "most delicate" in flavor. Ever helpful, he told me that I could judge the quality of the lungs by their color—they should be bright. He also said, in Mandy's translation, that I should order them from "a butcher of trust." My Paris butcher, M. Lechable, is definitely a butcher of trust, and he didn't even bat an eyelid when I ordered them. "Calf's?" he asked. "Yes, and ones that are bright, please." Then I added, "I understand they are more delicate." He overlooked the bright comment and agreed with me that veal lungs were the best. So far so good, but then I lost all credibility when I foolishly asked, "Do I have to buy two?" "Yes, madam," he replied with a smile, "they come in pairs." I decide not to ask if the trachea would still be attached or if he thought I should hang it over the edge of the pan when I cooked them.

When I picked up my lungs the next day, the package was a good size, but it weighed nothing. At home I unwrapped them carefully. They were rosy pink, they looked bright to me, and luckily there was no sign of the trachea. And they were solid, nothing like a semi-inflated balloon. I should have taken biology at school. I didn't bash them with a rolling pin, as Rico had made no mention of that.

Rico's recipe was very detailed, for which I was grateful—not all chefs are so precise. And even better, he'd emailed me step-by-step photographs. I was reassured that the lungs I'd purchased looked like those in Rico's shots; M. Lechable had not failed me. My soup looked just as good as the soup Rico served in the restaurant, except for one detail—his was topped with a magnificent, large dumpling. He hadn't sent me the recipe for that.

Would I make lung soup again? Yes, and I have; it is delicious. Was the lung an essential ingredient for flavor? I doubt it. It is certainly a way to make lung into a tasty dish, but I would happily replace it with tongue. So, if you are interested in trying this recipe and can't buy lungs, substitute a calf's tongue. If you can buy lungs, you'll have more than enough for this recipe—remember they come in pairs. Once they are trimmed, you can freeze them or brown them and braise them as you would any other meat.

Sour Lung Soup

SERVES 6

Of course I have modified Rico's recipe, and the portion sizes are now less Germanic, but I have kept the spirit. If you live in the United States, you could make this soup with a combination of heart and tongue. The tongue will mimic the softness of the lungs. Cook the whole tongue along with the heart and once it is cooked, peel it (see page 50) and let it cool.

1 pound / 450 g calf's lung

Coarse sea salt

1 pound / 450 g calf's heart, prepared (page 121)

3 tablespoons beef dripping or lard

1 onion, halved and thickly sliced

2 carrots, peeled and chopped

2 stalks celery with leaves, sliced

1 leek, halved lengthwise, rinsed well and sliced

3 stems flat-leaf parsley

1 fresh bay leaf

1 large sprig thyme

6 cups / 1.5 l water

6 black peppercorns, crushed

2 cloves

1/4 cup / 1 ounce / 30 g flour

A pinch of sugar

1 tablespoon white wine vinegar

2 cups / 500 ml Beef Stock (page 232)

6 cornichons, finely chopped

1 shallot, finely chopped

2 tablespoons capers, rinsed and finely chopped

2 canned anchovy fillets, rinsed and finely chopped

1 large clove garlic, finely chopped

1 lemon

1 tablespoon Dijon mustard

3 tablespoons chopped flat-leaf parsley

Cut the lung into 1 1/2-inch / 4-cm chunks, removing any large pieces of tube or cartilage as you go. Place the pieces in a large bowl, add 1 tablespoon of salt, and enough cold water to cover. Soak overnight in the refrigerator, changing the water a couple of times and replacing the salt. Weigh down the pieces of lung with a plate, as they float.

Remove the lung pieces from the refrigerator and drain well. Cut the heart into similar sized pieces; set aside.

In a large saucepan over medium heat, melt 2 tablespoons of the dripping. When hot, add the onion and cook, stirring from time to time until it begins to brown. Now add the carrots, celery, and leek, and stir to deglaze the pan with the moisture from the vegetables. Continue to cook until the vegetables soften slightly, then add the parsley stems, bay leaf, and thyme.

Add the pieces of heart and pour in the water. Bring to a boil over medium heat and then skim, reduce the heat so the liquid simmers, and

add the peppercorns and cloves. Continue to simmer, uncovered, for 30 minutes. Then add the pieces of lung, return to a boil, skim, and lower the heat. Place a heatproof plate or lid from a smaller saucepan on top of the lungs to weight them down and simmer for 1 1/2 hours.

Remove a piece of lung and heart and cut them through the center; the lung will probably be a little pink in the center. Taste; if they are tender, use a slotted spoon to transfer the pieces to a bowl and leave to cool. If not, continue to cook until they're tender. Strain the cooking liquid through a sieve into a bowl, let cool, and then remove the fat. Save the fat for another use. You will have about 4 cups / 1 l of cooking liquid.

Place the remaining dripping in a saucepan over medium-low heat. Add the flour and sugar and cook, stirring constantly, until the flour turns light brown; the mixture will resemble pureed chickpeas. Remove the pan from the heat and whisk in the vinegar and about 1 cup / 250 ml of the strained cooking liquid, whisking until smooth. Whisk in the remaining liquid and enough of the stock to make 6 cups / 1.5 l of liquid in total.

Return the pan to medium heat and bring to a boil, whisking, then lower the heat so the soup simmers. Stir in the cornichons, shallot, capers, anchovies, and garlic and simmer, partially covered, for 30 minutes.

Meanwhile, cut the lung and heart into thin short strips, removing any cartilage and wrinkly skin from the lungs, and fat from the heart, as you slice. Set the strips aside. Finely grate the zest of the lemon and squeeze 2 tablespoons of the juice; set aside separately.

Add the sliced lungs and heart to the soup and stir in the lemon juice and mustard, and cook until heated through. Stir in the parsley and lemon zest, check the seasoning, and serve.

Inside Story—Intestines

Chitterlings are intestines, most often pork, although beef and lamb intestines are available too. At first impression they might not seem something you would want to eat, but all of us who have eaten good quality sausages have eaten intestines.

Intestines are used for sausage casings and also for the filling of the French sausages called *andouille* and *andouillette* (see page 166). They can also be the main ingredient in a dish. In Asia, they serve them with noodles; in Britain, they are cooked and plaited and eaten cold with vinegar or fried in lard. Throughout the eastern Mediterranean, they are wrapped around skewers and slowly cooked on a spit over charcoal.

The word *chitterling* dates from the late thirteenth century, and its origins are unclear. The word may come from the Old English word *cieter*, meaning "intestine," or it could be linked to a German word for intestine, *kutel*. While the correct term is chitterlings, in the southern United States the word is abbreviated to *chitlins*, or even *chits*. There are also known by the euphemisms "Kentucky oysters" and "wrinkled steak."

The institution of slavery divided American society in many ways: one line of division was between the foods people ate. The hindquarters and the loins of pigs went to the plantation owners, while the chitterlings and other odd bits were left for the slaves. This division of people by what they ate gave chitlins political and cultural overtones. In the southern United States, chitlins became the quintessential soul food, a symbol of identity and oppression. There have been attempts to reclaim this culinary heritage by celebrating chitlins with festivals (see page 167).

Before working on this book, my experience of intestines was limited to the cleaned salt-packed hog casings I use for sausage making and the *andouille* and *andouillette* sausages I eat in France. I wanted to try cooking fresh intestines, so I asked my pork supplier to keep some for me, as he is always sold out by my usual market time of 8 a.m. There are many ethnic communities living in Toronto who appreciate intestines.

Chitterlings vary in taste and texture from earthy, gutty, and chewy to mild and very tender, depending on how they have been cleaned and cooked. Strong or mild, they benefit from being well seasoned, and despite seeming like there is nothing at all to them, they are quite rich. You may not be tempted to eat them unless they are wrapped around a delicious sausage mixture or already cooked, but then again you may, like me, be curious enough to try cooking them yourself.

Everything I read wasn't encouraging me to tackle the cleaning and cooking of chitterlings myself. Old charcuterie books tell you to take the warm intestines from the slaughtered pig straight to the river to rinse and clean them with plenty of water. I was convinced that cleaning chitterlings was going to be a messy, smelly, and time-consuming job, plus I live far from a river.

Well, the intestines I bought were not warm and they'd been flushed out at the abattoir, so I was pretty sure they wouldn't still contain anything I couldn't—or didn't want to—handle. Cowardly, I ordered a mere pound (450 g). When I picked them up, I was given a small plastic bag filled with a soft, creamy pink, innocuous-looking mass.

How to Choose

Your choice of casings and chitterlings will depend upon where you live. Cleaned casings for sausage making are usually about 1 1/2 inches / 4 cm in diameter, although you can get them smaller and larger depending on the animal and which part of the intestine you buy. Intestines get larger in diameter as they exit the animal. They are either packed in salt or brined; the salt-packed intestines will keep in your refrigerator or freezer for at least six months, while those packed in brine must be used up within a month.

Intestines meant for cooking, called chitterlings, are pork intestines. They are often available precooked and only need heating up in a sauce or frying. Uncooked intestines are usually slit, cleaned, and cut into lengths. You can buy these fresh or frozen.

So know what type of intestines you are buying, either for sausage making or cooking, and deal with a reputable supplier.

How to Prepare and Cook

Intestines for sausage casings need only to be soaked, then rinsed before use to remove the salt. Check they are not split by slipping one end of the casing over a tap and letting the water run through the casing like a hose. If they have any smell, soak them in water with a squeeze of lemon juice for a couple of hours.

> Good butchers are as rare as well-made chitterlings.
> A. A. GILL

With chitterlings to cook, the first step is to rinse and soak them in a bowl of cold water for a couple of hours. In Toronto, my intestines came attached to a fatty membrane that made them look more like an ocean creature than something out of a land animal—it was the mesentery. This frilly membrane holds the intestines together and to the inside of the animal. It is mostly fat and can be cut up and rendered (see page 229). My 1 pound / 450 g of chitterlings yielded 12 yards / 11 meters when detached from the mesentery, and they had a slight funky smell, but much less than I anticipated. In Australia, I bought intestines that were larger and were cut into 1 foot / 30 cm pieces and there was no mesentery attached. I prepared them the same way as my Toronto chitterlings and there was no difference in the final texture or taste.

The next step is to cut the intestines into manageable pieces of about 1 foot / 30 cm and to pull off any remaining fat. Rinse the chitterlings by slipping one end over a tap and running water through them. Then use a pair of scissors to cut them open lengthwise; they are slippery to handle. Inside the intestines is a mucous membrane, a pink lining that some people scrape off, but this is what gives them their flavor. Place the opened chitterlings in a bowl of cold water, add a squeeze of lemon, and set aside until ready to use.

Drain the intestines well; now they can be cooked like tripe. I suggest making the Beginner's Tripe (page 140), replacing the beef stock with veal or chicken stock. Or cook them in court bouillon (page 21), replacing the cinnamon stick with 6 crushed allspice berries and the star anise with a blade of mace or a good pinch of ground mace, and adding three cloves of peeled garlic. Bring them to a boil over medium heat, skim off the froth, then simmer the chitterlings until tender. Like tripe, the cooking time for chitterlings is variable: they will probably take about two hours, but the first batch I poached were tender in just over an hour, so pay attention and check them often. Drain them well. You will notice they have shrunk and wrinkled, earning their "wrinkled steak" moniker. Now they are ready to add to a sauce; try them with or instead of tongue in Spicy Tongue Tacos (page 53).

ANDOUILLE, ANDOUILLETTE, AND THE FIVE A'S

Intestines are common as sausage casings, but sometimes they provide both the casing and the filling of the sausage, as with the French *andouille* and *andouillette*.

The larger of these two intestine sausages, the *andouille,* is salted, smoked. and eaten cold like salami. The most celebrated is the *andouille de Guéméné* from Brittany. Its skin is dark black from smoking, and the inside of the sausage is made up of concentric circles of intestines, resembling the growth rings of a tree stump. The popular *andouille de Vire* from Normandy is also dark skinned, but its interior is a patchwork of meat and intestines that recalls a piece of pale pink marble.

> *La politique, c'est comme l'andouillette, ça doit sentir un peu la merde mais pas trop.*
>
> *Politics is like an andouillette, it should smell a little like shit but not too much.*
> EDOUARD HERRIOT

Smaller in diameter, *andouillettes* are grilled and eaten hot with mustard and fries; the best known come from the town of Troyes in the Champagne region. While intestines are the main ingredient, often pieces of pork belly and mesentery are added to the mix in these sausages. So revered are *andouillettes* in France that in the 1960s the Association Amicale des Amateurs d'Andouillette Authentique (or, "the friendly association of lovers of real *andouillettes*"), was founded. The membership, consisting mainly of food writers, meets regularly to taste and grade these sausages. Their point system is based on the number of A's a sausage warrants, from one to five. Only the handmade sausages merit a high score, and currently there are eight producers whose sausages have the top ranking of five A's. Both the producer and the restaurants that serve these sausages proudly display their ranking.

And what do *andouilles* and *andouillettes* taste like? Well, they smell stronger than they taste, so it is a matter of taking the plunge. As with foods like Munster cheese and white truffles, the smell is part of the experience, but it belies the strength of the sausage. If you are a novice, start with *andouille de Guéméné.* The fact that is it smoked and served cold mitigates the gutty smell and earthy flavor. If you enjoy *andouille,* you can move on to an *andouillette.* One sausage is usually enough, because despite being made mainly from intestines, they are rich and satisfying.

> *They are . . . the internal tubes that lead digested food of the animal on its final journey from the stomach and back into the outside world.*
> HUGH FEARNLEY-WHITTINGSTALL

EMINENT ENTRAILS

With a population of just over four hundred souls, it would seem unlikely that the small town of Salley, South Carolina, could achieve any kind of fame, but it has. Since 1965, Salley has been home to the Chitt'lin Strut, a festival celebrating chitterlings.

Each year on the first Saturday after Thanksgiving, over 30,000 people invade the town to celebrate the pig in all its forms and parts, but particularly its intestines. As with any festival worth its salt, there are rides, a parade, a strut contest (a sort of sexy dancing à la Michael Jackson), a hog calling competition, and—yes, you guessed it—a chitterling eating competition. Last year's winner ate his way through 2 pounds / 900 g of chitterlings in less than ten minutes. If that sounds like a few too many chitterlings for you, visitors can simply buy a small portion of boiled or fried chitterlings to snack on. The general consensus is that if it's your first time eating chitterlings, you should order them fried.

> Although we suggest that you clean the intestines before using, many ethnic cultures prefer them to be left alone. The undigested food within the intestines is regarded as a delicacy, much like the tomalley of the lobster.
> JANA ALLEN AND MARGARET GIN

SON-OF-A-BITCH STEW

With a name like son-of-a-bitch, this could only be a cowboy dish. Son-of-a-bitch stew was one of the more celebrated dishes served by chuck wagon cooks in the western states of America.

Made when a milk-fed calf was killed, it was a way to use all the highly perishable parts: the brain, tongue, sweetbreads, heart, liver, and marrow gut, which gave the stew its distinctive flavor. The marrow gut is neither marrow nor gut, but the tube that connects the calf's last two stomachs and is filled with partially digested milk. This milky filling looked to some like bone marrow, hence the name *marrow gut*. Every chuck wagon cook had his own recipe: some added onions, chiles, and even tomatoes, while others claimed that vegetables ruined the stew. Even the name was varied, with the "son-of-a-bitch" replaced by the name of a politician, lawyer, or local celebrity—someone who, in the cook's opinion, was a real son of a bitch. The cowboys of the western United States were not the only ones to eat marrow gut; the Mexicans make a dish of *tripas de leche* and serve it with tortillas and salsa.

> A son-of-a-bitch may have no brains and no heart and still be a son-of-a-bitch. But if it don't have no guts, it's not a son-of-a-bitch.
> COWBOY SAYING

Udderly Delicious

During the Renaissance, Italian cook Bartolomeo Scappi stuffed ravioli with a mixture of cow's udder, cheese, eggs, sugar, and spices and served the dish at the papal table in Rome. The recipe is in his book, *Opera*, published in 1570. When Samuel Pepys recorded his dinner on Thursday, 11 October 1660, cow udder was a popular dish in London. He doesn't describe how it was prepared but probably it was in the traditional English way—slices fried in butter and served with small white turnips, their bitterness balancing the udder's richness.

> *After we had done there Mr. Creed and I to the Leg in King Street, to dinner, where he and I and my Will had a good udder to dinner, and from thence to walk in St. James Park, where we observed the several engines at work to draw up water, with which sight I was very much pleased.*
> SAMUEL PEPYS

Probably you're like me, and never even thought about eating this odd bit. I discovered cow's udder on top of a salad at the Paris restaurant Le Ribouldingue. At first I thought it was bacon, but it didn't have the distinct layer of fat or the saltiness of bacon, and the taste was mild but rich. I was intrigued and set out to find the raw material, so to speak.

My local Paris market has an excellent *tripier*, a butcher who specializes in odd bits; it's my favorite stall, and everyone else's, it seems. Every Friday there is a long line that snakes around the stall and past the adjoining fish seller. As I wait in line I scan the refrigerated counter trying to see if there are lamb sweetbreads or testicles among the regular offerings of brains, liver, heart, tripe, and calf's feet. I'd never noticed udder. I asked the man serving if he had any udder, and he pointed to the tray perched on top of the coun-

ter. There was the udder in all its glory—or rather lack of it. It was a large hunk of gray meat resembling a whole cooked liver but with the texture of corned beef; it wasn't at all appetizing. The server explained that udder is always sold cooked, and you buy it by the slice.

That makes perfect sense when you think about how large an udder is. Udders can range from 12 to 50 pounds / 5.5 to 22.7 kg, with an average one weighing in around 20 pounds / 9 kg—not something you want to deal with in a domestic kitchen. It is even difficult for professional processors or tripe dressers (see page 146) to handle. First, it must be carefully cleaned of any remaining milk so that the milk doesn't spoil and ruin the taste of the meat. Then it takes six to eight hours of cooking to make it tender. During this time, much of its fat is rendered, and the udder loses up to three-quarters of its weight.

As with many other odd bits, udder has fallen from favor, and Pepys's dinner was its last moment of true glory. While Hannah Glasse (1747) gives recipes for roasting and stuffing udder, it gradually disappeared from cookbooks. In her book *British Cookery* (1984), Jane Grigson laments its passing and the waste of this good, edible animal part by turning it into pet food. Udder, also known as *elder* in England, is still sold in the northwest of the United Kingdom. In the Liguria region of Italy, it is a common filling for pasta, while the people in Belgium are fond of smoked *pis de vache* and I can find *tétine de vache* in my market and at least one restaurant in Paris. If you live in the United States, you won't be able to find udder: like lungs, the USDA doesn't think it is suitable food for humans.

If you are cooking outside North America, there are various ways to try udder: have your supplier slice it very thinly like a quality ham, and then fry it in butter until crisp and serve it on a salad. Or buy a thicker piece and cut it into cubes, coat them in flour, egg, and bread crumbs and fry them. Serve the pieces hot with a good, sharp mustard.

Or better yet, if you see it on a restaurant menu, don't hesitate to order it—the flavor is mild and rich. In thick pieces, its soft texture will remind you of tongue, and while it is slightly chewier and not as fine as tongue, it is good to eat. And you'll be doing your bit to help save a disappearing food.

Powerful Kidneys

Mr Leopold Bloom ate with relish the inner organs of beasts and fowls. He liked thick giblet soup, nutty gizzards, a stuffed roast heart, liver slices fried with crustcrumbs, fried hencod's roes. Most of all he liked grilled mutton kidneys which gave to his palate a fine tang of faintly scented urine.
JAMES JOYCE

What Leopold Bloom appreciated most about kidneys understandably turns the rest of us off this odd bit. It is very hard for most people to overlook the function of kidneys in the body. I have cooked many kidneys; my first job as a cook in a large hotel in Melbourne was preparing breakfast, and the mixed grill including kidney was very popular. Of all the kidneys I've cooked, only once did I detect the scent associated with their function, and that was over thirty years ago in London. You need to disassociate the organ from its role in the body and approach it without prejudice: remember, we eat eggs without giving them a second thought.

All kidneys have the same distinctive texture and their taste, while strong, varies with the age of the animal. If you're a kidney novice, start with the kidneys of veal, lamb, or poultry. Veal kidneys have as much protein as a T-bone steak and they are a good source of iron. If, after try-

ing them, you still don't like kidneys, you can still cook them. Just add diced kidneys to meatloaf, pâtés, or hamburger mixtures.

A casing of fat protects the kidneys inside the animal's body. This fat is special because it is firmer than the rest of the animal's fat, with a brittle crystalline structure. It is highly valued for making pastries and puddings. Pork kidney fat is called leaf lard, and beef and veal kidney fat is suet (see page 229). Rendered kidney fat is also excellent for deep-frying.

How to Choose

As with any odd bit, you must be sure of the provenance and freshness of kidneys. If you can buy them in their overcoat of fat or still with their protective membrane, do so. The fat and the membrane prevent the kidneys from drying out. Kidneys come in pairs, a fact often forgotten with larger veal and beef kidneys, as the two parts of these larger, multilobed kidneys are sold individually. While veal and beef kidneys are multilobed, all other animal and poultry kidneys are distinctively kidney shaped—think kidney bean, rounded on one side and concave on the other. Their size is related to the size and age of the animal.

Kidneys should be firm and shiny with no dry or discolored spots and no smell. Pork, poultry, game, and beef kidneys are reddish brown, while veal kidneys are paler, pinky brown. Buy kidneys whole, as they will be in better condition than those already sliced or chopped. Ask your butcher to prepare them or do it at home just before cooking. Keep kidneys refrigerated for up to two days or freeze.

How to Prepare and Cook

It's not difficult to remove the fat from kidneys: just make a cut in the fat and pull it away from the kidney, cutting the connective tissue between it and the fat. The hard, brittle fat comes away easily. Keep the fat to render (see page 229) or, with veal and beef kidney fat, instead of rendering you can simply grate it finely for use.

Next, remove the membrane covering the kidney by making a shallow slit on the rounded side of the kidney to split the membrane, then pull it off with your fingers, cutting it free where it is attached to the core. Often kidneys are sold with the membrane already removed.

> I knew to waste anything was about as close to a sin as a chef gets. . . . Once you've determined not to waste offal, you must learn to cook it. Often, these items are smelly, composed of fibrous cells, or have an overly powerful taste, all of which must be accounted for in the cooking process.
> THOMAS KELLER

Kidneys can be cooked whole, especially small poultry or rabbit kidneys. If grilling them, butterfly them first by cutting along the rounded side toward the core and opening up like a book, leaving the fat core intact to baste the kidney as it cooks. For sautéing, cut the kidney completely in half and cut out the fat core. With veal and beef kidneys, cut them into pieces following the natural pattern of the lobes. Rinse the kidneys and pat dry.

Beef and pork kidneys can be soaked in cold salted acidulated water—1 1/2 teaspoons of lemon juice and about 1 teaspoon of coarse sea salt per cup / 250 ml of water—for up to an hour before cooking to reduce their strong taste. Drain and pat dry before cooking.

When cooking kidney you have two choices: fast and still pink in the center or long and slow—anywhere in between will leave you with hard, chewy kidneys. Veal, lamb, and poultry kidneys are best when left pink in the center, while beef and pork are better suited to slow-cooked preparations.

A serving portion will depend on how much you love kidneys and the size of the animal. Remember you will lose some of the weight with cleaning. One pork kidney is about the equivalent of about two lamb kidneys, about 1/2 pound / 225 g. A veal kidney generally ranges from 1 pound / 450 g to 1 1/2 pounds / 700 g.

> A trained chimp can steam a lobster. But it takes love, and time and respect for one's ingredients to deal with pig's ear or a kidney properly. And the rewards are enormous.
> ANTHONY BOURDAIN

Devilled Kidneys and Mushrooms

SERVES 2 AS A MAIN COURSE OR 4 AS AN APPETIZER

This is a good introduction to kidneys, because you can increase the amount of mushrooms and reduce the amount of kidneys. The devilled flavors are a mixture of sweet and hot that match the kidneys perfectly and I'm sure will win you over. It's simple and fast to prepare, and you can use an apple jelly or apricot jam if you have no red currant jelly on hand. Serve this as an appetizer over toast or with rice or pasta as a main course.

4 slices bacon

8 lamb's kidneys, prepared, halved and fat core removed (see opposite)

Coarse sea salt and freshly ground black pepper

1/2 tablespoon unsalted butter

1 shallot, diced

3 portobello mushrooms, stems removed, cut into 1-inch / 2.5-cm pieces

1/4 cup / 60 ml dry sherry

1 1/2 tablespoons red currant jelly

1 tablespoon mustard powder

1 tablespoon Worcestershire sauce

2 teaspoons sherry vinegar

A good pinch cayenne pepper

2 tablespoons whipping (35%) cream

2 tablespoons chopped flat-leaf parsley

Preheat the oven to 200°F / 100° C.

In a large frying pan over low heat, cook the bacon slices until they are crisp and the fat has ren- dered. Leaving the bacon fat in the pan, transfer the cooked bacon to a plate lined with paper towels to drain, then chop into small pieces. Pat the kidneys dry and season them with salt and pepper.

Add the butter to the pan and increase the heat to medium. When the butter starts to foam, add the kidneys, letting them color lightly on all sides, about 4 minutes. Using a slotted spoon, transfer them to a plate and keep warm in the oven.

Add the shallot to the pan and cook, stirring, until it softens and begins to color lightly. Add the chopped mushrooms and stir to coat with the fat; once they begin to stick to the pan, pour in the sherry. Stir to deglaze the pan, lower the heat, and continue to cook until the mushrooms are soft.

Whisk together the jelly, mustard powder, Worcestershire, vinegar, and cayenne and add to the pan along with the kidneys and all their juices. Stir in the cream and cook gently until the kidneys are just pink and the sauce is reduced. Check the seasoning and add more cayenne if desired.

Serve sprinkled with the bacon pieces and chopped parsley.

Alternatives: Veal or pork kidneys

DANGEROUS ODD BITS

In southern Sudan, there is a dish called *marrara*. It is a mixture of raw odd bits that includes kidneys, lungs, the trachea, and the rumen of goats and sheep. It doesn't sound appetizing to me, and its consumption is not recommended. In this part of Africa, there is a disease called Marrara syndrome that is the result of eating this combination of raw odd bits. Marrara syndrome causes a reaction in the upper respiratory tract that results in itching in the throat and nose, deafness, tinnitus, and facial palsy.

Grilled Lamb's Kidneys with Rosemary Anchovy Butter

SERVES 2 AS A MAIN COURSE OR 4 AS AN APPETIZER

Lamb is often paired with rosemary and anchovies, and these flavors are perfect with lamb kidneys. You could serve these kidneys with grilled lamb chops, or you could use this flavored butter on grilled lamb's liver. If you have lots of both rosemary and patience, you can sharpen the ends of eight rosemary branches and use them instead of skewers. I use metal skewers, as my rosemary is never sharp or strong enough to skewer a kidney. If you use wooden skewers, soak them in water for about half an hour before skewering the kidneys. You can cut the kidneys in half instead of butterflying them if you prefer. Serve these with some grilled new potatoes.

> 1/3 cup / 2 1/2 ounces / 75 g unsalted butter, softened
>
> 4 canned anchovy fillets, rinsed and chopped
>
> 1 lemon
>
> 2 large sprigs rosemary
>
> Freshly ground black pepper
>
> 8 lamb's kidneys, prepared (see page 170)
>
> Coarse sea salt
>
> 3 tablespoons olive oil

Place the butter in a small bowl and add the anchovies and a squeeze of lemon juice. Remove the rosemary leaves from the stems, discard the stems, and chop the leaves finely. Add 2 teaspoons of chopped rosemary to the butter and set the remainder aside. Season the butter with freshly ground black pepper and, using a fork, blend together until thoroughly mixed. Check the seasoning and then place the butter on a piece of parchment paper or plastic wrap and form into a 4-inch / 10-cm sausage. Refrigerate until ready to use.

> *Hij is een jager in hart en nieren—literally, "he is a hunter in his heart and kidneys": he devotes himself to hunting*

Butterfly or halve the kidneys leaving the fat core intact. Using 8 small metal skewers, skewer the kidneys and place them in a shallow dish. Sprinkle the remaining chopped rosemary over both sides of the kidneys. Drizzle with olive oil, turning to coat, and cover and refrigerate the kidneys for up to an hour.

Remove the kidneys and the butter from the refrigerator. Preheat the grill or broiler to medium. Unwrap the butter and cut into 8 slices.

Season the kidneys lightly with salt and pepper. Place the kidneys cut side down on the grill for 3 minutes, turn, and cook the kidneys for another 2 minutes, or until pink in the center. Serve with a slice of butter on top.

Alternatives: Use 1 pound / 450 g of chicken livers or 4 pork kidneys halved (treat each half like a butterflied lamb kidney). Replace the anchovies with 1 teaspoon mustard powder to serve with the pork.

Veal Kidney in Gin-Mustard Cream Sauce

SERVES 2

My husband is the serious kidney lover in our family. I think he'd be happy to eat kidney three times a week. He loves to order it in Paris, and William, the owner of our neighborhood restaurant, always tries to have veal kidney on the menu when we are in town. A former butcher, William is very particular about the kidneys he buys and so should you be. At William's, kidney is always prepared the same way: whole in a mustard cream sauce and *rosé*—or pink—in the center. This is my husband's version of the recipe, although I doubt William's chef, Johnny, uses any gin in his recipe. My husband cuts the kidney into pieces, making the cooking time easier to judge. Serve these over rice or noodles.

1 pound / 450 g veal kidney, prepared (see page 170)

Coarse sea salt and freshly ground black pepper

2 tablespoon beef dripping or lard

1 shallot, finely chopped

2 tablespoons gin

1/2 cup / 125 ml Veal Stock (page 233)

1/2 cup / 125 ml whipping (35%) cream

2 tablespoons Dijon mustard

Cut the kidney into even-sized pieces, following the lobes, removing the fat core as you cut. Pat dry and season well with salt and pepper.

Place a large frying pan over medium-high heat. Add half the dripping and when it's hot, quickly brown the kidney pieces in batches and transfer them to a plate.

Lower the heat to medium, add the remaining fat and the shallot, and cook, stirring, until softened, about 3 minutes. Pour in the gin and the stock, bring to a boil, and deglaze the pan, using a wooden spoon to scrape up the browned bits from the bottom. Continue to boil until the sauce is reduced and syrupy. Add the cream and reduce again until thickened.

Lower the heat and return the kidneys and their juices to the pan. Stir in the mustard and allow the kidneys to heat through. Check the seasoning and serve.

Alternative: Lamb kidney

Meat and Kidney Braise

SERVES 6

Beef kidney slowly braised adds depth to this beef stew and becomes tender with the long slow cooking. You can adjust the ratio of meat to kidney up or down, and of course you can make it without kidney. Usually I serve it with mashed potatoes or over noodles, but if I have the time and energy I top it with Leaf Lard Pastry and use my pie bird to make a pie. This mixture can be made in advance and reheated or topped and baked. You can also top this with the rosemary biscuit topping from the

Lamb Cobbler (page 75). Serve with a salad or green vegetable.

21/4 pounds / 1 kg beef shoulder

1 pound / 450 g trimmed beef kidney, prepared (see page 170)

Coarse sea salt and freshly ground black pepper

3 tablespoons beef dripping or lard

10 large sprigs thyme

6 stems flat-leaf parsley

4 fresh bay leaves

2 stalks celery

2 large sprigs rosemary

2 onions, halved and thickly sliced

1 pound / 450 g cremini mushrooms, halved

1 cup / 250 ml red wine

2 cups / 500 ml Beef Stock (page 232)

1 small celery root (celeriac)

1 tablespoon Worcestershire sauce

1 tablespoon mustard powder

Leaf Lard Pastry (page 87)

1 egg

Preheat the oven to 325°F / 160°C.

Cut the beef into 1 1/2-inch / 4-cm pieces and divide the kidney into pieces following the lobes and removing the fat core. Pat the meat and kidney dry and season well with salt and pepper. In a flameproof casserole or Dutch oven with a lid, melt 1 tablespoon of the dripping over medium-high heat. Add the meat in batches and brown, adding more dripping as necessary. Transfer the meat to a plate. Lower the heat to medium and brown the kidney pieces, then transfer to a plate. Meanwhile tie the thyme, parsley, bay leaves, celery, and rosemary into a neat bundle with kitchen twine.

Add the onions to the pan and cook, stirring, until softened slightly, 3 to 5 minutes. Add the mushrooms and red wine and deglaze the pan, using a wooden spoon to scrape up the browned bits from the bottom. Return the meat and kidney with their juices to the pan, add the herb bundle, pour in the stock, and bring to a boil, stirring. Cover the meat with a piece of wet parchment paper and the lid, transfer to the oven, and cook for 1 1/2 hours.

Meanwhile, trim, peel, and cut the celery root into 1-inch / 2.5-cm chunks and keep in a bowl of acidulated water until ready to use.

Uncover the pan and remove the parchment paper, stir in the celery root, and continue to cook, uncovered, until the meat and celery root are tender, about 1 hour.

Remove and discard the herb bundle. Using a slotted spoon, transfer the meat, kidney, and celeriac into a 9 by 12-inch / 23 by 30-cm baking dish or a 10 cup / 2.5 l pie plate.

Whisk the Worcestershire and mustard together and stir into the sauce. Bring to a boil and boil for 3 minutes, then check the seasoning. Pour the sauce over the mixture in the dish; it should be about 1/2 inch / 1 cm from the top. Nestle a pie bird in the middle of the dish and let cool. At this point you can leave the stew to cool completely, then refrigerate, covered, up to 4 days before serving. Before proceeding, bring to room temperature.

Roll out the pastry on a floured work surface to about 1/2 inch / 1 cm larger than the surface area of the baking dish. Cut a strip of pastry 1/2 inch / 1 cm wide from the outside edge and fit it around the rim of the dish; this forms a collar to anchor the pastry top. Whisk the egg with 1 teaspoon of water and brush the pastry strip with some of the egg mixture. Top the pie with the remaining pastry, draping it over the bird. Cut a slit to allow the bird to emerge from the pie and press the edges to seal. Brush the top of the pie with some of the egg mixture and refrigerate for 30 minutes.

Preheat the oven to 425°F / 220°C.

Remove the pie from the refrigerator and place it on a baking sheet; brush again with the remaining beaten egg. If you are not using a pie bird, cut a slit in the center of the pie to allow the steam to escape. Bake until the pastry is golden brown and the filling hot, about 45 minutes.

Alternatives: Lamb shoulder and lamb kidneys or pork shoulder and soaked pork kidneys

FOUR

The Back End: Conventional and Beyond Belief

While the middle of the animal is the richest source of odd bits, the back end has its share. Shanks are returning to the spotlight, thanks to their current popularity on restaurant menus. Yes, shanks are found at the front too, but hind shanks are bigger and meatier, so I'm classifying them as back end parts. Inside the shank and leg bones is another delicious odd bit, bone marrow. Bones liberated of their meat are no longer relegated to the stockpot but roasted and proudly enjoyed as a dish in their own right.

Tails are the other obvious odd bit to include here, but not all animals are equally endowed. Sheep, at least the ones we are familiar with, have their tails docked, leaving nothing behind worth eating. In some places, sheep keep their tails and they are added to stews, but it is only fat-tailed sheep (see page 199) that have tails really worth considering. Pig's tails, while mostly bone, have enough tasty fat and skin to add texture to braised dishes. When cooked and then fried, they make a great fatty snack. For a meal of tail, you must turn to beef or oxtail, which has a good quantity of delicious, unctuous meat. I am happy to say that oxtail is slowly losing its odd bit status.

That's about it, you might think, for the rear of the animal. But in this chapter I am also including odd bits that will surprise and even shock the less adventurous eater: testicles, blood, and skin. Eating animal testicles is often tied to proving or improving one's masculinity, which is obviously of no interest to me, but that wasn't the reason I'd never eaten them prior to working on this book. I'd simply never seen them for sale in a butcher's or listed on a menu. So when I did see them on a restaurant menu in Paris, I ordered them without hesitation. I discovered an odd bit that was mild in flavor with a wonderful mousse-like texture.

The two other odd bits I mentioned—blood and skin—could have been included in any of the earlier chapters. They are here because there is more space. Blood—and before you think "vampires," consider that animal blood is a highly nutritious food. Many cultures depend on it for their survival, and for the cook it is a magical liquid in the kitchen, with the power to enrich and thicken sauces. I've taken blood to new culinary heights—or lows depending on your point of view. The second is skin, which is an organ. We all love crispy pork skin on a roast and pork cracklings, but skin is so much more than a crunchy snack, as we'll see.

> . . . I was talking to Marco Pierre White about how brilliant oxtail is, but how difficult it is to get people to try it in restaurants, because their perception of it is as something too robust and difficult to eat.
> GIORGIO LOCATELLI

So in this chapter you'll find both odd bits that are quickly becoming mainstream and some that will take longer to become conventional—if they ever do.

Shapely Shanks

Let's start with the most conventional and familiar odd bit at the back of the animal: the shank. The shank is the section between the knee and the ankle of the animal. Shanks are also called knuckles, shins, and hocks (the term *hock* comes from the old English word *hohsinu,* meaning *hamstring,* which is commonly applied to pork shanks). Every animal has four shanks, two at the front and two bigger and meatier ones at the back. The shank is a mixture of meat, fat, and connective tissue that requires long cooking but yields flavorful,

succulent meat. It also has a section of leg bone, so shanks are a source of bone marrow.

For most of us, the Italian dish osso buco was probably our first introduction to shank and is still the most familiar shank dish. Osso buco is a slice of braised veal shank where both the meat and the bone marrow are equally important parts of the dish—yet many of us still ignore the marrow. Lamb shanks are becoming popular on restaurant menus and in home kitchens because their size makes them a perfect single portion, but lamb marrow is often overlooked.

Beef shin is a large cut, and it's usually sold as boneless stewing meat, with the bones sold separately as marrow bones. But braising slices of beef shank on the bone means you can enjoy both the meat and the marrow and have a much more flavorful sauce.

Pork hocks are the most versatile shank because you can buy them not only fresh, but also smoked and cured. Smoked hocks are excellent for flavoring soups, stews, bean dishes, and sauerkraut (page 186).

Shanks, whether whole, sliced, or boneless pieces, are a perfect odd bit for braising. Look for shanks from other animals like goat and game; they are a good way to introduce yourself to a new meat.

How to Choose

Apart from following the general advice for selecting meat, your choice will be dictated by taste and size. Shanks from smaller animals are a good size for single servings. Shanks from large animals are sliced, and the meatiest slices are those just below the knee. It is often difficult to buy equal-sized pieces, so consider cooking a whole shank or a large piece of veal or beef shank. It makes an impressive dish that is easy to serve because the meat will simply fall off the bone. To be sure the shank fits into your pan, you may want to follow my method. I take a piece of string the length of my Dutch oven with me to the butcher and measure the shank with my string. If it is too big I ask my butcher to saw off a piece from the ankle or thin end where there is less meat so the shank fits my pan. Make sure when the butcher cuts the shank bone that the marrow is exposed at one end; then you will be able to scoop it out when the shank is cooked.

How to Prepare and Cook

Shanks are straightforward to prepare. For whole shanks, make a cut at the narrow end to free the meat and tendons from the bone. This allows the meat to slip down the bone in one piece as it cooks.

For an impressive presentation, shanks can be frenched. Frenching is simply paring the meat back from the top 2 to 3 inches / 5 to 7.5 cm of the thin, ankle end of the bone so that after cook-ing a clean bone juts out of the cooked meat. It is easy to do yourself, but you can ask your butcher to do it for you.

When shank is sliced, the membrane that encircles the slices causes the pieces to curl as they cook. To prevent this from happening, make a couple of cuts through the membrane before browning the slices.

Pork hocks come with the skin; if I am cooking them whole I leave it on, but when they are cut into slices I prefer to remove the skin, and add it to the dish for texture and flavor (see page 228).

All shanks require lengthy cooking, and you can substitute them in any slow-cooked dish. If you decide to cook boneless pieces, ask your butcher for the bones and add them to the pan, as they will give you a rich unctuous sauce—and of course you'll have the marrow.

Don't worry if your whole shanks weigh a bit more or less than called for; it won't dramatically affect the recipe.

Spiced Lamb Shanks with Gingered Lentils

SERVES 4

While frenching the shanks is not necessary, it does dress this dish up and makes the final presentation more impressive. Remember that people eat with their eyes too, and the carrots and the orange lentils also make this dish look good. Toasting the spices in a pan until fragrant releases their volatile oils and improves their flavor. I love all sort of lentils and these gingered ones match well with the mixture of spices in the lamb. You can make the lamb ahead and reheat it, but the lentils should be cooked just before serving.

4 lamb shanks, about 1 pound / 450 g each, frenched (see above)

Coarse sea salt and freshly ground pepper

3 tablespoons rendered lamb fat or lard

4 carrots, peeled and sliced

1 onion, halved and sliced

1 stalk celery, sliced

2 tablespoons fennel seeds, toasted

2 tablespoons coriander seeds, toasted

continued

12 green cardamom pods, crushed and seeds removed

1 teaspoon cumin seed, toasted

8 garlic cloves, crushed

Two 5-inch / 13-cm cinnamon sticks

1/4 teaspoon chile flakes

2 cups / 500 ml fruity white wine like Gewürztraminer

1 lemon

1 1/3 cups / 8 3/4 ounces / 250 g split orange lentils or masoor dal

One 1-inch / 2.5-cm piece fresh ginger, peeled and diced

2 1/2 cups / 625 ml water

3 tablespoons chopped flat-leaf parsley

Preheat the oven to 300°F / 150°C.

Pat the lamb shanks dry and season with salt and pepper. In a heavy flameproof casserole or Dutch oven, heat 2 tablespoons of the fat over medium-high heat. Brown the lamb shanks, in batches if necessary, and transfer to a plate. Add the remaining fat and the carrots, onion, and celery, then lower the heat and continue to cook until the vegetables soften slightly.

Meanwhile, place the fennel, coriander, cardamom, and cumin seeds in a spice grinder or mortar and grind to a powder. Stir the ground spices into the vegetable mixture and add the garlic, cinnamon sticks, and chile flakes. Pour in the wine and bring to a boil, then deglaze the pan using a wooden spoon to scrape up the browned bits from the bottom.

Remove the zest from the lemon in large strips and add to the pan with the shanks and any juices. Set the lemon aside. Cover the shanks with a piece of wet parchment paper and the lid and transfer to the oven. Cook for 1 hour, then turn the shanks, cover, and cook for another hour.

After 2 hours, uncover the pan and remove the parchment paper and cook for another 30 to 45 minutes, turning once, until the lamb is very tender but not falling off the bone.

Meanwhile pick over the lentils and rinse them in a sieve under cold running water.

Place the lentils in a saucepan and add the diced ginger and water. Place over medium heat and bring to a boil, reduce heat, cover, and simmer, about 15 minutes, stirring from time to time, until the lentils are very soft.

Puree the lentils with an immersion blender or in a food processor, and season with salt and pepper. Return to the pan and keep warm over low heat.

Place the shanks in a serving dish, and cover loosely with aluminum foil to keep warm. Remove the garlic, cinnamon sticks, and lemon zest from the cooking liquid and discard. Pour the sauce into a large measuring cup; you should have about 2 cups / 500 ml. Let stand for 5 minutes, and then skim off any excess fat. Set the fat aside for another use and return the liquid to the pan. Bring to a boil and boil until reduced to about 1 1/4 cups / 310 ml, and check the seasoning.

Pour the sauce over the shanks, sprinkle with the parsley, and serve with the lentils.

Alternatives: Lamb neck and shoulder; goat, pork, or venison shanks

Shank's pony: When I was a child my relatives used this expression to answer the question "How did you get there?" It meant they'd walked.

Classic Beef Stew

SERVES 6

There are countless permutations of beef stew in almost every cuisine. Instead of boneless pieces of beef, I cook slices of beef shank with the bone. Browning two or three slices is a lot less tedious than a pile of cubed meat. Once the dish is cooked, I divide the shank slices into serving portions. Serve with Bone Marrow Dumplings (page 192).

2 cups / 500 ml red wine

3 pounds / 1.4 kg beef shank, cut into 1^1/$_2$-inch / 4-cm slices, prepared (see page 179)

4 large onions, halved and sliced

2 stalks celery, sliced

3 cloves garlic, crushed

3 stems flat-leaf parsley

2 sprigs thyme

1 fresh bay leaf

^{1}/$_4$ teaspoon black peppercorns

Coarse sea salt and freshly ground black pepper

^{1}/$_4$ cup / 1^3/$_4$ ounces / 50 g beef dripping or lard

4 carrots, peeled and cut into 1^1/$_2$-inch / 4-cm pieces

1 tablespoon tomato paste

2 cups / 500 ml Beef Stock (page 232)

8 ounces / 225 g portobello mushrooms, trimmed and quartered

^{1}/$_4$ cup chopped flat-leaf parsley

1 tablespoon red wine vinegar

Pour the wine into a large saucepan and bring it to a boil. Reduce the heat so the wine bubbles gently. Tip the saucepan slightly away from you and, using a long match, light the wine. Once the flames die out light it again and keep lighting it until it no longer flames. Set aside to cool.

Place the meat in a nonreactive baking dish or bowl, add one of the sliced onions, the celery, garlic, parsley, thyme, bay leaf, and peppercorns. Pour over the cooled wine and stir to mix. Leave to marinate for 3 hours on the counter or all day in the refrigerator; the marinade works slower in the colder temperature.

Preheat the oven to 300°F / 150°C.

Remove the meat from the marinade and pat dry. Strain the marinade, keeping the solids and liquid separate. Pour the liquid into a saucepan and bring to a boil; continue to boil until it is reduced by half, then set aside.

Season the meat with salt and pepper. In a large, deep Dutch oven or flameproof casserole heat half the fat over medium high-heat and brown the meat in batches, adding more fat as necessary. Transfer the browned pieces to a plate.

When all the meat is browned, add the remaining onions, the carrots, and the vegetables and herbs from the marinade to the pan. Stir; the moisture from the vegetables will begin to deglaze the pan. Continue to cook, stirring the vegetables until the onions soften slightly. Add the tomato paste, stir, and cook for a minute. Pour in the reduced liquid and bring to a boil, using a wooden spoon to deglaze the pan by scraping any browned bits from the bottom.

Add the stock, return the shank slices with any juices to the pan, and bring to a boil. Cover the shanks with a piece of wet parchment paper and the lid and transfer to the oven for 2 hours.

Uncover and remove the paper. Add the mushrooms and continue to cook for another hour or until the beef is very tender.

Check the seasoning and the consistency of the sauce: it should coat the meat. If the sauce is too thin, remove the meat and vegetables and keep warm, and boil the sauce to reduce it. Add the parsley and red wine vinegar and serve.

Alternatives: Beef shoulder or cheeks; oxtail

Whole Veal Shank with Saffron

SERVES 4 TO 6

The popularity of osso buco means that we rarely see whole veal shanks. I prefer to cook veal shanks whole, as then I don't have to search for equal-sized slices and my guests can eat as much or as little meat as they want. Also cooking a whole shank is easier, as you only have one piece of meat to brown. The only caveat is the size of your pan. The saffron and cream combine to make a rich, perfumed sauce. Serve this with Potato Gnocchi (page 38) or Bone Marrow Dumplings (page 192), which will add an extra layer of marrowy richness.

1 veal shank, about 4 pounds / 1.8 kg, prepared (see page 179)

Coarse sea salt and freshly ground black pepper

2 tablespoons olive oil

1 tablespoon unsalted butter

1 onion, chopped

1 carrot, peeled and chopped

2 stalks celery, sliced

4 cloves garlic

1 large sprig thyme

1 fresh bay leaf

$1/4$ teaspoon saffron threads

2 teaspoons tomato paste

$1/2$ cup / 125 ml dry white wine

$1\,1/4$ cups / 310 ml Veal Stock (page 233)

$1/4$ cup / 60 ml (35%) whipping cream

One hour before cooking, remove the shank from the refrigerator and pat dry.

Preheat the oven to 300°F / 150°C. Season the shank with salt and pepper.

In a large, heavy flameproof casserole or Dutch oven, heat 1 tablespoon of the olive oil and the butter over medium-high heat. Brown the shank and transfer to a plate.

Add the remaining olive oil and the onion, carrot, and celery. Lower the heat and cook, stirring from time to time, until the vegetables are softened, about 10 minutes. Add the garlic, thyme, bay leaf, saffron, and tomato paste, stir, and cook for a couple of minutes.

Pour the wine into the pan and bring to a boil, deglazing the pan by scraping up the browned bits from the bottom. Add the stock and return the shank to the pan with any juices, cover with a piece of wet parchment paper then the lid and transfer to the oven. Cook for 1 hour, then turn the shank, cover, and cook for another hour.

Uncover the shank, remove the parchment paper, and continue to cook for 30 minutes, or until the meat is very tender, almost falling off the bone. Carefully transfer the shank to a platter, and loosely cover with aluminum foil to keep warm.

Strain the cooking liquid through a sieve into a bowl, pressing on the vegetables to extract all the juice; discard the vegetables. Let the cooking liquid stand 5 minutes, then skim off any excess fat and set the fat aside for another use. Return the cooking liquid to the pan and place over medium-high heat. Bring to a boil, and continue to boil until the liquid is reduced to 1 cup / 250 ml. Stir in the cream and check the seasoning.

Spoon the sauce over the shank and serve with the gnocchi. The meat will fall off in big chunks, and don't forget the bone marrow—it will slide right out of the bone.

Alternatives: Slices of veal shank, veal cheeks, veal shoulder, or veal breast

Wild Boar Shanks with Cranberries and Chocolate

SERVES 4

I love wild boar, but in Canada the only boar available isn't wild at all—it's farmed. As a result, it doesn't have the same gaminess as European boar, but farmed shanks are a good size for one per person. Unfortunately, no one seems to want this cut—they are all deboned and ground, so I must order them in advance from my supplier. The role of the chocolate in this recipe is not to flavor but to thicken and enhance the sauce. Start this recipe a day in advance as the shanks marinate overnight. Serve with pureed parsnips.

3 cups / 750 ml red wine

4 boar shanks, about 1 pound / 450 g each, prepared (see page 179)

1 large onion, halved and sliced

1 large carrot, peeled and diced

2 stalks celery with leaves, sliced

1 clove garlic, crushed

6 large juniper berries, crushed

2 large sprigs rosemary

2 sprigs thyme

1 fresh bay leaf

1/4 teaspoon black peppercorns

1/4 cup / 60 ml plus 3 tablespoons red wine vinegar

3 tablespoons olive oil

Coarse sea salt and freshly ground black pepper

2 tablespoons lard

2 ounces / 60 g fatty pancetta, diced

A piece of pork skin

1/3 cup / 2 1/4 ounces / 65 g sugar

1 cup / 3 1/2 ounces / 100 g fresh or frozen cranberries

1 ounce / 30 g dark (70%) chocolate, chopped

Pour the wine into a large saucepan over high heat and bring it to a boil. Reduce the heat so that the wine simmers, then tip the saucepan away from you and light the wine with a long match.

Let the wine burn; then when the flames die out, light the wine again. Continue until the wine no longer lights and then remove the pan from the heat and let the wine cool completely.

Place the shanks in a large deep bowl; add the onion, carrot, celery, garlic, juniper berries, rosemary, thyme, bay leaf, and peppercorns. Pour 1/4 cup / 60 ml of the vinegar and the olive oil into the cooled wine and then pour the mixture over the shanks. Turn to coat, cover, and refrigerate overnight, turning from time to time.

Preheat the oven to 300°F / 150°C.

Remove the shanks from the marinade, pat them dry, and season them with salt and pepper. Strain the marinade and set the liquid and the vegetables aside.

In a large, deep, heavy flameproof casserole or Dutch oven, heat the lard over medium-high heat and brown the shanks, in batches if necessary. Transfer the browned shanks to a plate.

Add the pancetta to the pan, lower the heat, and cook until its fat is rendered. Add the vegetables with the herbs and spices from the marinade to the pan and cook until the onion begins to color. Pour in the marinade liquid, bring to a boil and deglaze the pan, using a wooden spoon to scrape up the browned bits from the bottom.

Return the shanks to the pan with any juices, then cover with the pork skin and the lid. Transfer to the oven and cook for 2 1/2 hours, or until the meat is almost falling off the bone, turning the shanks once or twice.

While the shanks are cooking put the sugar and the remaining 3 tablespoons of vinegar in a small pan over low heat and stir to dissolve the sugar. Add the cranberries and cook, stirring from time to time, until the cranberries pop and the mixture has a jamlike consistency. Strain the mixture through a fine sieve, pressing on the fruit to extract all the juice; you should have about 1/4 cup / 60 ml. Keep the liquid and discard the residue in the sieve.

Discard the pork skin and transfer the shanks to a plate and cover loosely with aluminum foil to keep warm. Strain the cooking liquid through a sieve and let it stand for 5 minutes, then skim off any excess fat and set the fat aside for another use. Discard the vegetables. Return the liquid to the pan and bring it to a boil over high heat. Boil until reduced to about to 1 1/2 cups / 375 ml.

Remove from the heat and whisk in the chocolate and strained cranberry mixture. Check the seasoning, pour over the boar shanks, and serve.

Alternatives: Elk shank, venison shanks, or pork hocks

Sweet and Sour Pork Hocks with Savoy Cabbage and Capers

SERVES 3 OR 4

Sweet and sour flavors go well with pork, and one of its natural allies in the vegetable kingdom is cabbage. I use fresh hocks but smoked ones would work, and you won't need to brown them. Taste the dish at the end of cooking so you can balance it with a little more vinegar if necessary. Serve with boiled potatoes.

> 6 pork hock slices, about 2.8 pounds / 1.3 kg, prepared (see page 179)
>
> Coarse sea salt and freshly ground black pepper
>
> 2 to 3 tablespoons lard
>
> 1 onion, chopped
>
> 1 carrot, peeled and sliced
>
> 1 stalk celery, sliced
>
> 1/3 cup / 2 1/4 ounces / 65 g sugar
>
> 1/3 cup / 75 ml white wine vinegar
>
> 1/2 savoy cabbage, cored and sliced, about 10 cups / 2.5 l
>
> 1/2 cup / 3 1/2 ounces / 100 g capers packed in vinegar, drained

Preheat the oven to 300°F / 150°C.

Pat the hock slices dry and season well with salt and pepper.

In a heavy flameproof casserole or Dutch oven, heat 2 tablespoons of the lard over medium-high heat. Brown the slices, in batches if necessary, and transfer to a plate. Add the remaining lard, if necessary, and the onion, carrot, and celery, then lower the heat and continue to cook until the vegetables soften slightly.

Stir in the sugar and vinegar and deglaze the pan, using a wooden spoon to scrape up any browned bits from the bottom. Stir until the sugar dissolves and bring to a boil. Add half the shredded cabbage and the capers and stir to mix. Add the hock slices with any juices, then cover them with the remaining cabbage, the skin from the hock slices, and a piece of wet parchment paper; put the lid on the pan and transfer to the oven. Cook for 1 1/4 hours, then stir and cover again and cook for another 1 1/4 hours.

Uncover, remove the parchment, and continue to cook until the meat begins to fall off the bones, about 30 minutes. Check the seasoning and add a little more vinegar if necessary.

Alternatives: Pork neck or shoulder; wild boar shanks

Haralds's Sauerkraut

SERVES 8

My husband is the sauerkraut expert in our house. He cooked this recipe, based on his mother's, in Paris for the local *charcutier* and his wife. He was quite chuffed when our guests proclaimed it the best *choucroute* they'd ever eaten. *Choucroute* is the French word for sauerkraut; and the French version often lacks depth and is too acidic for my husband's taste.

When testing again for this book, he made one of his best renditions using our homemade pickled cabbage. I recommend trying your hand at making sauerkraut cabbage; it is ridiculously simple and immensely satisfying. However, that means you'll need to be thinking about cooking this dish at least a month in advance. You can make this dish with quality store-bought sauerkraut—not canned. Half of the sauerkraut cabbage is rinsed to remove some of its acidity. Taste your sauerkraut and decide whether you need to rinse more or less. If you make the sauerkraut cabbage you won't need to add the caraway seeds to this recipe. You'll need a heavy flameproof casserole or Dutch oven big enough to hold the sauerkraut and hocks. Serve the sauerkraut and knackwurst with boiled potatoes and mustard—nothing else is necessary.

> 4 quarts / 4 1/2 pounds / 2 kg Homemade Sauerkraut Cabbage (page 188) or quality prepared sauerkraut
>
> 1/4 cup / 1 3/4 ounces / 50 g duck fat or lard
>
> 4 onions, halved and sliced
>
> 3 large sweet apples, peeled, cored, and sliced
>
> 10 juniper berries, crushed
>
> 1 tablespoon caraway seeds (optional)
>
> 3 1/2 pounds / 1.6 kg smoked pork hocks
>
> 3 cups / 750 ml medium-dry Riesling
>
> 8 knackwurst sausages, about 1 3/4 pounds / 800 g

Preheat the oven to 325°F / 160°C.

Place half the sauerkraut in a colander and rinse well under cold running water; set aside.

In a very large, heavy flameproof casserole or Dutch oven, melt the duck fat over medium-high heat. Add the onions and cook, stirring, until slightly softened but not colored. Add the apples and continue to cook, stirring, for about 5 minutes. Add the washed and unwashed sauerkraut and stir to mix with the apples and onions. Stir in the juniper berries and caraway seeds, if using.

Nestle the hocks into the sauerkraut, pour over the wine, cover and transfer to the oven. Cook for 2 hours, then turn the hocks. If there is still a lot of liquid in the pan, uncover and cook for another hour; if not, only uncover for the last 30 minutes. The sauerkraut is cooked when the cabbage becomes golden on the top and most of the liquid has evaporated. Remove the hocks and cut the skin, fat, and meat into large chunks, then stir through the cabbage.

Bring a large saucepan of water to a boil, drop in the sausages, turn off the heat, and allow them to poach until heated through. Drain. Serve the sauerkraut with the sausages.

THREE-STAR ODD BITS

While writing this book, my husband and I had a wedding anniversary with a zero at the end. When there is a zero involved, important dates take on even more meaning, so we decided to celebrate with dinner at a well-known restaurant in Paris. We had followed the chef Eric Frechon from his first restaurant in the depths of the nineteenth arrondissement to his luxurious quarters in the Hôtel le Bristol, where he had finally won his three Michelin stars. The evening was perfect—superlative service, great wine and food—but for me, the highlight was my main course: *tête de veau*. Just to see this common bistro dish listed on a three-star menu was a surprise, so I had to order it. (Also, I am always looking for another recipe to add to my odd bits repertoire.) Well, in true Frechon style, he had taken this simple food and elevated it into a dish worthy of his three-star rating. Calf's head is readily available at butcher shops throughout Paris and often turns up on the menu at two of our local restaurants. The head is boned out and stuffed with a mixture that includes veal and tongue in pieces or ground, and then the head is poached. In my neighborhood market, shoppers specify whether they want it with or without the tongue. All you or the local cook have to do is fry up a slice and serve it with *ravigote* sauce, made from oil and vinegar blended with capers, onions, and herbs.

I knew Frechon would not be buying his *tête de veau* already prepared, but I didn't expect to be presented with a dish that looked more like it belonged in a pastry store than a butcher shop. My *tête de veau* resembled a mille-feuille: layered between a "pastry" of thinly sliced potatoes was a filling of calf's head. There was soft yielding tongue, chewy snout, creamy brain, succulent cheek, and rich skin. Then this veal mille-feuille, was "iced" with the green *ravigote* sauce and decorated with baby capers and a tiny, perfect dice of cornichons, shallots, red onion, egg yolk, and egg white that had probably taken an apprentice hours to prepare. The plate was finished with two streaks of red pepper coulis. Technically complex, spectacular, and absolutely delicious. Although I managed to get the recipe, I won't be whipping it up any time soon. This is exactly the type of food you want a Michelin-starred chef to cook for you.

Homemade Sauerkraut Cabbage

MAKES 6½ POUNDS / 3 KG

I learned how to make this at a Weston A. Price meeting. Part of this group's philosophy is the consumption of nutrient-dense foods like quality animal fats, and when my book *Fat* was published, the head of the Toronto chapter, Patricia Meyer, invited me to a meeting where she demonstrated how to make sauerkraut. It was so simple I couldn't believe that I hadn't made it before. The only work is shredding the cabbage. You can make any amount you like: the recipe below yields the amount that my glass jar holds. You need a large jar with a narrow neck that forms a shoulder, and a small jar that fits inside the neck of the larger jar. Fill the smaller jar with stones or water to use as a weight to submerge the cabbage in the brine. The fermentation changes the sugar in the cabbage to acid that results in a delicious tangy vegetable that it is full of vitamin C and enzymes that aid digestion.

1 large cabbage about 6½ pounds / 3 kg
3 tablespoons coarse sea salt
1 tablespoon caraway seeds

Remove one large leaf from the cabbage, rinse, and set aside. Cut the remaining cabbage into quarters, rinse, and remove the cores. Shred the cabbage and place it in a large bowl. Add the salt and, using your hands, mix together well and leave for about 5 minutes, or until the cabbage starts to release its liquid. Now mix in the caraway seeds.

Pack the cabbage into the clean jar, filling the jar just to the shoulder and pushing down on the cabbage to eliminate as much air as possible. The cabbage will release water, which will form a brine with the salt (this will take an hour or so). Cover the shredded cabbage with the whole cabbage leaf and then place the smaller jar on top. This will force the liquid up to submerge the cabbage completely. Remove any cabbage shreds that are above the level of brine. Set the large jar in a pan or dish to catch any overflow and cover with a clean towel. If for some reason the salt and cabbage does not make enough brine to cover the cabbage, add some of the brine (see page 22), made only with the salt and water to the jar.

Leave the jar on the counter for 1 to 3 weeks. The cabbage needs an ambient temperature of 64 to 68°F / 18 to 20°C to ferment: below this range the cabbage won't ferment, and above it the cabbage will spoil.

While the cabbage is fermenting, press down on the small jar at least once a day to make sure the cabbage is covered with the brine. The cabbage will bubble as it gives off carbon dioxide, and a white froth will form on the surface of the brine: skim this off every day and discard. When no more froth appears, check the flavor of the cabbage: it should be ready to eat; its level of acidity is a matter of taste. The longer you leave it, the more acidic it will be. Remove the small jar, discard the leaf, seal the jar, and refrigerate for up to 9 months.

Getting to the Marrow

> *... the rather mucilaginous matter that fills bone and is considered a particular delicacy by cannibals.*
> WAVERLEY ROOT

Obviously Bourdain and Root share very different views of bone marrow. If Root were alive today, he would no doubt be surprised at the growth in popularity of roasted marrow bones. I love bone marrow, and it is encouraging to know that this odd bit once consigned to the soup pot, tossed to the dog, or thrown in the garbage is now finally being appreciated as a dish in its own right.

Our ancestors held marrow in high regard; for them, particularly those who lived in marginal areas, it was an important food source. Marrow is the main ingredient in pemmican, a food that was key to the survival of early explorers in northern Canada, the Arctic, and Antarctica. Medieval cooks preferred their bone marrow sweet, adding it to puddings and pastries, while Georgian diners so loved to eat it straight from the bone that they commissioned specially designed silver spoons just for the task of scooping the marrow from the bone. Queen Victoria was another bone marrow lover, reputedly eating it every day. The queen lived to the age of eighty-one, and no doubt she, like most Victorians, regarded marrow as a health food. Many people avoid marrow because it is fat, but it should be remembered that marrow is 69 percent unsaturated fat. It is also a very nutritious food, containing iron, phosphorus, vitamin A, and trace amounts of thiamin and niacin. There is even more good news for marrow lovers: science has shown that the fat of ruminants contains substances that boost and maintain our body's immune system. So the Victorians were right—marrow is a health food and definitely way too good for the dog.

While all animals have marrow in their bones, birds have less, because many of their bones are hollow so that they can fly. Veal and beef marrow are the most popular because of their very mild flavor and the higher ratio of marrow to bone. Marrow is more versatile than you might think. Apart from eating it straight from the bone, you can use it like you would any other fat, adding it to dumplings, hamburgers, and dessert. It is also an excellent fat for sautéing and frying.

> *After eating the Roast Bone Marrow and Parsley Salad at St. John [restaurant], I declared it my always and forever choice for my 'Death Row Meal', the last meal I'd choose to put in my mouth before they turned up the juice.*
> ANTHONY BOURDAIN

There is another type of animal marrow that is less common; this is the pith or spinal marrow. This is found in the spinal column, and it's the marrow you see in neck and oxtail slices. It is edible and is usually enjoyed with the meat and bone rather than separately.

How to Choose

Veal and beef marrow are the most popular, as bovine leg bones contain the most marrow. The bones can be cut to any length you want; ask your butcher for pieces cut from the center of the leg bone, where the ratio of marrow to bone is highest. Make sure the marrow is accessible at both ends of the bone, especially if you plan on extracting the marrow before cooking. It is hard to judge how much marrow you will get from any bone, and it ranges widely depending on the thickness of the bone: a 3-inch / 7.5-cm bone will yield anywhere from 3/4 to 3 ounces / 20 to 90 g, but usually it averages around 1 1/2 ounces / 40 g.

Buy extra bones to be sure you have enough. Bone marrow freezes well in or out of the bone.

You can also have the bones cut lengthwise: this makes the marrow easy to get at with any spoon—no need for a silver Georgian one.

The bones should already be free of meat and should smell clean and faintly meaty. The marrow itself should be whitish pink in color; don't worry if you can see blood spots on the surface of the marrow—that's normal.

How to Prepare and Cook

There are various methods to extract raw marrow from the bones. Recently, I learned a new one from my friend chef Albert Ponzo. I now use this method all the time, but the marrow must be accessible at both ends of the bone.

Leave the marrow bones on the counter at room temperature for about 15 minutes; the marrow should just begin to soften slightly. Now run a small, flexible knife between the marrow and bone at each end, to free the marrow from the bone as much as possible. Pick up the bone and, using your thumb, push the marrow from the thin end toward the fat end out of the bone. Don't start at the thick end. The marrow will be soft and will tend to squish under the force of your thumb, but persist and eventually the marrow will emerge from the bone in one piece.

If the bones are cut lengthwise, run a knife along either edge of the cut bone, and let sit at room temperature until slightly softened, then ease the marrow out.

To remove the blood from the marrow, place the marrow bones or extracted marrow in a bowl of ice water with 1 teaspoon of coarse sea salt per cup / 250 ml of water. Refrigerate for 12 to 24 hours, changing the water 4 to 6 times and replacing the salt each time. Drain and refrigerate until you are ready to cook the marrow. Use within 24 hours or freeze the drained marrow bones or marrow for up to 3 months.

To roast marrow bones, drain them, pat the bones dry, and place them standing up or cut side up in a roasting pan in a preheated 450°F / 230°C oven. Roast them for 15 to 25 minutes, until the marrow has puffed slightly and is warm in the center. To test, insert a metal skewer into the center of the bone, then touch it to your wrist to gauge the marrow's temperature. There should be no resistance when the skewer is inserted, and some of the marrow will have started to leak from the bones. Always serve roasted bone marrow very hot.

One way to horrify at least eight out of ten Anglo-Saxons is to suggest their eating anything but the actual red fibrous meat of a beast. A heart or kidney or even a sweetbread is anathema. It is too bad, since there are so many nutritious and entertaining ways to prepare the various livers and lights. They can become gastronomic pleasures instead of dogged voodoo, so that when you eat a stuffed baked bull's heart, or a grilled lamb's brain or a 'mountain oyster,' you need not choke them down with the nauseated resolve to be braver or wiser or more potent, but with plain delight.
M. F. K. FISHER

Bone Marrow Dumplings

MAKES 6 TO 8 DUMPLINGS

I don't like cooking dumplings on top of a stew. There never seems to be enough room for them to expand, so I cook them separately. While salted water will do, they will have much more flavor if you cook them in a stock that matches the meat they accompany. You can also add fresh herbs like thyme and parsley if serving them with the Classic Beef Stew (page 181). This recipe can be doubled if you like dumplings, but you might need to add an extra tablespoon of cold water to the dough to achieve the right consistency. These dumplings are also delicious, and very light, when made with finely grated suet instead of bone marrow.

> 2/3 cup / 2 ounces / 60 g bone marrow, extracted and soaked (see page 190)
>
> 1/2 cup / 2 ounces / 60 g flour
>
> 1/2 teaspoon baking powder
>
> 3/4 cup / 2 ounces / 60 g fine fresh bread crumbs
>
> 1 teaspoon finely chopped shallot
>
> Fine sea salt and freshly ground black pepper
>
> 1 egg
>
> 2 cups / 500 ml Beef Stock (page 232) or water

Drain and finely chop the bone marrow and set aside.

Sift the flour and baking powder into a bowl and stir in the bone marrow, bread crumbs, shallot, and 1/2 teaspoon of salt. Whisk the egg and stir it into the flour mixture to make a stiff dough. Tip the dough onto a floured surface and knead gently. Divide the dough into 6 to 8 equal pieces and roll each piece into a ball. Set aside.

In a wide saucepan over medium heat, bring the stock to a boil and season with salt and pepper if necessary. Add the dumplings, lower the heat so the stock simmers, cover the pan, and cook gently until the dumplings have doubled in size and are cooked through, about 20 minutes.

Remove the dumplings from the liquid with a slotted spoon and serve in a soup or stew, with a roast, or alongside cooked vegetables.

> *. . . the shank, if sawed into cross-sections, has an advantage; the core of the bone is filled with delicious and nutritious marrow. When the meat is done, you can scoop out the marrow with a small fork or spoon and eat it.*
> RICHARD OLNEY

Bone Marrow and Mushroom Custard

This is a rich treat, so serve it as an appetizer with a sharp peppery salad to balance the richness. The custards must be chilled for several hours to firm up. However, they are best served at room temperature, so don't forget to take them out of the refrigerator at least thirty minutes in advance.

> 2 tablespoons / ^{1}/$_5$ ounce / 5 g dried porcini mushrooms
>
> ^{1}/$_4$ cup / 60 ml boiling water
>
> About 5 ounces / 140 g bone marrow, extracted and soaked (see page 190)
>
> 1 cup / 250 ml whole milk
>
> 3 large sprigs thyme
>
> ^{1}/$_2$ teaspoon fine sea salt
>
> Freshly ground black pepper
>
> 2 eggs, beaten

Place the mushrooms in a small bowl and pour over the boiling water. Let them soak for 30 minutes.

Preheat the oven to 325°F / 160°C.

Remove the mushrooms from the soaking liquid, squeeze dry, and place in a small saucepan. Strain the soaking liquid through a fine sieve into the pan and discard the debris. Drain the marrow and add it to the pan with the milk and thyme and season with the salt and pepper. Place the pan over medium heat and bring just to a simmer, then lower the heat and poach the marrow at a very gentle simmer for 5 to 7 minutes, until it no longer looks raw. The marrow will shrink and melt into the milk. Set aside to cool slightly and remove the thyme sprigs.

Pour the milk and marrow mixture into a blender and blend. Add the eggs and blend again.

Place six ^{3}/$_4$-cup / 175-ml ovenproof ramekins in a roasting pan, then divide the bone marrow mixture among the ramekins. It should come to about ^{1}/$_2$ inch / 1 cm from the lip. Pour enough boiling water into the pan so that it comes halfway up the ramekins. Bake the custards for 25 to 30 minutes, or until they are set but still wobbly in the center. Transfer the custards from the pan to a cooling rack and when cool, refrigerate for several hours or overnight.

To serve, remove the custards from the refrigerator about 30 minutes before serving. Run a small knife around the edges of the ramekin, then turn out onto a small serving plate and add the salad.

What's in the marrow is hard to take out of the bone.

Salad with Warm Bone Marrow Croutons

SERVES 4 TO 6

Recipe ideas come at odd times, but most often during meals with friends who love food. I was having lunch with Kim Sunée, author of *A Trail of Crumbs,* and we were greedily eating, sharing tastes, and talking about the food. When she described eating deep-fried bone marrow, I swooned. Why hadn't I thought of that? Well, after some experimentation I decided it was better and easier to shallow-fry it. The result is a very rich dish that definitely needs acid to balance it. I suggest treating the fried bone marrow pieces as an extreme crouton—three or four will be enough on top of a peppery salad like watercress or, even better, baby mustard greens. But I could just pop these little fritters as a snack with drinks, while citing the Victorians: "It's a health food, you know."

About 5 ounces / 140 g bone marrow, extracted and soaked (see page 190)

Fine sea salt and freshly ground black pepper

1/4 cup / 1 ounce / 30 g flour

1 egg, beaten

2/3 cup / 1 3/4 ounces / 50 g fresh bread crumbs

1 teaspoon mustard powder

Olive oil or lard

10 to 12 cups / 2.5 to 3 l mixed salad greens

Haralds's Vinaigrette (page 196)

Drain and slice the marrow into equal slices about 1/2-inch / 1-cm thick and season with salt and pepper.

Prepare 3 shallow dishes: 1 with the flour, 1 with the egg, and 1 with the bread crumbs. Season the beaten egg with salt and pepper and mix the mustard powder into the bread crumbs.

Dip the seasoned marrow slices into the flour, then the egg, and finally the bread crumbs, making sure each piece is very well coated with crumbs. If the marrow isn't well coated, it may melt as it cooks. Keep the marrow cool; if your kitchen is warm or your hands are too hot, the marrow will begin to soften. Return the bread-crumbed marrow slices to the refrigerator to firm up.

Preheat the oven to 200°F / 100°C. Place a baking sheet lined with paper towels in the oven.

Set a small frying pan over medium heat and pour in enough olive oil to cover the bottom of the pan. When the oil is hot, add half the marrow slices and cook until golden brown, about 2 minutes per side. Transfer to the baking sheet, sprinkle with salt, and keep warm in the oven.

Drain the fat from the pan, wipe it clean, and pour in more olive oil to fry the second batch of marrow. Transfer to the baking sheet and sprinkle with salt.

Trim, rinse, and spin dry the salad greens, and then place them in a large salad bowl and toss them with enough of the vinaigrette to coat. Divide the salad between the plates and top with the warm marrow croutons.

If man was immortal, imagine what his butcher's bill would be.

WOODY ALLEN

Marrow and Sweet Peas

SERVES 4

As much as I love digging in to a roasted marrow bone, I also like to serve marrow out of the bone, and matched with fresh sweet peas. The bone marrow enriches the peas and this is a good way to introduce the unconvinced to its pleasures.

As it is always hard to judge just how much marrow your bones will yield, I always buy extra—bone marrow freezes well and is good to add to a sauce or to make dumplings (see page 192). You will need about 1³/4 pounds / 800 g of peas in the pod.

2 cups / 9 ounces / 255 g shelled peas

Coarse sea salt

About 5 ounces / 140 g bone marrow, extracted and soaked (see page 190)

1 shallot, finely chopped

3 tablespoons Veal Stock (page 233)

Freshly ground black pepper

1 tablespoon finely shredded mint leaves

Blanch the peas in boiling salted water, then drain and refresh under cold water. Place them in a bowl of ice water and set aside.

Drain and slice the bone marrow into 1/2-inch / 1-cm rounds, setting aside any offcuts or imperfect slices.

In a frying pan over medium heat, add the marrow offcuts and the shallot. Cook, stirring, until the shallot softens and the marrow melts. Increase the heat to medium-high and add the marrow slices and cook, turning once, until translucent and no longer pink, about 3 minutes.

Meanwhile, drain the peas, and add them and the stock to the pan and cook just until warmed through. Season with salt and pepper, stir in the mint leaves, and serve.

Haralds's Vinaigrette

MAKES ABOUT 1 CUP / 250 ML

While I like sharp vinaigrette, sometimes a little sweetness is good with bitter greens. This is my husband's recipe. He uses the same raspberry syrup that is popular in Europe as the basis for summer drinks. The syrup is available in Eastern European grocery stores.

1 tablespoon raspberry syrup

1 tablespoon Dijon mustard

1 tablespoon balsamic vinegar

1 teaspoon wine vinegar

Coarse sea salt and freshly ground black pepper

3/4 cup / 175 ml extra virgin olive oil

1/2 clove garlic, crushed

In a glass measuring cup, whisk together the raspberry syrup, Dijon mustard, and vinegars. Season with salt and pepper and slowly whisk in the olive oil. Add the garlic clove and whisk again.

NUMBLE . . . UMBLE . . . OR HUMBLE PIE?

You are probably familiar with the expression *to eat humble pie,* but did you know that it was originally a *numble pie?* The phrase *to eat humble pie* is relatively modern, dating from the nineteenth century, but in the middle of the twelfth century a numble pie was a pie made from venison *numbles,* the loins of a deer. Language is constantly changing, and some time later the *n* was dropped and the word became *umbles.* The pie changed too: no longer was it made from a prime cut of venison but with the deer's entrails instead.

Umble pie was very popular with hunters, who believed that eating the deer's heart, liver and intestines would give them strength. As the forests and hunting grounds of Europe were taken over by the aristocracy, hunting ceased to be a traditional right open to all and was restricted to the nobility. Peasants who had supplemented their diet with wild game could now only hunt in the employ of the property owners or risk being arrested for poaching. The nobility preferred the prime cuts and left the numbles or umbles for their servants. These humble servants enjoyed umble pie, which led to a further confusion between the words *umble* and *humble.* Add to this linguistic muddle the practice of many English dialects to drop the letter *h* in front of words, and *umble* came to be thought of as the same word as *humble.* The result: umble pie became humble pie and was thought of as a lower-class food.

> *Offal offers us a chance to pay our respects, in a full and holistic manner, to animals we've raised for meat. The nose-to-tail approach to using the animals we kill for food must . . . be a central tenet of the contract of domestication and good husbandry. Waste is not acceptable. It's all or nothing.*
> HUGH FEARNLEY-WHITTINGSTALL

Today when you *eat humble pie,* you get nothing to chew on. No longer does it refer to a real pie, but it simply means either to apologize or, worse, to be humiliated. The comedown of the esteemed *numbles pie* to a figurative *humble pie* reflects the decline in odd bits' prestige.

A Bit of Tail

I grew up eating oxtail stew; for me it was just another piece of meat. Not until I was in Chicago handing out samples of braised oxtail in a food market to promote my first book, *Bones,* did I realize that people thought it very strange to eat this odd bit. Almost no one would sample my oxtail until I started to call it braised beef; then everyone wanted to try it.

I admit the word *ox* might be off-putting, so be assured that oxtail is no longer from oxen, or castrated beef, but from regular cattle. This odd bit has a good coating of fat and rich gelatinous meat that is perfect for braising.

> The sinewy meat on an oxtail responds particularly well to braising. The gentle lengthy cooking softens and gently melts the gelatinous tendons that extend the length of the tail, thus keeping the meat moist and succulent . . .
> RICHARD OLNEY

Pig's tails, while not as meaty as oxtail, contain lots of fat and gelatin; this makes them a good addition when braising lean meats, like rabbit and game, or in soups and with beans. For those who like rich, fatty, finger-licking snacks, roasted pig's tails are perfect.

In older cookbooks, and in other cuisines, there are recipes for sheep's tails but most sheep raised in North America have short or docked tails, leaving nothing to eat. However, more than a quarter of the world's sheep population are fat-tailed sheep. These sheep are found in Central Asia, North Africa, the Middle East, and northern India, and they are aptly named. Either wide and fat like a beaver's, or long and thick like a kangaroo's, the tails of fat-tailed sheep can equal one-sixth of their body weight. The tails are prized for their soft, succulent subcutaneous fat, which is used for flavoring and cooking from South Africa to the Middle East and China.

I am still on a quest to try a fat lamb tail; I have recently learned that some sheep producers are raising them in North America, so my quest may be nearing its end.

How to Choose

Oxtail is a long, tapered piece of red meat covered in a layer of creamy fat. You can buy it whole, but it is more practical cut into thick slices, which are progressively smaller as the tail tapers to its end. The best pieces are the first few meaty ones close to the animal's rump, but most likely your butcher or supplier will sell you the whole tail. Keep the small end pieces for making stock, or cook them along with the rest of the tail and use them to make Oxtail Ravioli (page 204). An average oxtail weighs about 3⅓ pounds / 1.5 kg and yields enough meat for four, with leftovers. Oxtail keeps refrigerated for at least forty-eight hours and freezes well.

> There are two kinds of tail, the bony ones from ox and pig that have rich meat on them or the fatty ones from fat-tailed sheep that have no bone and are highly valued in the Arab world.
> ANISSA HELOU

Pig's tails are not, as you might imagine, curly. They can be long or short and fat with just a slight bend. They come with their skin and part of the spine still attached. They are fatty with some meat and lots of gelatin, and they add fat and texture to dishes like Pig's Tail and Rabbit Stew (page 206). They should be smooth, pale pink, and slightly damp but not sticky, and they usually weigh from 7 to 8¾ ounces / 200 to 250 g each.

How to Prepare and Cook

If the oxtail is whole, you can cut it into sections yourself. You will notice indentations on the tail that indicate the cartilage; at these points, you can cut through the tail. If the tails are very fatty, trim off some of the fat, but as most of the fat melts during the long cooking and keeps the meat succulent, I prefer to leave it on. Chilling the stew overnight will set the fat on the top of the stew, and the excess can easily be removed and kept for another use.

Tails need long, slow cooking to render them tender. They contain lots of collagen that gives a wonderful lip-smacking quality to the sauce and makes them a good ingredient in soups, with beans, or in any slow-cooked beef stew recipe.

Pig's tails need a scrub and a rinse under cold running water. They can be cooked whole or in pieces, and marinating them overnight in Spiced Seasoning Salt (page 28) or brining them (see page 22) before cooking improves their flavor. You can add them uncooked to soups, stews, and beans or poach them in a court bouillon, as you would with feet (see page 100). Once cooked, pig's tails can be crisped up in a hot oven and served as a snack, glazed with a sauce like ribs, or added to a dish of cooked lentils.

Oxtail Noodle Soup with Caramelized Onion and Star Anise

SERVES 8

I have wonderful memories of eating pho on the streets of Saigon, sitting in a makeshift restaurant set up at the side of the road. Even although it was hot and humid, the soup with the addition of fresh herbs and bean spouts was refreshing. I can eat pho in any season. This recipe is not the soup I had in Vietnam; instead of a garnish of thinly sliced beef, I've added the shredded meat from the cooked oxtail to the soup. I like to use udon noodles (dried Japanese wheat noodles), but the choice of noodle is up to you.

3 pounds / 1.4 kg oxtail, cut into 2-inch / 5-cm pieces
Coarse sea salt and freshly ground black pepper
12 cups / 3 l cold water
2 whole star anise
One 5-inch / 13-cm cinnamon stick
1 serrano chile, split lengthwise
2 large onions, halved and thinly sliced
1 tablespoon beef dripping or lard
1/4 cup / 60 ml dry sherry

2 tablespoons dark soy sauce
1/2 to 3/4 pound / 225 to 350 g daikon
11/3 pounds / 600 g dried udon noodles
6 green onions, thinly sliced
1 lime, cut into wedges
Hot chile paste, optional
Fresh Thai basil leaves
Bean sprouts

Preheat the oven to 400°F / 200°C.

Pat the pieces of oxtail dry and season well with salt and pepper. Place them in a single layer in a roasting pan and cook for about 40 minutes, turning occasionally, until they are dark golden brown all over. Transfer the oxtail pieces to a large stockpot. Leave the oven on and set the pan aside.

Add 10 cups / 2.5 l water of the water to the oxtail with the star anise, cinnamon stick, and chile pepper. Place over medium-low heat, and bring to a boil.

Meanwhile, add the onion slices to the roasting pan, stir to coat in the fat rendered from the oxtail, adding extra fat if necessary, and return to the oven. Roast for 15 to 20 minutes, stirring often until the onions are soft and golden.

Transfer the onions to a bowl and set aside. Place the roasting pan over low heat, add the sherry, and deglaze the pan by scraping up the browned pieces with a wooden spoon. Add this mixture to the oxtails and bring to a boil, then skim, lower the heat, and simmer gently, uncovered, for 3 to 4 hours, or until the largest pieces are very tender and meat is beginning to fall off the bone.

Strain the mixture through a sieve into a large bowl and set the oxtail pieces aside to cool. Discard the star anise, cinnamon stick, and chile. Skim the fat off the cooking liquid and set the fat aside for another use. When the oxtails are cool enough to handle, pull off the meat and shred it. Don't let the oxtails get too cold, as the meat will be harder to separate from the bones.

Pour the skimmed liquid into a clean saucepan, add the shredded meat, caramelized onions, and soy sauce. Peel the daikon and cut into $1/2$-inch / 1-cm dice, and add to the soup. Simmer until the radish is cooked but still slightly crunchy, about 15 minutes. Check the seasoning.

Meanwhile, fill a large saucepan three-quarters full with water and bring to a boil over high heat. When boiling, add the noodles, stir, and return to a boil. Add 1 cup / 250 ml of the remaining cold water, stir the noodles, and return to a boil again. Add the remaining 1 cup / 250 ml of cold water and stir. When the water boils again, test the noodles as you would pasta. If the noodles are not cooked, continue to simmer, testing often.

Drain the noodles and divide them among 8 large warmed soup bowls. Ladle over the soup and scatter with the green onions. Serve with the lime, chile paste, basil, and bean sprouts.

Spring Tails

SERVES 6

We usually think of oxtail as rib-sticking winter food, but it also matches well with fresh peas, making it a perfect dish for those fickle spring days when the weather can suddenly turn cool again. To have six good sized pieces, you will have to buy two oxtails, leaving you with extra pieces. So there are two recipes here: Spring Tails, and the beginning of the Oxtail Ravioli (page 204). If you don't want to make the ravioli, you can use the extra oxtail in the Salad of Beef Cheeks (page 34), or add them to the Beef Stock (page 232). You will need a bit more than $2 1/4$ pounds / 1 kg of peas in the pod to give you enough shelled peas. This recipe is a two-day affair, so start at least a day before you want to serve it. Serve with steamed new potatoes.

2 oxtails, about 6 pounds / 2.8 kg, cut into 2-inch / 5-cm pieces

Coarse sea salt and freshly ground black pepper

3 tablespoons beef dripping or lard

1 large carrot, peeled and diced

1 onion, chopped

1 stalk celery with leaves, sliced

3 cloves garlic, finely chopped

5 large sprigs flat-leaf parsley

5 large sprigs thyme

2 fresh bay leaves

3 cups / 750 ml Pinot Noir

continued

3 cups / 14 ounces / 400 g shelled peas

1 tablespoon unsalted butter

1 Vidalia or other sweet onion, halved and sliced

1 tablespoon sugar

1 tablespoon black currant jelly or red currant jelly

1 cup / 15 g chervil leaves

Preheat the oven to 300°F / 150°C.

Pat the pieces of oxtail dry and season well with salt and pepper.

In a heavy flameproof casserole or Dutch oven, melt the fat over medium-high heat and brown the oxtail in batches, transferring the browned oxtail to a plate. When all the oxtail pieces are browned, lower the heat to medium, add the carrot, chopped onion, and celery to the pan and stir. Continue to cook until the vegetables soften slightly, then add the garlic, parsley, thyme, and bay leaves. Pour in the red wine and bring to a boil and deglaze the pan, using a wooden spoon to scrape up the browned bits from the bottom of the pan.

Return the browned oxtail pieces to the pan, placing the larger pieces on the bottom and the smaller ones on top. Cover the oxtail with a piece of wet parchment paper and the lid and transfer to the oven. Cook for 3 to 4 hours, or until the meat is beginning to part company with the bones.

Set aside enough of the larger oxtail pieces to serve 6 and keep the remaining pieces for ravioli or beef cheeks salad. Remove the meat from the smaller pieces as soon as they are cool enough to handle; once cold, the meat will be harder to remove. Refrigerate or freeze the shredded meat until ready to use. Strain the cooking liquid through a sieve and let cool; discard the debris in the sieve. Cover and refrigerate the cooking liquid and the larger oxtail pieces separately overnight.

Remove fat from the cooking liquid and set aside for another use. Tip out the jellied liquid and cut off the cloudy top and bottom sections and place them in a measuring cup. Place the clear jellied liquid in a saucepan over low heat to melt. When it's liquid, set aside 2 cups / 500 ml and add any of the remaining clear liquid to the cloudy jelly in the measuring cup and either set aside for the ravioli or cheek salad, or refrigerate or freeze for another use.

Preheat the oven to 250°F / 120°C.

Place the large oxtail pieces in a baking dish, and pour over the 2 cups / 500 ml of clear melted liquid. Cover with aluminum foil and transfer to the oven. Cook for 1 hour, or until heated through, turning once.

Meanwhile, blanch the peas in boiling salted water and then refresh under cold running water. Set aside in a bowl of ice-cold water.

Melt the butter in a frying pan over low heat, add the sweet onion, and sprinkle with the sugar. Cook gently, stirring until the sugar is melted and the onion is softened.

Remove the hot oxtail pieces from the oven. Transfer the pieces to a hot serving dish. Pour the liquid from the oxtail into the frying pan with the onion and stir in the currant jelly. Drain the peas and stir them into the pan; check the seasoning. When the peas are hot, remove the pan from the heat and stir in the chervil. Pour the peas, onions, and sauce over the oxtail pieces and serve.

Alternatives: Beef or lamb shanks, beef cheeks, or beef or lamb shoulder

As animals store reserve fat in their tails, a winter oxtail is an unexpectedly meaty joint.
DOROTHY HARTLEY

THE ORIGIN OF OFFAL

Many odd bits are also classed as offal. The word *offal* has a confusing history. It came into the English language in the fourteenth century from the Dutch word *afval,* which literally translated means "off-fall." *Offal* was first used for waste and garbage. Then during the fifteenth century, the word's meaning was expanded to include the organs that fall off or out of the animal when it is eviscerated. So offal had two meanings: waste and the collective term for an animal's internal organs. Unfortunately, this led to many people thinking of these odd bits as garbage.

Other languages don't have this negative association; for example, the French use the word *abats* for animal organs and *abattis* for poultry odd bits, and their words for waste—*déchets, detritus, ordures*—are not related at all. So while people continued to enjoy offal, its linguistic connection with garbage didn't help its image. Perhaps language has played a part in many English speakers' dislike of odd bits? Later, the definition of offal expanded beyond the internal organs to include the animal's head, feet, and tail, stigmatizing these tasty odd bits too. Perhaps we should all use the American term, variety meats—it would be more positive. It has no connotations of garbage and it accurately describes this collection of very varied and different animal parts.

> *Ask any chef of any three-star Michelin restaurant what their favorite single dish to eat is and you will often get an answer like 'confit of duck' or 'my mother's pied cochon' or 'a well-braised shank of lamb or veal.'*
> ANTHONY BOURDAIN

Oxtail Ravioli

With oxtail, you often end up with lots of small pieces of tail that are not large enough to serve. Sometimes I use them for stock, but often I cook them with the larger pieces and then take the meat off the bone to make this ravioli. You will need about 1 pound / 450 g for this recipe. If you have a little more or less, don't worry; this recipe is very flexible. If peas aren't in season, use good quality frozen ones, and if it is fava season use them instead of peas. Just over 1 pound / 450 g of peas in the pod should yield enough shelled peas.

As for the pasta, you could make your own, but I prefer to use good quality dried Italian egg pasta sheets. This is not a traditional ravioli. Instead I place a cooked lasagna noodle in the dish, add the filling, and fold the noodle over.

This recipe can be prepared ahead, even the pasta. Drain the cooked pasta well and then brush the sheets lightly with olive oil to keep the sheets from sticking together; keep the peas in a bowl of cold water. Reheat the sauce, adding a little extra wine or water if it starts to stick, drop the cooked pasta into boiling water to reheat, and add the drained peas to the reserved sauce to reheat.

2 tablespoons fat from cooking oxtail or beef dripping

1 onion, finely chopped

1 stalk celery with leaves, finely chopped

1/2 carrot, peeled and finely chopped

2 cloves garlic, finely chopped

About 1 pound / 450 g deboned, cooked oxtail, shredded

1/2 cup / 125 ml sauce from Spring Tails (page 201)

1/2 cup / 125 ml red wine

1 tablespoon tomato paste

Coarse sea salt and freshly ground black pepper

2 tablespoons chopped flat-leaf parsley

6 lasagna sheets, preferably egg pasta

1 cup / 250 ml Beef Stock (page 232)

1 cup / 4 1/2 ounces / 130 g shelled peas, blanched and refreshed

1 cup / 15 g chervil sprigs

In a large frying pan over medium heat, melt the fat. When the fat is hot, add the onion, celery, and carrot and cook, stirring from time to time, until the vegetables begin to caramelize. Add the garlic, shredded oxtail, and the sauce and wine, and stir in the tomato paste; season with salt and pepper. Let the sauce simmer, uncovered, for 30 minutes. Stir in the parsley.

Meanwhile, bring a large saucepan of water to a boil over high heat. Add some salt and the lasagna sheets, stir, and return to a boil. Adjust the heat so the water boils gently, and cook for 10 to 12 minutes, or until the lasagna is tender. Drain well.

Heat the stock in a frying pan over medium heat, check the seasoning, stir in the peas, and cook until heated through, then stir in the chervil sprigs.

Place 1 drained lasagna sheet on each of 6 warm shallow pasta bowls, top with the oxtail mixture, then fold the sheet over to enclose the mixture. Spoon over the pea sauce and serve immediately.

Alternatives: Cooked beef cheek, shoulder, or shank

Pig's Tail and Rabbit Stew

SERVES 6

I love rabbit, but it is a lean meat and always benefits from some extra fat. By cooking it with pig's tails, you add fat and flavor and improve the texture of the sauce. The pig's tails are enhanced by marinating them overnight in salt. As they take longer to cook than the rabbit, they are cooked for 1 1/2 hours before adding the rabbit. If your guests are pig's tail lovers, just cut the cooked tails in half; otherwise pull the off the skin, fat and any meat you can find, dice it, and add it back to the stew. Thyme is a wonderful match with rabbit. I like to imagine my rabbits hopping across fields of wild thyme, but I doubt any of the rabbits I buy have ever grazed on thyme. No matter, I can add it. If your rabbit comes with its head, add it with any trimmings to the stew. If you can only buy rabbit in pieces, they'll work too. This recipe can also be made ahead and reheated. Serve with boiled potatoes or noodles.

When I make this recipe in France, I use one leek, as French leeks are mostly white topped with green. In Toronto, however, the reverse is true—there the leeks are mostly green with a little white at the root end, so I use two.

3 pig's tails, about 1 1/3 pounds / 600 g

3 tablespoons Spiced Seasoning Salt (page 28)

2 carrots, peeled

2 stalks celery

1 leek, rinsed well and separated into white and green parts

3 cloves garlic, germ removed

1/4 teaspoon black peppercorns

6 large sprigs thyme

1 fresh bay leaf

3 cups / 750 ml dry sparkling cider

3 tablespoons flour

Coarse sea salt and freshly ground black pepper

1 rabbit, about 3 pounds / 1.4 kg, cut into 6 pieces, liver and kidneys set aside (see opposite)

1/4 cup / 1 3/4 ounces / 50 g lard or duck fat

2 onions, halved and sliced

1 tablespoon unsalted butter

1 tablespoon fresh thyme leaves

Preheat the oven to 250°F / 120°C.

Place the pig's tails in a glass dish and sprinkle with the seasoning salt, turning to coat. Cover and refrigerate overnight.

Rinse the pig's tails and place them in a small, heavy flameproof casserole or Dutch oven. Add the rabbit head, if you have it, and any offcuts from portioning the rabbit. Slice 1 of the carrots, 1 of the celery stalks, and the green of the leek, and add to the pan with 2 of the garlic cloves and the peppercorns. Add 3 of the thyme sprigs, the bay leaf, and cider. Place over medium heat and bring to a boil, cover the meat with a piece of wet parchment paper and the lid, and transfer to the oven.

Cook for 1 1/2 hours; the tails should just be tender but not falling off the bone. Using a slotted spoon, remove the tails from the pan and place them on paper towels to drain. Strain the liquid into a large measuring cup, discarding the rabbit offcuts and vegetables. Let stand for 5 minutes, then skim off any excess fat and set the fat aside for another use.

Increase the oven temperature to 350°F / 180°C.

Place the flour in a shallow dish and season with salt and pepper. Dip the rabbit pieces in the seasoned flour, tossing to coat, and shake off the excess.

In a large, heavy flameproof casserole or Dutch oven over medium-high heat, melt 3 tablespoons of the lard and brown the rabbit pieces in batches, transferring the browned pieces to a plate.

Meanwhile, cut the remaining carrot into 1/4-inch / 6-mm slices and cut the remaining celery stalk in half lengthwise, then slice. Cut the white part of the leek into 1-inch / 2.5-cm slices.

Lower the heat to medium, add the drained pig's tails, and cook for several minutes, until they begin to pop and spit, then transfer to the plate with the rabbit pieces.

Add the remaining fat to the pan with the sliced onions, stirring to coat with the fat. Add the sliced carrot, celery, and leek and the remaining garlic and thyme sprigs. Cook, stirring, for 5 minutes, or until the onion has softened slightly.

Pour in the skimmed pig's tail cooking liquid and bring to a boil; add the rabbit pieces and top with the pig's tails. Cover the tails and rabbit with a piece of wet parchment paper and the lid, transfer to the oven, and cook for 1 hour. Uncover and remove the parchment paper and cook for about 30 minutes, or until the rabbit is tender.

Using a slotted spoon, transfer the rabbit pieces to a warm platter and loosely cover with aluminum foil to keep warm. Transfer the pig's tails to a board and discard the thyme sprigs.

Bring the cooking liquid to a boil and continue to boil for 10 minutes, or until it coats the back of a spoon. Meanwhile, remove the meat and fat from the tails and cut into pieces. Add the rabbit, tail meat, and fat back to the pan, check the seasoning, and sprinkle with the thyme leaves. Keep warm.

Cut the liver into 3 pieces and the kidneys in half, season with salt and pepper. Melt the butter in a frying pan over medium-high heat and sauté the liver and kidneys until just cooked; add them to the stew.

One could go on forever with stews, braises, casseroles: The permutations are enormous, and I can't think of one that couldn't be cooked in advance.
NIGELLA LAWSON

CUTTING UP A RABBIT

Cut off the head and neck, if the butcher hasn't already, and set them aside to cook with the pig's tails. Remove the liver; you can leave the heart and lungs attached to the ribs. Turn the rabbit onto its stomach and cut the front legs from the rib cage. Cut the rib cage from the body in one piece by slicing through the backbone where the ribs end and the loins begin. The rib cage has little flesh and lots of small bones; split it in two or more pieces and keep it for the stockpot with the heart and lungs. Cut through the backbone at the point where the hind legs join and separate the back legs by cutting on either side of the backbone. Finally, attack the meaty midsection, known as the saddle. There are thin skin flaps attached to either side of this piece; trim them off. Turn over the saddle so you can see where the kidneys are, and then cut the saddle into two or three equal pieces without damaging the kidneys. Keep all the trimmings for cooking.

Tail and Tongue Stew

SERVES 6

This dish is a good way to make tongue converts, provided they like oxtail. There is a lot of beefy oxtail to distract them from the tongue, but I guarantee that once they try the tongue they'll be won over. After its long cooking in the sauce, the tongue is so tender it just melts in your mouth. The tomatoes supply the necessary acidity to balance this rich dish and, like many of the recipes in this book, this dish is best made ahead. This allows the excess fat to be removed, and the flavors improve and meld as it sits. The tongue is tastier if brined, so start this recipe a couple of days ahead.

This stew simply needs gentle reheating before serving, making it a perfect dish for winter entertaining. You can make this recipe without the tongue, replacing it with more oxtail. Serve with Mustard Mashed Potatoes (see opposite).

3^1/$_3$ pounds / 1.5 kg oxtail, cut into 2-inch / 5-cm pieces

Coarse sea salt and freshly ground black pepper

2 tablespoons beef dripping or lard

2 carrots, peeled and chopped

1 large onion, chopped

3 stalks celery with leaves, sliced

2 cloves garlic

1^1/$_4$ cups / 310 ml red wine

One 28-ounce / 796-g can San Marzano tomatoes

1 veal tongue, about 1^1/$_2$ pounds / 700 g, brined (see page 50)

4 stems flat-leaf parsley

2 fresh bay leaves

1 large sprig thyme

1 cup / 15 g flat-leaf parsley leaves

Preheat the oven to 300°F / 150°C.

Pat the oxtail dry and season with salt and pepper.

In a heavy flameproof casserole or Dutch oven, heat half the dripping over medium-high heat and brown the oxtail in batches, adding more fat if necessary, and transferring the browned pieces to a plate.

Add the carrots, onion, celery, and garlic to the pan and cook, stirring, until the vegetables are slightly softened, about 5 minutes. Pour the wine into the pan, bring to a boil, and deglaze the pan, using a wooden spoon to scrape up the browned bits from the bottom. Stir in the tomatoes with all their juice and return to a boil, breaking up the tomatoes with a spoon.

Place the tongue in the pan and then add the oxtail pieces, packing tightly. Add the parsley stems, bay leaves, and thyme and cover the meat with a piece of wet parchment paper and the lid. Transfer to the oven and cook until the tongue can be easily pierced with a skewer, about 3 hours. Remove the parchment paper and the tongue. Set the tongue aside to cool slightly.

Return the uncovered pan to the oven and continue to cook the oxtail until it is coming away from the bone, about another hour. Meanwhile, peel the tongue while it is still warm (see page 50). Remove the cooked oxtail pieces from the sauce and allow to cool. Strain the sauce into a bowl, pressing hard against the solids to extract all the juice. Discard the solids and let the sauce cool.

Remove the oxtail meat from the bones. Place the meat and peeled tongue on a plate. When the meat and sauce are cool, cover and refrigerate overnight. The next day, remove the excess fat from the sauce and set aside for another use; you should have about 2 to 2^1/$_4$ cups / 500 to 560 ml of sauce. Place the sauce in a heavy flameproof casserole or Dutch oven.

Preheat the oven to 300°F / 150°C.

Cut the oxtail into chunks. Slice the tongue in half lengthwise, then cut into 1/2-inch / 1-cm pieces and add to the pan. Cover and transfer to the oven until heated through, about 1 hour.

Meanwhile, chop the parsley leaves. Remove the pan from the oven, check the seasoning, and then sprinkle with chopped parsley and serve.

Alternatives: Beef shin, chuck, or cheeks; lamb neck, shanks, and tongues

Mustard Mashed Potatoes

SERVES 6

Mashed potatoes are always a good accompaniment to any saucy dish, and mustard is a good foil to a rich dish like the Tail and Tongue Stew (see opposite). These are really pureed potatoes, as they are put through a food mill. I'm prepared to take this extra step because the texture is better, but if you just want to mash, that's fine too. The amount of mustard is a matter of taste; the puree should taste of potato first, then mustard. I bring Dijon mustard back from France as it more potent than the Dijon mustard that is exported, so you might want to add an extra spoonful.

2 pounds / 900 g baking potatoes
1 fresh bay leaf
Coarse and fine sea salt
1/2 cup / 125 ml hot whole milk
3 tablespoons Dijon mustard
3 tablespoons / 1 1/2 ounces / 45 g unsalted butter, diced

Peel the potatoes and cut them into large chunks. Place them in a large saucepan, cover with cold water, and add the bay leaf. Cover the pan and bring to a boil over high heat, add 1 teaspoon of coarse salt, then uncover the pan and lower the heat to a gentle simmer. Continue cooking the potatoes until they are very soft but not falling apart, 15 to 20 minutes depending on the potato and the size of the chunks.

Drain the potatoes very well and remove and discard the bay leaf. Pass them through a food mill using the fine grill and return them to the pan. Place the pan over low heat and, using a wooden spoon, stir until the moisture from the potatoes evaporates and they begin to stick to the bottom of the pan.

Remove the pan from the heat and beat in about half the milk, and then beat in the mustard and butter. Add enough of the remaining milk to make a soft puree, and then check the seasoning.

If you are not serving the puree immediately, you can keep it warm in a water bath. Place a buttered heatproof bowl over a pan of barely simmering water. Spoon the puree into the bowl and then cover with a lid. The potatoes will keep this way for up to 1 hour. Stir before serving.

Testicles: Yes, Balls

> *I wanted to eat as many pieces of sheep as possible. We managed muscles, sweetbreads, tongue, liver, brains and balls. The brains were everything you always imagined sheep's brains would be: soft and stupid and nice enough to feed cows. The tongues took some bleating, but sadly my balls were overcooked and had become granular, like old school rubbers.*
>
> A. A. GILL

I know this might be a hard sell, especially if you've had an experience like A. A. Gill, but properly cooked these odd bits are tasty, tender, and, surprisingly, very mild in flavor. Testicles are a legitimate food and should not be thrown away. In agricultural societies around the world, animals were traditionally castrated in the early summer, as only few males were required to ensure the next generation. This meant that testicles were seasonal, and as there was a limited supply, they were commonly mixed with other odd bits to make a dish.

Bartolomeo Scappi, chef to Pope Pius V and a lover of odd bits, gives a recipe for a pie in his cookbook, *Opera* (1570):

> *Boil four bull's testicles together with salt. Cut into slices and sprinkle with salt, pepper, nutmeg and cinnamon. Then, in a pie crust, place layers of sliced testicles alternated with mince of lamb's kidneys, ham, marjoram, cloves and thyme.*

The English cook Robert May (1685) mixes both poultry and lamb testicles with ox palates, sweetbreads, marrow, and cockscombs in a dish with chicken, pigeon, artichokes, and pistachios—a plethora of odd bits. While both these recipes sound delicious, neither is very practical today.

I don't want to create a huge demand for testicles: there's no point. Only half the animals have them, and while today the supply is no longer seasonal, it is still limited. However, your butcher should be able to source them for you, and if you buy a whole or half animal you may end up with a pair, so if like me you are a curious and adventurous eater, you should try them at least once. In my experience men, perhaps naturally, are more squeamish than women. And if you have no desire to eat testicles, these recipes can be made using brains or sweetbreads.

How to Choose

As lamb testicles are the easiest for me to source, all my recipes were tested using them, but you could substitute beef, goat, or deer. The older the animal, the stronger the taste will be; I've eaten testicles from older rams and they had a distinct livery taste. Whatever animal they are from, they should be very fresh, firm, plump, and pink with their outer shiny skin intact and no smell.

There is no mistaking them: they look exactly like what they are, and there is an inevitable variation in size and weight. However, as they are sliced in the recipes, this won't matter. The testicles I've cooked ranged from $5^1/2$ to $10^1/2$ ounces / 155 to 300 g. They will lose up to $3^1/2$ ounces / 100 g of this weight during the cleaning and, yes, they always come in pairs.

You may be able to source poultry testicles, probably from chicken and turkey. They are small, so are mainly used as a garnish like cockscombs (see page 60). It is interesting to note that poultry testicles are located inside the bird.

Testicles freeze well, so if your only source is frozen, you'll have to rely on your supplier to guarantee the quality.

How to Prepare and Cook

Like all highly perishable odd bits, testicles should be cooked within twenty-four hours of purchase. If you have fresh ones and don't plan to cook and eat them straight away, then freeze them without preparing them. Thaw them out and follow the preparation instructions.

> And culinary novices—young cooks, heavily pierced and tattooed metalheads, thin, well dressed adventuresses, practitioners of 'extreme' eating who saw the night's fare, perhaps, as an extension of 'extreme' sports—all came looking excited but uncertain.
> ANTHONY BOURDAIN

Three layers of thin shiny skin protect the edible part of this gland, and they must be removed. Testicles are slippery, so hold one firmly in your hand, squeezing it very gently. Then, with a sharp knife, make a slit lengthwise to cut through the first two layers of skin. Slip your fingers underneath and peel the skin back, exposing the testicle covered by a final thin skin. The first two skins will still be attached along one side where there is also a tube. Pinch the third skin at this point and make a slit where the three skins meet to reveal the pale pink soft flesh underneath. This final skin is tightly attached, so carefully slip your finger between it and the flesh to avoid tearing it, and gently peel it back. Use the knife to cut the filaments that attach it to the soft flesh; if you just pull, you will tear the flesh. You will have a very soft pale pink egg-shaped morsel that is quite squishy and difficult to handle.

Drop the skinned testicles into cold salted water—about 1 teaspoon of coarse sea salt per cup / 250 ml of water—and refrigerate overnight, changing the water a couple of times and replacing the salt to help remove any traces of blood.

Many recipes have you peeling, slicing, and then cooking them, but you will have noticed that the flesh is so soft that they are very difficult to handle; blanching makes it easier.

The next day, drain the testicles and place them in a saucepan. Add enough cold water to cover them by at least 1 inch / 2.5 cm and add 1 tablespoon of white wine vinegar per testicle. Place the saucepan over medium heat and bring just to a boil, uncovered. Reduce the heat so that the water gently simmers and cook for 5 to 7 minutes, or until the testicles are resistant to the touch but with some spring and the juices run clear when they are pierced with a skewer.

Using a slotted spoon, transfer the testicles to a bowl of ice-cold water. Drain, then keep covered with water and refrigerated for up to 2 days.

There are two recipes here for you to discover how mild and versatile testicles are, and perhaps this will inspire the more adventurous among you.

While light in texture, testicles are rich and filling, and I think they are best served as an appetizer, so the average pair will serve four.

Testicles with Caramelized Onions and Double-Smoked Bacon

SERVES 4 AS AN APPETIZER

Yet again, a recipe that reveals the power of bacon. As testicles are very mild, they need to be matched with ingredients that give them flavor. Many smaller purveyors are making specialty bacon that is double smoked, and it adds smoky fatty flavor; however, any good quality bacon or even a good cured country ham would work.

1 tablespoon lard

2 red onions, halved and sliced

2 slices double-smoked bacon, cut into 1/4-inch / 6-mm slices

1 large sprig sage

1 tablespoon brown sugar

Coarse sea salt and freshly ground black pepper

1/2 cup / 125 ml Lamb Stock (page 234) or Veal Stock (page 233)

2 lamb testicles, prepared (see page 211)

2 tablespoons flour

3 tablespoons unsalted butter

12 fresh sage leaves

In a frying pan over medium heat, melt the lard. When it's hot, add the onions, bacon, sage sprig, and sugar, season with salt and pepper, and cook until the onions soften and begin to color. Add the stock and bring to a boil; deglaze the pan, using a wooden spoon to scrape up the browned bits from the bottom of the pan. Continue to cook until the stock is reduced by half, then keep warm.

Meanwhile, cut the testicles into quarters, season them with salt and pepper, and toss them in the flour, shaking off the excess.

Melt the butter in a frying pan over medium heat; when it is foaming, add the floured testicles and the sage leaves and cook, turning, until the testicles are golden and the sage leaves are crisp, about 8 minutes.

To serve, divide the onion mixture among the plates and top with the testicles and sage leaves.

The final chummy attraction for critics was the menu: it had tons of offal on it. Nothing attracts us like the soft internal bits. If you eat a lot, you end up eating colon, udder, and testicles, sucking weird glands and licking lungs. We live for the vibrant vitals, without bone or muscle. I know you think it's disgusting, but actually, it makes us all very, very good in bed.
A. A. GILL

MYTH, REALITY, AND EUPHEMISMS

It is understandable that primitive peoples believed that eating an animal's genitals would enhance their own sexual prowess. They also thought that eating an animal's heart would make them brave, its brain more intelligent.

Today, while you may have to be brave to eat a heart, I doubt that anyone thinks that consuming this muscle will make them more courageous, yet the myth around testicles endures. The Chinese use them as medicine to improve sexual performance, and the Spanish prize the testicles of bulls killed at the *corrida* or bullfight, considering them to be an especially potent aphrodisiac. Even those who may not believe in the power of testicles to improve their sexual performance think that eating them is proof of their masculinity.

As a result, there is a daredevil macho approach to cooking this odd bit, and its consumption is often accompanied by much snickering, smirking, and knowing nods. A Serbian, Ljubomir Erovic, who calls himself the "king of balls," is a self-proclaimed expert on the subject. He has written a book exclusively devoted to cooking testicles. Erovic also organizes an annual World Testicle Cooking Championship in Serbia that draws competitors, mainly men, from all over Europe, who cook their way through a ton of testicles. The dishes include testicle goulash, testicle moussaka, pizza topped with testicles, and testicles in a béchamel sauce flavored with herbs. This "king of balls" claims the tastiest testicles are from bulls, horses, and ostriches, while horse and sheep testicles are the most powerful aphrodisiacs.

Despite Erovic's bold claims, there is no evidence that he is correct. In an attempt to stop illegal poaching of protected species, the Wild Life Conservation Society strongly discounts the idea that you can increase your testosterone levels or improve your sex life by eating animal testicles. Most testicles available in legitimate markets come from prepubertal animals and have naturally low levels of testosterone, so consuming them will have no effect on the levels in your body. Testicles from older mature animals have higher testosterone levels, but you would need to eat copious amounts every day for it to have even have the slightest effect. And while it might make your workout in the gym a little easier, it still won't improve your sex life. The other problem is that the testicles from older animals do not make very good eating.

Every language has various euphemisms for this part of the anatomy in and out of the kitchen. Fries is the accepted term for lamb and beef testicles when they appear in recipes, but this can be confusing. (In Australia, lamb's fry, which sounds similar, refers to a lamb's liver not its testicles). Older English recipes use the word *stones,* especially for lamb and poultry testicles. In French recipes, they are called *animelles* or, more commonly, *rognons blancs,* or "white kidneys." The Italians prefer the term *giorelli,* meaning "jewels." The Spanish have two polite terms for testicles in the culinary sense: *criadillas* and *huevos de toro* or "bull's eggs." Oddly, Americans have several names for testicles (perhaps it is the combination of cowboy culture and puritanical beginnings): they include prairie or mountain oysters, cowboy caviar, and swinging beef.

Crispy Testicles with Onion, Pepper, and Caper Sauce

SERVES 4 AS AN APPETIZER

By coating the testicles in fresh bread crumbs and frying them, you add a crisp texture to the soft testicle. The red pepper adds some sweetness, while the capers add acidity to balance the testicles' richness. This is a good introduction to this unusual odd bit; served as an appetizer, it is not overwhelming, and it looks good too.

1 large red bell pepper, stemmed and seeded

1 onion, halved and thinly sliced

1 clove garlic, germ removed, thinly sliced

1 sprig thyme

1/4 cup / 60 ml water

2 tablespoons olive oil

1 tablespoon capers, rinsed

Coarse sea salt and freshly ground black pepper

2 lamb testicles, prepared (see page 211)

2 tablespoons flour

1 egg, beaten

2/3 cup / 1 3/4 ounces / 50 g fresh bread crumbs

2 tablespoons unsalted butter

1 tablespoon chopped flat-leaf parsley

Cut the pepper into quarters and then slice thinly from the shorter side. Place the pepper, onion, garlic, thyme, water, and olive oil in a frying pan. Cover, place over medium heat, and cook for 10 minutes, or until the vegetables soften. Remove the thyme, stir in the capers, and season with salt and pepper. Set aside.

Cut the testicles into 1/2-inch / 1-cm slices and season with salt and pepper. Place the flour in a shallow dish, pour the egg into another shallow dish, and place the bread crumbs in a third shallow dish. Toss the slices of testicles in the flour, then in the egg, and then coat well with the bread crumbs.

In a frying pan over medium heat, melt the butter. When it begins to foam, add the breaded testicles and cook until golden, about 4 minutes on each side.

Meanwhile, reheat the onion and pepper mixture, add the parsley, and spoon onto a warm serving plate. Top with the crisp golden testicle slices and serve.

> *It's the melting quality of various sorts of offal that really gets me going. And generally one would find something perky in the way of a sauce or dressing to accompany them. The contrast is delicous.*
> SIMON HOPKINSON

Vital Blood

Homer's *Odyssey*, written around 800 BCE, has one of the earliest literary descriptions of blood pudding (see page 218). I am not sure how many of us would see a dinner of a goat's stomach filled with blood and fat as a sign of good luck, but Ulysses did. While blood is a very old food, today its consumption is more likely to trigger images of vampires than of brave warriors or nourishing meals. Blood is an odd bit with strong emotional overtones. It was thought to be the essence or soul of an animal and, as a result, cultures either celebrated it or banned its consumption totally. Blood is an excellent source of nourishment and, like milk, can be taken from the animal without killing it. For this reason, it became an essential food for many peoples living in harsh climatic conditions.

In Tanzania and Kenya, the Masai herders travel long distances with their animals in search of pasture, during which time they live almost exclusively on a diet of blood and milk from their animals. To remove the blood, they use an arrow specially designed so it doesn't penetrate the animal's neck too deeply. They draw from 2 to 4 quarts / 2 to 4 liters of blood from the animal's jugular vein and then seal the wound. This blood is consumed fresh, often mixed with the animal's milk, providing a complete food. This is very practical in a subsistence farming society that is constantly on the move. In a hot climate, meat doesn't keep well, and killing the herd could lead to starvation, but by keeping their animals alive the Masai have a constant source of food. The animals are also a store of wealth for the Masai, and killing one of them for food would be like cashing in their shares; instead they prefer to take dividends.

The Masai are not alone in consuming blood; Berber tribes drank a mixture of raw blood and milk to relieve their thirst when water wasn't available. Other African tribes bled their animals and coagulated the blood by boiling it and turning it into cakes of solidified blood that could be cooked over an open fire. Before the arrival of Islam, Arabs made a dish made of camel's hair and blood.

> It is simply not decent to throw away such a valuable food source [blood] in a starving world.
> BIRGIT SIESBY

Marco Polo describes in detail the ability of Mongol warriors to traverse large distances quickly without being spotted. They didn't stop to make fire and cook their food, because firewood was scarce on the steppes and the smoke from a fire would reveal their location to enemies. Instead each man traveled with eighteen horses and survived by drinking their blood. Up to $1^1/4$ cups / 310 ml can be taken from a horse every ten days without endangering its health. This was also common practice among trappers and explorers in the early days of opening up North America. They either drank the animal's blood fresh or preserved it with salt to eat when other sources of food were in short supply. So you can see that blood is a very practical food. You can take 4 quarts / 4 liters of blood every two weeks from a well-nourished cow without causing the animal any harm. This yields the same amount of protein that you would get if you waited two and a half years to slaughter it.

In harsh northern climes where food was often scarce, both Scandinavians and the Irish survived on animal blood. The growing antlers of reindeer were a source for Laplanders, while in Ireland they turned blood into a national dish. The French writer Henri Misson de Valbourg wrote about his voyages through England, Scotland, and Ireland in the late seventeenth century in *Misson's Memoirs and Observations in his Trav-*

els over England (1690). In Ireland, he recalled eating "one of their most delicious dishes" made from blood mixed with milk and butter and flavored with herbs. He was describing *drisheen* (see page 222), a blood sausage very popular in County Cork. All over Ireland similar puddings were made: in Tipperary turkey or goose blood was the main ingredient, and in Tyrone and Derry they preserved blood by coagulating and layering it with salt.

In Asia, cooked blood is cut into cubes and sold as a snack or added to soup. A well-known Filipino dish, *dinuguan* (euphemistically called "chocolate meat"), is a stew of pork and tripe cooked in blood with vinegar and hot peppers. Blood is not restricted to savory dishes; the Italians use pork blood to make sweet chocolate desserts (page 226).

How to Choose

All animal blood is edible and can be used interchangeably in recipes, but you are not likely to have a choice. Pig's blood is most common, and it's the only kind I've regularly been able to obtain fresh. Check with your butcher or supplier to see if he can source it for you. Fresh blood should be bright red and have the consistency of liquid cream and no smell. If you can't buy it fresh, frozen blood is an alternative and once thawed works in all of the recipes. I know someone who slaughters their own chickens, so occasionally I can obtain poultry blood, but I can't say that I can tell a difference in the taste, and all animal blood has the same thickening properties. Asian markets are often a good source for fresh blood, and they are likely to have blood cakes, squares of coagulated blood that can be added to soups or stews. All of the recipes here use fresh liquid blood.

How to Prepare and Cook

Blood requires little preparation, but it does separate on standing. My supplier likens it to orange juice; "don't forget to give it a good shake before you use it," he tells me every time I buy it. I nod. His advice is good, but do make sure the container is well sealed before shaking it. The next step is to strain the blood through a fine sieve to remove any clots. Depending on the blood, this can take time, and you may need to rinse the strainer a couple of times during the process. Now the blood is ready to use.

Blood should be used as fresh as possible, preferably the day you buy it or within twenty-four hours. However, it will keep for a couple of days refrigerated if you add a splash of vinegar to stop it coagulating. Blood freezes well; just remember that liquid expands, so don't fill your containers too full. It will keep about three months frozen, and will be darker in color when thawed.

While fresh blood is bright red, it turns dark brown as it cooks. It is good to remember that blood stains and colors everything it touches. Blood's value is not only nutritional; it works like egg yolks to thicken mixtures. When cooking blood, treat it like a liquid custard mixture: you can heat it gently but don't boil it or else it will curdle.

And the most important question: what does blood taste like? Well, just like when you suck a cut finger. I only consume cooked blood, which is rich and unassertive, with a slight metallic taste right at the back of the mouth.

Black Pancakes

MAKES ABOUT 15 PANCAKES

These pancakes are so popular in Finland that you can buy blood pancake mix in the supermarket. I doubt any North American food manufacturer will be adding blood pancakes to their range of pancake mixes, but perhaps they should.

You might think that these wouldn't be very appetizing, but they are delicious and their very dark chocolate color makes them striking. The rye flour dominates the blood and removes any lingering metallic flavor, so this is a beginner's blood recipe. In Finland, lingonberry jam is a popular topping, so I serve them with Red Currant Sauce. These pancakes, even with the shallots in the mixture, can be sweet or savory. Pair them with bacon and/or syrup for breakfast, or serve them as an appetizer. While I was eating them, I thought of topping them with smoked fish and sour cream, or duck confit.

Made into smaller rounds, about 1 1/2 inches / 4 cm in diameter, they would make a great base for all different sorts of toppings for hors d'oeuvre.

1 cup / 4 ounces / 125 g rye flour

1 cup / 250 ml pork blood, prepared (see page 217)

1/2 cup / 125 ml whole milk

1 egg

1 tablespoon molasses

1/2 teaspoon fine sea salt

1/4 teaspoon dried oregano

Freshly ground black pepper

1/4 cup / 2 ounces / 60 g unsalted butter

1 shallot, finely chopped

Red Currant Sauce (see opposite), syrup, or lingonberry jam

Place the flour in a bowl. Whisk together the blood, milk, egg, and molasses. Add the salt, oregano, and pepper and then whisk into the flour until the mixture is smooth. Cover the batter and let it rest for at least 30 minutes at room temperature.

Meanwhile, heat 2 tablespoons of the butter in a small frying pan over medium-low heat. Add the shallot and cook until softened and translucent. Let cool, then stir the shallot and butter into the batter.

Preheat the oven to 200°F / 100°C.

Place a heavy cast-iron pan over medium-high heat and when hot, add a little butter, and swirl it around the pan. Add the batter in 1/4 cup / 60 ml amounts to make 3 1/2-inch / 9-cm pancakes. Cook the pancakes until they darken around the edges and the surface begins to set, 2 to 3 minutes. Flip the pancakes over and cook on the other side. Transfer the cooked pancakes to a baking sheet and keep warm in the oven. Continue cooking until all the batter is used up.

Serve hot with Red Currant Sauce, syrup, or lingonberry jam. Or serve cold with different toppings.

'Listen to me,' said Antinous, 'there are some goats' paunches down at the fire, which we have filled with blood and fat, and set aside for supper; he who is victorious and proves himself to be the better man shall have his pick of the lot; he shall be free of our table and we will not allow any other beggar about the house at all.'

Ulysses hailed this as of good omen, and Antinous set a great goat's paunch before him filled with blood and fat. Amphinomus took two loaves out of the bread-basket and brought them to him, pledging him as he did so in a golden goblet of wine. 'Good luck to you,' he said, 'father stranger, you are very badly off at present, but I hope you will have better times by and by.'
THE ODYSSEY

Red Currant Sauce

MAKES ABOUT 1 CUP / 250 ML

A red currant bush thrives in my garden, so I have a guaranteed supply. These bright jewel-like, tart berries are becoming more popular, and I often see them at the farmers' market. The season is short, but luckily they freeze well.

Place them in a single layer on a baking sheet in the freezer. When frozen, pack into freezer bags: they will keep for 6 to 8 months. Frozen berries are easy to remove from their stems. Add them to recipes directly from the freezer.

1 cup / 6 ounces / 170 g red currants

1/4 cup / 1 3/4 ounces / 50 g sugar

2 tablespoons red wine vinegar

Remove the currants from their stems and place in a saucepan with the sugar and vinegar. Place over low heat and stir until the sugar dissolves, then continue to cook until the berries pop and soften.

Boudin Noir

SERVES 8 AS AN APPETIZER

I must admit to being a devotee of blood pudding, but not just any blood sausage will do. I try them everywhere I go. I don't like those filled with too much kasha or grain; I'm a purist—just blood, fat, and spices. Christian Parra makes one of my favorites, and my local restaurant in Paris serves it with cooked apple and a salad of baby arugula—perfection. My first attempt at making blood sausage went well; the filling just needed some extra spicing, so I very confidently began my second test. It was a disaster. I'd missed a small hole in the intestines and soon there was blood all over my kitchen—it looked like a crime scene from *CSI*. That set me off on my quest to cook the mixture without putting it into the sausage casing. This is the result: easier to make and much less messy.

1 pound / 450 g pork back fat, cut into 3/8-inch / 9-mm dice

1 pound / 450 g onions, finely chopped

2 cups / 500 ml pork blood, prepared (see page 217)

1/2 cup / 125 ml whipping (35%) cream

4 teaspoons / 1/2 ounce / 15 g coarse sea salt

1 teaspoon freshly ground black pepper

2 teaspoons piment d'espelette or ground chipotle pepper

1 teaspoon quatre épices

A generous pinch of ground nutmeg

4 small tart cooking apples

10 to 12 cups / 2.5 to 3 l baby dandelion or arugula leaves

Harald's Vinaigrette (page 196)

Place about 10 1/2 ounces / 300 g of the diced fat in a large frying pan over medium-low heat. Cook, stirring, until some of the fat begins to render. Add the onions, stir to coat in the fat, cover, and cook, stirring from time to time, for about 45 minutes, or until the onions become creamy and most of the fat melts. Uncover, add the remaining fat and cook, stirring, for about

continued

20 minutes, until the fat loses its whiteness and turns opaque and the moisture from the onions evaporates. Set aside to cool.

Preheat the oven to 325°F / 160°C.

Line a 9-inch / 23-cm square glass baking dish with plastic wrap overhanging on all sides and then evenly place the fat and onion mixture in the bottom of the dish.

Whisk together the blood, cream, salt, pepper, *piment d'espelette, quatre épices,* and nutmeg and then pour over the fat mixture. Place the baking dish in a roasting pan and add enough hot water to come three-quarters up the side of the baking dish.

Bake for 75 minutes or until the center is resistant to the touch and a skewer inserted in the center comes out clean. Remove the baking dish from the pan and place it on a cooling rack. When cool, remove the blood pudding from the dish using the plastic wrap to ease it out. Cut into squares any size you want; I usually cut it into 16 squares and serve 2 per person as an appetizer. Blood pudding freezes well.

To serve, preheat the oven to 350°F / 180°C.

Peel, quarter, core, and slice the apples and place them in a saucepan with a splash of water. Cover and cook over low heat until just soft. Keep warm.

Meanwhile, place a heavy, ovenproof frying pan over medium-high heat. Once hot, add the boudin squares topside down. Cook for 1 minute, then turn the squares over and place the pan in the oven for 10 minutes.

Meanwhile trim, rinse, and dry the dandelion greens and place them in a large salad bowl. Toss them with enough of the vinaigrette to coat.

Remove the pan from the oven and serve the squares with the cooked apple and salad.

Our ancestors knew the value of blood. They used the blood as food and as an offering to the gods.
BIRGIT SIESBY

BEGINNER'S BOUDIN

As the author of a cookbook about fat I am loath to suggest a less fatty variation of boudin, but I do understand that not everyone loves or appreciates fat as much as I do (they should read my book!). I don't want you to be intimidated by seeing a sausage dotted with large pieces of fat, so if a little less fat encourages you to try this recipe, so be it. I had this idea while dining at Daniel Boulud's restaurant DBGB Kitchen and Bar in New York. This restaurant specializes in hamburgers and sausages, and I was thrilled to see blood sausage on the menu and ordered it. A large slice arrived atop a pile of soft, creamy potatoes. Instead of the usual pieces of fat speckling the sausage there were pieces of pork. The sausage was tasty, if leaner than I like; however, that potato underneath contained more than enough fat to make up for any missing from the sausage. Sometimes it's just better to hide the fat.

So if you want to try a leaner version of the boudin, replace about 6 ounces / 170 g of the pork fat with diced pork belly. I can't bring myself to use pork loin like Boulud—it is just too lean—but a dice of the meaty section of a pork belly does the trick. Add it when you uncover the mixture and cook only until the moisture from the onions evaporates, then follow the Boudin Noir recipe (see page 219).

THE WORLD OF BLOOD SAUSAGES AND BEYOND

Blood sausage is also called black pudding. The name comes from the color of cooked blood, which is a dark chocolate color—almost black—depending on the blood. Early black puddings were mixtures of blood, meat, fat, and spices cooked in animal intestines or stomachs. When the pig was slaughtered, usually between Christmas and Easter, making blood sausage was a way to preserve this nutritious food, and almost every cuisine has its own blood sausage—*blutwurst* (Germany), *kashanka* (Poland), *kishka* (Hungary), *morcilla* (Spain), and black pudding (England). As noted earlier, when mixed with grains or milk, blood becomes a perfect food; in Central Europe toasted buckwheat or rice are often added to the filling, while in England oats are mixed in the blood.

In France, blood sausage, *boudin noir,* is a specialty. Rarely are cereals or grains included, but cream is, and depending on the region where it is made there are other additions. In Alsace, it's apples, spinach in Poitou, herbs and brandy in Lyon, and in the Paris region onions are common. There is even a sweet version of blood sausage in Pas-de-Calais that includes ginger, cloves, pepper, sugar, cinnamon, and raisins.

> *Who comes yonder puffing as hot as a black pudding?*
> ULPIAN FULWELL

Ireland is famous for its *drisheen,* a very popular dish in the town of Cork. At the end of the seventeenth century, Cork became an important center for the export of meat to England, Europe. and North America. This meant that there was a large supply of blood during the slaughtering season, from August to January. Cork residents didn't waste it; they made a blood sausage called *drisheen*. There were three varieties: sheep, beef, and tansy. Sheep *drisheen* was made from sheep's blood and cooked in sheep's intestine and beef was a mixture of sheep's and cow's blood in beef casings, as all cow's blood made the sausage too tough and dark. The third sausage was made from either sheep's or a combination of sheep's and cow's blood, and flavored with the bitter herb tansy. Like many traditional foods, *drisheen* is in decline. The O'Reilly family is the only producer of *drisheen* remaining in Cork, and they no longer make the sheep or tansy *drisheens*.

However, I hold out hope that blood pudding will become popular again. At its best, it is a rich, tasty sausage with a wonderful silken texture. Mortagne-au-Perche, a town in Normandy, boasts a long history of making charcuterie. While they make a dubious claim to have exported their blood sausage savoir faire to the United Kingdom and Germany, they do know how to celebrate this sausage. They founded a Confrérie des Chevaliers du Goûte-Boudin, a brotherhood of boudin lovers, who host an international competition for the best boudin. Every March they receive over seven hundred entries from around the world. Oh to be a judge.

> [The Irish] bleed their cows and boil the blood with some milk and butter that comes from the same beast; and this with a mixture of savory herbs is one of their most delicious dishes.
> HENRI MISSON DE VALBOURG

Blood is not only made into sausage: in the Philippines you can enjoy *dinuguan*, a stew of pork offal that includes heart, liver, intestines, and pancreas cooked in fat, hot peppers, with blood added to thicken it. Blood is often used to thicken stews, especially ones made with game. *Civet* is a thick, rich game stew made from any furred game—wild boar, venison, and rabbit, but most often hare. The meat is cooked slowly in a red wine sauce, and then thickened with the animal's blood just before serving. The name *civet* comes from one of the ingredients in this dish, small green onions, and the English took the word *civet* from the French during the eighteenth century. The more familiar coq au vin is traditionally thickened with chicken blood, and the French make *sanguette*, a dish of fried chicken blood or rabbit blood mixed with bacon, garlic, and parsley.

However, I think the Scandinavians are even more creative. As well as blood sausages and Black Pancakes (page 218), they make bread with blood, rye flour, and beer and season it with cloves, allspice, and ginger.

Blood Facts

- A 1,000-pound / 454-kg steer yields between 30 and 40 pounds / 13.5 and 18 kg of blood.
- A 225-pound / 102-kg hog will yield between 5 and 10 pounds / 2.25 and 4.5 kg of blood.
- A sheep will yield between 3 and 5 pounds / 1.4 and 2.25 kg of blood.
- A 4$1/2$-pound / 2-kg chicken will yield around 6 ounces / 170 g.

> These are the glory of the Midlands and the north-west in particular, with Bury as their Mecca. David and Richard Mabey describe the scene outside Bury market (In Search of Food), where the black pudding stalls sell nothing else. "Your order is brief and explicit: 'Three hot, please.' The man turns and pulls three steaming puddings from one of the big coppers which are bubbling away continuously. He slits each pudding and lets the two halves open like the pages of a book. He hands them over, you pay your money and then reach for the mustard— essential with hot black puddings."
> JANE GRIGSON

Brazilian Chicken

SERVES 6

While promoting my first two books, I met Brazilian journalist Olivia Silva Fraga and we kept in touch. I asked her for a recipe for *galinha ao molho pardo*, chicken in blood sauce, a specialty of Brazil. She talked to well-known chef and owner of Mocotó restaurant, Rodrigo Oliveira, and persuaded him to share his recipe with me, so I hope they don't mind the changes I've made. The original used a lot of chicken blood and was very rich. I have used less blood and substituted pig's as it is easier for me to get. Not sure about blood? You can still make this recipe and thicken the sauce with a little cornstarch; it will not give you the same richness, but it will taste almost as good. Serve with rice.

1 chicken, about 4 pounds / 1.8 kg

4 large limes

4 plum (Roma) tomatoes, peeled, seeded, and chopped

6 garlic cloves, sliced

1 large onion, halved and sliced

1 red bell pepper, seeded and chopped

2 teaspoons cumin seeds, toasted and ground

5 sprigs cilantro (coriander)

3 fresh bay leaves

1 cup / 250 ml red wine

Freshly ground black pepper

Coarse sea salt

2 tablespoons rendered duck fat or lard

1 tablespoon tomato paste

2 tablespoons pork blood, prepared (see page 217)

1/2 cup / 7 g cilantro (coriander) leaves

Cut the chicken into 8 pieces. Finely grate the zest from the limes, then squeeze the juice; you should have about 2/3 cup / 150 ml. Place the zest and juice in a large bowl, add the tomatoes, garlic, onion, red pepper, cumin, cilantro (coriander) sprigs, and bay leaves. Set 1 tablespoon of the wine aside and pour the remaining red wine into the bowl; season well with black pepper. Add the chicken pieces and stir to coat with the marinade. Cover and refrigerate for 3 hours.

Remove the chicken from the refrigerator. Take the chicken pieces from the marinade, pat dry, and season with salt and pepper. Strain the marinade, keeping the liquid and the vegetable-seasoning mixture separate.

Place a frying pan, large enough to hold the chicken pieces in a single layer, over medium-high heat and add the fat. When hot, add the chicken pieces skin side down in two batches, and brown on both sides, transferring the browned chicken pieces to a plate. When all the chicken is browned, add the vegetables and spices from the marinade and cook, stirring, for 5 minutes, or until softened slightly. Lower the heat, add the tomato paste, and cook for 2 minutes.

Pour in the liquid from the marinade and bring to a boil; deglaze the pan, using a wooden spoon to scrape up the browned bits from the bottom. Boil the liquid for 5 minutes, then return the chicken pieces with any juices to the pan. Lower the heat so the chicken simmers; cover, and cook for 20 minutes.

Uncover the pan, turn the chicken pieces over and continue to simmer, uncovered, for another 20 minutes, or until the chicken is cooked. Transfer the cooked chicken to a dish and keep warm.

Whisk the blood with the reserved wine and then whisk into the sauce over low heat. The sauce will thicken and turn dark brown. Return the chicken to the pan and reheat over low heat, making sure that the sauce doesn't boil, or else it will curdle. Turn the chicken pieces to coat with the sauce and heat through. Sprinkle with the cilantro (coriander) leaves and serve.

BLOOD NUTRITION AND TABOOS

In the past, people believed in the medicinal powers of animal's blood. In an edition of the French journal *Le Monde Illustré* published in 1890, there was an illustration of young women visiting the abattoir to drink fresh blood. Why? It was thought that it would prevent tuberculosis. Today we now know that consuming blood provides no protection against tuberculosis, but it is a rich source of iron and is very nutritious, containing about 20 percent protein by weight. Although blood has all the essential amino acids, some are only present in very small amounts; but by mixing blood with milk or a grain protein, the mix of essential amino acids greatly improves, making it an excellent food source. Oddly enough, in today's society, we don't consider blood as food and of the millions of animals slaughtered every year, very little of their blood makes it into our kitchens.

So why don't we eat more blood? There are strong taboos linked to the consuming of blood. In Genesis 9:2–4, it says:

and I have given them to you for food. From now on, you may eat them, as well as the green plants that you have always eaten. But life is in the blood, and you must not eat any meat that still has blood in it.

These words are the source of the taboo against eating blood, which is very strong in the Jewish religion. For meat to be kosher, it must have no blood in it, and meat is often soaked and salted after slaughter to remove any remaining traces of blood. Muslims and many early Christians took the same stance against consuming blood, believing that it was the life force of the animal. This belief that blood housed the animal's soul resulted in a completely different reaction in other cultures. The Nordic peoples thought if they drank the animal's blood they would imbibe the animal's qualities and strength. In the *Gesta Danorum,* a twelfth-century Danish tale, the great warrior Bjarke kills a giant bear and offers its blood to the younger Hjalte to drink. The blood fills the youth with the bear's strength and fighting spirit, which is revealed in the rest of the story.

Today, even outside of religion, there is a strong prejudice against eating blood. This has grown as animal slaughter has become highly industrialized and traditional dishes using blood have disappeared from our tables. Buying blood is difficult in many places and illegal in others. The result is that a valuable nourishing food source is wasted. Blood could be added to many foods, from hamburger and sausage to bread, making them tastier and improving their nutritive value. We should take heed of the example set by Finland, where frozen blood is available in supermarkets. There is no reason why properly inspected blood couldn't be in our supermarkets too, right there next to the frozen dinners and offering us a much healthier choice.

Sanguinaccio alla Napoletana

SERVES 6

This recipe comes to me from the renowned pastry chef and teacher Nick Malgieri. He adapted a Neapolitan sweet blood and chocolate cream from *Le Ricette Regionali Italiane* (1967) by Anna Gosetti della Salda, a goldmine of authentic recipes for obscure Italian specialties, he assures me. Della Salda notes that *sanguinaccio* is a typical carnival sweet in Italy. *Sanguinaccio* varies from region to region: in Calabria it includes almonds and cinnamon, while in Campania candied fruit is a popular addition.

Well, true to form I've adapted his recipe yet again—my excuses to both Nick and Anna. Each cook puts a stamp, sometimes deliberately, sometimes accidentally, on a recipe, and it was my taste buds that led me to add ginger. While I have included the candied fruits, they are optional, as I prefer the pudding without them.

> 3/4 cup / 5 1/4 ounces / 150 g sugar
>
> 1/3 cup packed / 1 ounce / 30 g alkalized (Dutch-processed) cocoa
>
> 2 tablespoons / 3/4 ounce / 20 g cornstarch
>
> 1/2 teaspoon ground ginger
>
> Pinch of fine sea salt
>
> 1 cup / 250 ml whole milk

1/2 cup / 125 ml pork blood, prepared (see page 217)

Finely grated zest of 1 orange

3 1/2 ounces / 100 g candied fruit, finely diced (optional)

Place the sugar in a bowl, then sift in the cocoa and cornstarch. Add the ginger and salt, then gradually whisk in the milk until the mixture is fairly smooth. Pour in the blood and whisk to combine.

Pour the mixture—which will be a crimson color—into a saucepan and place over medium heat. Stir constantly with a spatula to make sure the mixture doesn't stick to the sides of the pan. Continue to stir until the mixture thickens and approaches a boil. The color will change from burgundy to dark chocolate and will become shiny and smooth. It will look like melted chocolate. Remove the pan from the heat.

Stir in the orange zest and candied fruit, if using. Transfer the mixture to a bowl and stir it again to distribute the fruit. Press a piece of plastic wrap on the surface to prevent a skin forming, cool, and refrigerate. Serve in small dishes with whipped cream.

Chocolate Blood Ice Cream

SERVES 6

This recipe grew out of the Sanguinaccio alla Napoletana (above). I found it fascinating how the cooked blood mixture is like a custard and had a rich chocolate taste when combined with the cocoa. While others loved the pudding texture of the *sanguinaccio*, I didn't, so I decided to turn it into an ice cream. The result is a rich, chocolate-tasting ice cream that is delicious and good for you. I doubt anyone will guess the secret ingredient, and served cold it doesn't seem quite so rich.

Make the *sanguinaccio* without the candied peel and add 2 tablespoons of Grand Marnier with the grated orange zest. After refrigerating overnight, stir, then churn the mixture in an ice cream maker according to the manufacturer's instructions.

Skin and Fat Exposed

The best parts of a pork roast for many are the cracklings, or roasted skin. Pork skin makes up a little over 6 percent of the carcass weight and is inexpensive.
CALVIN SCHWABE

Who doesn't like deep-fried pork rinds? Pork skin is delicious when cooked crisp and crunchy, but pork skin cooked long and slow is also tasty, and its consistency is soft and chewy. This is the texture that you find in headcheese and *cotechino,* a large Italian pork sausage that is a specialty of the Emilia-Romagna region. *Cotechino* is a fresh sausage made from ground cooked pork skin, fat, and meat. The inclusion of cooked skin gives the sausage a wonderful creamy, sticky texture. Its name is derived from *cotenna,* the Italian word for skin.

Cotechino sausages appear at my local market around New Year's, the traditional time to eat them. Poached and served with lentils, they supposedly guarantee good health and luck for the coming year. They are also part of the Italian dish *bollito misto,* which also includes odd bits like ox tongue and half a calf's head.

di cotica—literally, "the skin": a response to an overstatement

You may not like the texture of soft, chewy, sticky *cotechino* or be bothered with frying pork rinds, but that doesn't mean you should ignore pork skin. When you are cooking odd bits that don't have bones, the sauce can often lack substance and that is why many recipes in this book include a foot to improve the texture of the sauce. However, feet are not always readily available, but pork skin is, and it's not a bad substitute. Pork skin has lots of collagen and when it's added to a dish it will help add a lip-smacking quality to the sauce. Remove as much fat as you can from the skin before using and keep it for rendering.

Fat

While I have covered this topic extensively in another book, I want to mention it very briefly here. Many might try to argue that fat doesn't qualify as an odd bit, but alas my experience tells me otherwise. We are all familiar with fat in general, but different types of fat confuse us, even those who work in butcher shops. I was given fat trimmed from beef ribs in place of suet. So here is a recap. Knowledge is power.

Pork Fat

Back fat is the layer of fat found just below the skin on the back, shoulder, and rump of the animal. It is sold in pieces, usually with the skin attached.

Leaf lard is the fat that encases the pig's kidneys; it is prized for pastry making because of its brittle crystalline structure.

Both back fat and leaf lard can be rendered and used for cooking, frying, and pastry.

Caul fat is a spidery web of fat that encloses the pig's intestines. It is great for wrapping around lean meats or mixtures of ground meat.

Poultry Fat

Duck fat is the most readily available poultry fat and is sold already rendered. It is simple to render your own using the skin and the fat found inside the bird.

Beef Fat

Suet is the the fat that encloses the bovine kidneys. It can be rendered or just finely grated and added to a dish or used to make pastry.

Dripping is the fat from roasting beef; it has a beefy flavor and is good for cooking and to spread on sandwiches.

Tallow is a general term for rendered fat from cattle or sheep. It is a very stable fat, and beef tallow is an excellent medium for frying.

Bone marrow, the fat from inside the animal's bones, is discussed in depth on page 189.

Rendering Fat

Cut the fat into 1-inch / 2.5-cm pieces, removing any traces of meat and blood, or the papery membrane and kidney from suet.

Put the diced fat in a heavy flameproof casserole or Dutch oven and add about 1/3 cup / 75 ml water per 1 pound / 450 g of fat. The water keeps the fat from burning before it begins to melt. Place the pan, uncovered, over very low heat on the stovetop or in a 250°F / 120°C oven. If you are rendering on the stovetop, you will have to stir the fat often. In the oven, stir the fat after 30 minutes, then at 45 minutes, and then every hour, watching carefully as the fat begins to color. As you stir the fat, press the pieces against the side of the pan to help them melt. The rendering can take from 4 to 8 hours, depending on the quantity of fat and the size of the pieces. Not all the fat will liquefy; some pieces of connective tissue will remain solid. As soon as the pieces in the pan start to color, remove the pan from the oven and let cool slightly. Strain the liquid fat into clean containers.

Let the fat cool completely, then cover and store in the refrigerator for up to 2 months or in the freezer for a year. Animal fat is generally very stable, but, like all fats, it will eventually turn rancid.

FIVE

———

Basic Recipes: Odd Stocks

Essential to cooking, stock is the foundation of soups and sauces, and it adds depth of flavor to braised meats and other dishes. You can make specific stocks or multi-purpose white and brown stock.

Stock is simple to make and is a good way of using the whole animal, especially odd bits like shank, neck, feet, tail, and head. You can use only odd bits or mix them with bones. If you don't add some bones, make sure to include feet in your mixture of odd bits.

Up until recently I always simmered my stock on top of the stove, but now I place my stockpot in the oven at 250°F / 120°C and leave it to cook overnight. I don't have to worry about trying to keep it barely simmering, and the final

stock is very clear. You need a big oven to do this, and you can of course continue to cook it on top of the stove—just be sure it simmers very gently.

Stock can be made in any quantity: these recipes are based on the perfect amounts for my own 10-quart / 10-liter stockpot, but you can halve, double, or quadruple the recipe. Keep the stock refrigerated or frozen. If room is tight in your freezer, concentrate the stock before freezing it (see page 234).

Beef Stock

MAKES 6 TO 7 CUPS / 1.5 TO 1.75 L

To make a beef stock, roast the odd bits, including a cow's foot, oxtail, or shank, before simmering them in water. The result is a darker, stronger flavored stock.

1 large onion, unpeeled, cut into wedges

2 carrots, sliced

1 stalk celery, sliced

1 leek, trimmed, quartered, and rinsed well

4 1/2 pounds / 2 kg mixed beef odd bits, cut into 2- to 3-inch / 5- to 7.5-cm pieces

3 quarts / 3 l cold water

1 large tomato, halved

6 garlic cloves, unpeeled

Mushroom trimmings (optional)

3 stems flat-leaf parsley

3 large sprigs thyme

1 fresh bay leaf

1/4 teaspoon black peppercorns

Preheat the oven to 425°F / 220°C.

Scatter the onion, carrots, celery, and leek over the bottom of a large roasting pan. Rinse the odd bits well under cold running water, pat dry, and place them on top of the vegetables.

Roast for 1 hour, or until the odd bits are well browned, turning them once or twice. Remove from the oven and lower the oven temperature to 250°F / 120°C.

Using tongs, transfer the odd bits and vegetables to a large stockpot. Discard any fat from the roasting pan. Add 2 cups / 500 ml of the water to the pan and bring to a boil over medium heat, deglazing the pan by scraping up the browned bits from the bottom. Pour this liquid into the stockpot and add the tomato, garlic, mushroom trimmings, parsley, thyme, and bay leaf. Add the remaining cold water, making sure it covers the odd bits—use more water if necessary. Place over low heat and bring slowly to a simmer. As soon as the stock begins to simmer, remove it from the heat and, using a soup ladle, skim off any scum that has risen to the surface. Add the peppercorns and transfer to the oven and leave to cook 8 hours or overnight, skimming from time to time if you're awake.

Remove the pot from the oven and let it stand for 10 minutes. Strain the stock through a sieve into a large bowl. Discard the debris left in the sieve, and cool the stock quickly by placing the bowl in a larger bowl or sink filled with ice water; stir occasionally as it cools.

Refrigerate the stock overnight to allow the fat to rise to the top and any debris to sink to the bottom. Remove the fat and set it aside for another use and discard the debris at the bottom of the bowl. The stock will keep for up to 3 days in the refrigerator or frozen for up to 6 months.

Veal Stock

MAKES 6 TO 7 CUPS / 1.5 TO 1.75 L

Veal stock can be used in any veal dish as well as in place of chicken and pork stock. Use only veal odd bits, including a calf's foot or pieces of shank, and don't roast them or the vegetables. Place the odd bits and vegetables in the stockpot with the tomato, garlic, mushroom trimmings, parsley, thyme, and bay leaf and all the water. Bring to a boil over low heat, skim, add the peppercorns, then transfer to the oven and cook as for Beef Stock (see opposite).

Poultry Stock

MAKES 6 TO 7 CUPS / 1.5 TO 1.75 L

While you can roast the odd bits and vegetables in the oven to give a more robust flavor to the stock, as with Beef Stock, I prefer just to simmer the odd bits. This yields a stock with good flavor that won't overpower other flavors, making it versatile enough that it can be used almost anywhere stock is required. Don't hesitate to mix and match the odd bits of different birds, and don't forget to add some feet.

4^1/$_2$ pounds / 2 kg poultry odd bits, cut into 2- to 3-inch / 5- to 7.5-cm pieces

1 onion, unpeeled, cut into wedges

2 carrots, sliced

2 stalks celery, sliced

2 leeks, trimmed, quartered, and rinsed well

3 cloves garlic, unpeeled

6 stems flat-leaf parsley

1 fresh bay leaf

1 large sprig thyme

3 quarts / 3 l cold water

Large strip lemon zest

^{1}/$_4$ teaspoon black peppercorns

Preheat the oven to 250°F / 120°C.

Rinse the odd bits well under cold running water and place them in a large stockpot along with the onion, carrots, celery, leeks, garlic, parsley stems, bay leaf, and thyme. Pour in enough of the cold water to cover the odd bits, place over low heat, and bring slowly to a boil. As soon as the stock begins to simmer, remove from the heat and, using a soup ladle, skim off any scum that has risen to the surface. Add the lemon zest and peppercorns, transfer to the oven, and leave to cook 8 hours or overnight, skimming from time to time if you are awake.

Remove the pot from the oven and let it stand for 10 minutes. Strain the stock through a sieve into a large bowl. Discard the debris left in the sieve, and cool the stock quickly by placing the bowl in a larger bowl or sink filled with ice water; stir occasionally as it cools.

Refrigerate the stock overnight to allow the fat to rise to the top and any debris to sink to the bottom. Remove the fat and set it aside for another use, and discard the debris at the bottom of the bowl. The stock will keep for up to 3 days in the refrigerator or frozen for up to 6 months.

Lamb Stock

MAKES 6 TO 7 CUPS / 1.5 TO 1.75 L

There is a widespread misconception that lamb stock is greasy and strong, but while lamb stock may not be as versatile as veal or poultry, it adds depth to lamb dishes. Be sure to include some pieces of neck or shank.

4$^1/_2$ pounds / 2 kg lamb odd bits, cut into 2- to 3-inch / 5- to 7.5-cm pieces

1 large onion, unpeeled, cut into wedges

1 large carrot, sliced

2 stalks celery, sliced

1 leek, trimmed, quartered, and rinsed well

1 whole head garlic, unpeeled, separated into cloves

3 flat-leaf parsley stems

1 fresh bay leaf

1 large sprig thyme

1 sprig rosemary

3 quarts / 3 l cold water

$^1/_4$ teaspoon black peppercorns

Follow the same method as for Poultry Stock (page 233), adding the rosemary along with the other herbs.

Concentrated Stock

MAKES 1$^1/_2$ CUPS / 375 ML

Often I don't have the room for one more container of stock in my freezer, so I make frozen concentrated stock cubes. As the stock boils, the water evaporates to concentrate the stock's flavor. (This technique of boiling to reduce the liquid is also a way to boost the flavor of an insipid stock, but only if there is no salt in it. If salt is added before reducing the stock, the final concentrated stock will be too salty.) The wider the saucepan, the faster the liquid will evaporate, but it will still take at least fifteen to twenty minutes. The saucepan must be deep enough to prevent the stock from boiling over. Watch the stock carefully toward the end of the cooking time as it can boil up quite dramatically.

6 cups / 1.5 l unsalted stock

Before starting, pour 1$^1/_2$ cups / 375 ml water into the saucepan you plan to use. This will show you the quantity of the concentrated stock you're aiming for. Discard the water.

Pour the stock into the pan and bring to a boil. Continue to boil until it is reduced by about three-quarters, about 15 minutes. Pour the stock into a glass measuring cup to see if it has reduced to 1$^1/_2$ cups / 375 ml. If not, return it to the saucepan and continue to reduce it further. The stock will become syrupy and darken in color.

Pour the reduction back into the measuring cup and allow it to cool slightly. Then pour the reduced stock into ice cube trays and place in the refrigerator to chill. I usually end up with 24 cubes, each about 1 tablespoon. When cold, the cubes will set like jelly and can be popped out of the trays and stored in bags in the freezer.

These stock cubes are 4 times as strong as the original stock. You can use them without water to boost the flavor of soups and sauces, or reconstitute them in place of stock, adding 3 tablespoons of water along with each cube.

Bibliography

Alexander, Stephanie. *The Cook's Companion.* Melbourne: Viking, 1996.

Allen, Jana, and Margaret Gin. *Innards and Other Variety Meats.* San Francisco: 101 Productions, 1974.

Arndt, Alice. *Culinary Biographies.* Houston: Yes Press Inc., 2006.

Ayto, John. *The Diner's Dictionary.* Oxford: Oxford University Press, 1993.

Behr, Edward. "The Andouillette of Troyes: Primary Sausage." *The Art of Eating,* No. 78, 2008.

Berthiaume, Guy. *Les roles du mageiros. Etude sur la boucheries, la cuisine et le sacrifice dans la Grece ancienne.* Montreal: Presses de l'Université, 1982.

Bertolli, Paul. *Cooking by Hand.* New York: Clarkson Potter, 2003.

Bocuse, Paul. *La Cuisine du Marché.* Paris: Flammarion, 1980.

Bogue, Robert Herman. *The Chemistry and Technology of Gelatin and Glue.* New York: McGraw-Hill, 1922.

Boxer, Arabella. *A Visual Feast.* London: Random Century, 1991.

Brillat-Savarin, Jean-Anthelme. *The Physiology of Taste*, translated by M. F. K. Fisher. Washington, D.C.: Counterpoint, 1994.

Brown, Lynda. "Elder: 'A Good Udder to Dinner.'" *Petits Propos Culinaires,* No. 26, July 1987.

Buren, Raymond. *Le Boudin: Récits et recettes de la cuisine du sang.* Paris: Jean-Paul Rocher, 1998.

Camdeborde, Yves, and Sébastien Lapaque. *Des Tripes et Des Lettres.* Paris: Les Éditions de l'Épure, 2007.

Carrington-Smith, Denise. "Mawson and Mertz: A Re-evaluation of their ill-fated mapping journey during the 1911–1914 Australasian Antarctic Expedition." *Medical Journal of Australia,* Vol. 183, November 12, 2005.

Carroll, Lewis. *The Adventures of Alice in Wonderland & Through the Looking-Glass.* London: Weidenfeld and Nicolson, 1949.

Cassell's Household Guide: Being a Complete Encyclopedia Domestic and Social Economy. London: Petter and Galpin Cassell, 1869.

Child, Julia, Louisette Bertholle, and Simone Beck. *Mastering the Art of French Cooking.* New York: Knopf, 1961.

Cole, Bernard. *Gelatine—Consumer Information.* http://www.gelatin.co.za

Colquhoun, Kate. *Taste: The Story of Britain Through Its Cooking.* London: Bloomsbury, 2007.

Conran, Terence, and Caroline Conran. *The Cook Book.* New York: Crown, 1980.

David, Elizabeth. *A Book of Mediterranean Food.* London: Dorling Kindersley, 1988.

Davidson, Alan, ed. *On Feasting and Fasting.* London: Macdonald Orbis, 1988.

———. *The Oxford Companion to Food.* Oxford: Oxford University Press, 1999.

de Pomiane, Edouard, translated by Philip and Mary Hyman. *French Cooking in Ten Minutes.* New York: McGraw-Hill, 1978.

Detienne, Marcel, and Jean-Pierre Vernat. *La cuisine du sacrifice en pays grec.* Paris: Gallimard, 1979.

Dickens, Charles. *The Old Curiosity Shop.* London: Penguin, 2000.

Durand, Jean-Louis, and Annie Schnapp. "Boucherie sacrificielle et chasses initiatiques," in C. Berard, et al., eds., *La cité des images*. Paris: Fernand Nathan, 1984.

Dyson-Hudson, Rada, and Neville Dyson-Hudson. "Subsistence Herding in Uganda." *Scientific American*, Vol. 220, No. 2, February 1969.

Ezard, Teage. *Ezard: Contemporary Australian Food*. Melbourne: Hardie Grant, 2003.

Fasman, Jon. "With your heart in my mouth." *The Economist: Intelligent Life*, October 18, 2007.

Fearnley-Whittingstall, Hugh. *The River Cottage Cookbook*. London: HarperCollins, 2001.

———. *The River Cottage Meat Book*. London: Hodder and Stoughton, 2004.

Fernández-Armesto, Felipe. *Near a Thousand Tables*. Toronto: Key Porter Books, 2002.

Fisher, M. F. K. *With Bold Knife and Fork*. New York: Paragon Books, 1968.

Fitzgibbon, Theodora. *A Taste of Ireland: Irish Traditional Food*. London: Pan Books, 1976.

Flandrin, Jean-Louis, and Massimo Montanari, eds. *Food: A Culinary History*. New York: Columbia University Press, 1999.

Gill, A. A. *Table Talk: Sweet and Sour, Salt and Bitter*. London: Weidenfeld and Nicolson, 2007.

Grigson, Jane. *Charcuterie and French Pork Cookery*. London: Penguin, 1978.

———. *Jane Grigson's Book of European Cookery*. New York: Atheneum, 1983.

———. *The Observer Guide to British Cookery*. London: Michael Joseph, 1984.

Halici, Nevin. *Nevin Halici's Turkish Cookbook*. London: Dorling Kindersley, 1989.

Hartley, Dorothy. *Food in England*. London: Little, Brown, 2003.

Helou, Anissa. *The Fifth Quarter*. Bath: Absolute Press, 2004.

Henderson, Fergus. *Nose to Tail Eating*. London: Bloomsbury, 2004.

Herbst, Sharon Tyler. *The New Food Lover's Companion*. New York: Barron's, 2001.

Hickman, Martin. "Britain gets an offal taste of austerity." *The Independent*, September 11, 2008.

Hopkins, Jerry. *Strange Foods*. Hong Kong: Periplus, 1999.

Hopkinson, Simon. *Roast Chicken and Other Stories*. London: Ebury Press, 1994.

Joyce, James. *Ulysses*. New York and London: Garland Publishing, 1984 (originally published 1922).

Kamman, Madeleine. *The New Making of a Cook*. New York: William Morrow, 1997.

Kingsolver, Barbara. *Animal, Vegetable, Miracle*. New York: HarperCollins, 2007.

Keller, Thomas. *Bouchon*. New York: Artisan, 2004.

Kurlansky, Mark. *Salt: A World History*. New York: Knopf, 2002.

Lang, George. *The Cuisine of Hungary*. New York: Atheneum, 1985.

Lawson, Nigella. *How to Eat*. New York: Wiley, 2000.

Leipoldt, C. Louis. *Leipoldt's Cape Cookery*. Cape Town: W. J. Flesch, 1989.

Lemnis, Maria, and Henryk Vitry. *Old Polish Traditions in the Kitchen and at the Table*. Warsaw: Interpress, 1981.

Lobel, M. & Sons. *Meat*. New York: Alpha Books, 1971.

Locatelli, Giorgio. *Made in Italy*. London: Fourth Estate, 2006.

Luard, Elizabeth. *The Old World Kitchen: The Rich Tradition of European Peasant Cooking*. New York, Bantam, 1987.

———. *Sacred Food: Cooking for Spiritual Nourishment*. Chicago: Chicago Review Press, 2001.

McDougall, Hamish. "Beauty of the Beast." *Sunday Herald Sun Magazine*, May 16, 2010.

McGee, Harold. *On Food and Cooking*. New York: Scribner, 1984.

McNeil, F. Marian. *The Scots Kitchen*. Edinburgh: Mercat Press, 2004.

Mennell, Stephen. *All Manners of Food*. Oxford: Blackwell, 1985.

Montagné, Prosper. *Larousse Gastronomique*. London: Hamlyn, 1961.

Morton, Mark. *Cupboard Love*. Toronto: Insomniac Press, 2004.

Noël, Noëlle. *La Cuisine Ariegeoise Traditionelle: Les Recettes Authentiques*. Nîmes, France: Christain Lacour, 2000.

Olney, Richard, ed. *The Good Cook Series: Outdoor Cooking.* New York: Time-Life Books, 1979.

———. *The Good Cook Series: Preserving.* New York: Time-Life Books, 1979.

———. *The Good Cook Series: Variety Meats.* New York: Time-Life Books, 1979.

Parra, Christian. *Mon Cochon de La Tête aux Pieds.* Paris: Editions J'ai lu, 2001.

Pollan, Michael. "Farmer in Chief." *New York Times,* October 12, 2008.

Prusiner, Stanley B. "Detecting Mad Cow Disease." *Scientific American,* July 2004.

Raichlen, Steven. *The Barbecue Bible.* New York: Workman, 1998.

———. *How to Grill.* New York: Workman, 2001.

Rombauer, Irma and Marion Becker. *Joy of Cooking.* New York: Bobbs-Merrill, 1978.

Root, Waverley. *Food.* New York: Simon and Schuster, 1980.

Rossetto Kasper, Lynne. *The Splendid Table: Recipes from Emilia-Romagna, the Heartland of Northern Italian Food.* New York: Morrow, 1992.

Ruhlman, Michael, and Brian Polcyn. *Charcuterie: The Craft of Salting, Smoking, and Curing.* New York: W. W. Norton & Company, 2005.

Sage, Adam. "Recipes for the recession bring offal back into fashion in France." *London Times,* November 20, 2008.

Saveur Magazine. Saveur Cooks Authentic Italian. San Francisco: Chronicle Books, 2001.

Schwabe, Calvin W. *Unmentionable Cuisine.* Charlottesville: University Press of Virginia, 1999.

Severson, Kim. "Young Idols with Cleavers Rule the Stage." *New York Times,* July 8, 2009.

Siesby, Brigit. "Blood Is Food." *Petits Propos Culinaires* No. 4, February, 1980.

Spicer, Susan, with Paula Disbrowe. *Crescent City Cooking.* New York: Knopf, 2007.

Smith, Andrew F. *The Oxford Companion to American Food and Drink.* Oxford: Oxford University Press, 2007.

Stern, Steven. "Take Half a Ton of Beef . . ." *New York Times,* October 1, 2008.

Tannahill, Reay. *Food in History.* New York: Stein and Day, 1973.

Tolstoy, Leo. *War and Peace.* Translated by Richard Pevear and Larissa Volokhonsky. New York: Knopf, 2007.

Trotter, Charlie. *Charlie Trotter's Meat & Game.* Berkeley: Ten Speed Press, 2001.

Vié, Blandine. *Testicules.* Paris: Les Éditions de l'Épure, 2005.

Vileisis, Ann. *Kitchen Literacy.* Washington, DC: Island Press, 2008.

Villemur, Michèle. *Plats Canailles.* Paris: Aubanel, 2006.

Visser, Margaret. *The Rituals of Dinner.* Toronto: HarperCollins, 1991.

———. *The Way We Are.* Toronto: HarperCollins, 1994.

Walker, Harlan, ed. *Oxford Symposium on Food and Cookery 1994: Disappearing Foods.* Totnes: Prospect Books, 1995.

Walters, Mark Jerome. *Six Modern Plagues and How We Are Causing Them.* Washington, DC: Island Press, 2003.

Weber, Nicolas Fox. *The Bauhaus Group: Six Masters of Modernism.* New York: Knopf, 2009.

Wheaton, Barbara Ketcham. *Savoring the Past: The French Kitchen and Table from 1300 to 1789.* New York: Touchstone, 1966.

White, Florence. *Good Things in England.* London: Futura, 1974.

Willan, Anne. *French Regional Cooking.* New York: Morrow, 1981.

———. *Great Cooks and Their Recipes.* Maidenhead: McGraw-Hill, 1977.

———. *La Varenne Pratique.* Toronto: Macmillan, 1989.

———. "The Slippery Subject of Variety Meats." *The Greenbrier Food Symposium,* 2000.

Wrangham, Richard. *Catching Fire.* New York: Basic Books, 2009.

Wright, Clarissa Dickson. *Food: What We Eat and How We Eat It.* London: Ebury Press, 2000.

Acknowledgments

With this book I complete my trilogy, *Bones*, *Fat*, and *Odd Bits*. I doubt there will be a skin book but I hope that one day these three books will be sold as a boxed set wrapped in vellum.

I am happy to say that "odd bits" was an easier subject to sell than animal fat. I'd cheekily mentioned the idea to Aaron Wehner at Ten Speed before *Fat* was published. He believed like me, it was a subject that should to be tackled and I was thrilled to work with him and his team again. I was happy when HarperCollins Canada was also willing to tackle the subject. Agent extraordinaire, devotee of tongue, Liv Blumer never doubts my contrarian ideas. She is always there for me, thank you Liv. Thanks also to Bill Blumer, my knight errant who, as my champion, fights tirelessly for justice on my behalf.

The love of good food brings people together initiating and sustaining friendship, and I would like to express my gratitude to friends, colleagues and strangers who generously took time to answer my questions, share their knowledge, pass on recipes, and search out information for me.

In North and South America, I would like to thank Allison Boomer, David Brown, Laura Calder, Ian Campbell, Lesley Chesterman, Michael Clampffer, Naomi Duguid, David Field, Brenda Garza, Gunter Gruener, Steve Isleifson, Raghavan Iyer, Don Kerstens, Ihor Kuryliw, David Leite, Nick Malgieri, Patricia Meyer, Lieve De Nil, Brian Polcyn, Albert Ponzo, Dr. Chris Raines, Miriam Rubin, Olivia Silva Fraga, Mark Scarbrough, Michele Scicolone, Ron Smyth, Walter Staib, Oksana Slavyutich, Andrew Smith, Kim Sunée, Keijo Tapanainen, Heather Trim, Nach Waxman, Bruce Weinstein and Andrew Zimmerman.

In Europe, I extend thanks to Bénédict Beaugé, Marie-jose Bablot, Rico Buchholz and Mandy Hegewald, Franck and Lise Courtès, François and Caroline Gerard, Cyril and Maryse Lalanne, Melinda Leong, Bruno Neveu, Patrick and Eliane Suzanne, Franceso Tripoli, Hanno and Christine Rinke.

In Australia, thanks are due to Jane and Craig Agnew, Sally and Ken Coles, Robyn McAlister, Claudine McLagan and Cherry Ripe.

Thank you to my friends, who willingly ate their way through this book often with trepidation but always with a sense of adventure; Isabelle Cochard, Colin Faulkner, David Field, Rob and Daniela Fiocca, François and Caroline Gerard, Eric and Marie-line Incarbona, Val and Ilze Lapsa, Karen Lim, and Vincent Wong.

And to Mathew Cosgrove, who corrected grammar and spelling mistakes that an army of others missed, thank you for making this book so much better.

While knowledge and experience are fundamental to good cooking, a cook is nothing without quality ingredients and in this case often hard to find ones. So I'd like to thank all my suppliers, especially Elizabeth and Eric Bzikot at Baa Sheep, Wayne Kienitz of Wayne's Meat Products, Leila Batten of Whitehouse Meats, Peter Sanagan of Sanagan's Meat Locker, and Stephen Alexander of Cumbrae Farms. Thank you also to my Paris butcher, Joël Lachable who is passionate about meat and a big merci beaucoup to the team at La Triperie Groussard, the temple of odd bits in my local market.

I was lucky to work again with the wonderful team at Ten Speed. Thank you to Jenny Wapner for editing my words with talent, care and humor and to copy editor Clancy Drake who kept her pen sharp and steady to the last word. The design team that worked magic on *Fat* succeeded again, making odd bits look delectable; a big thank-you to photographer Leigh Beisch, food stylist Dan Becker, and prop stylist Sara Slavin. And thank you to designer Betsy Stromberg for creating a stylish and beautiful package for my words and recipes.

As always I owe the biggest debt of gratitude to my husband, Haralds Gaikis, he has now survived three books. Writing a book especially as the deadline approaches requires intense concentration and focus that is not much fun for those living with you. He endured that and the endless meals of odd bits, offering insightful comments and recipe ideas. Love you, Haralds, I couldn't have done it without you.

Jennifer McLagan
Toronto, 2011

Index

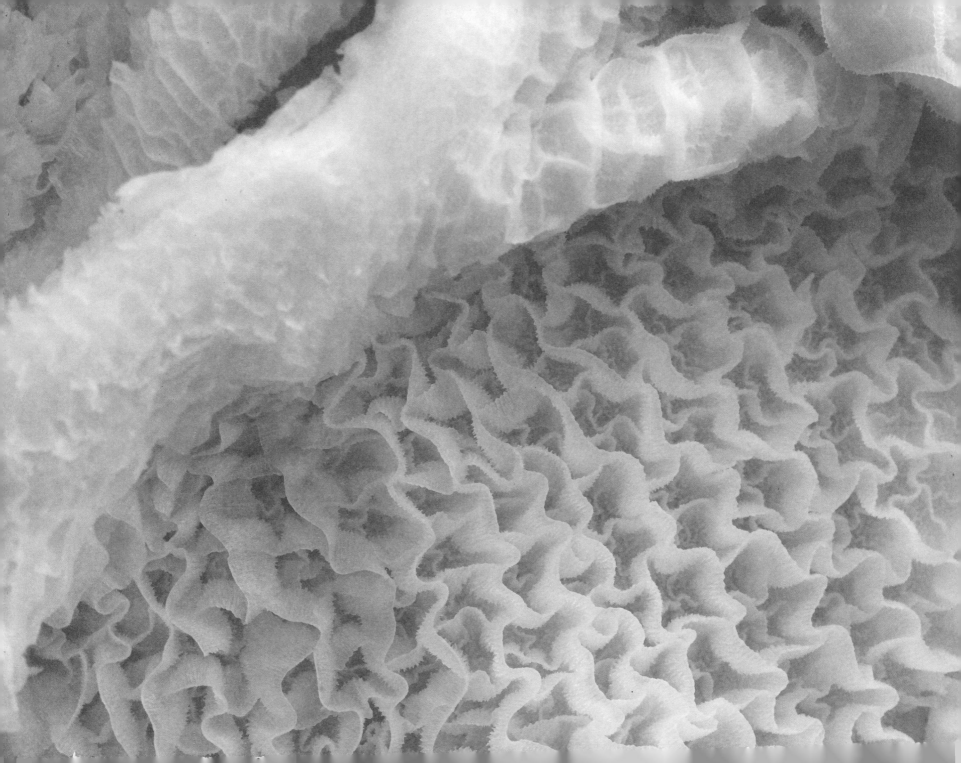